Genevieve Preer

SHOOTING BACK

To Peter
Love,
Genevieve
May 1992

SHOOTING BACK

A Photographic View of Life by Homeless Children

SELECTED BY JIM HUBBARD

Introduction by Dr. Robert Coles

CHRONICLE BOOKS • SAN FRANCISCO

Library of Congress
Cataloging-in-Publication Data
Hubbard, Jim, 1942 –
Shooting back : a photographic view of life by homeless children / by Jim Hubbard : with an introduction by Robert Coles.
p. cm.
ISBN 0-8118-0019-9
1. Homeless children – Washington (D.C.) – Pictorial works. 2. Inner cities – Washington (D.C.) – Pictorial works. I. Title.
362.7'08'6942 – dc20
91-14982 CIP

Distributed in Canada by
Raincoast Books,
112 East Third Avenue,
Vancouver, B.C.
V5T 1C8

Chronicle Books
275 Fifth St.
San Francisco, CA
94103

Book design:
John Sullivan &
Dennis Gallagher,
Visual Strategies S.F.

For more information on Shooting Back, Inc. please write or call:

Shooting Back, Inc.
1901 Eighteenth St. NW
Washington, D.C. 20009

(202) 232-5169

Printed in Hong Kong

10 9 8 7 6 5 4 3 2 1

ACKNOWLEDGMENTS

We want to express our gratitude to the mothers and fathers of the children we have worked with for allowing us into their lives and the lives of their children. The pictures in this book were also made possible by the enormous time and energy given by hundreds of volunteers. To name everyone would take many pages, but we are eternally grateful to every one of the volunteers who helped the children of Shooting Back show their talent and vision in these pages.

Several individuals, because of their tireless and compassionate efforts, must be mentioned: Betsy Frampton of the Glen Eagles Foundation for having faith in us; Laurie, Sue and Mitchell Kuff, for their enormous generosity; Nancy Sanford for her time and talent; our tireless friend Robin Smith who produced the Shooting Back video that has appeared on PBS and travels with the Shooting Back exhibit.

A special warm and heartfelt thanks to my wife, Sherry, and my two beautiful and wonderful daughters, Hanna and Priya. A warm and special thanks first to Mary Ellen Hombs, who creatively and faithfully helped organize the Shooting Back Education and Media Center in Washington, D.C. — we would not have been able to establish a long-term program and center for the children without her help — and also to my Project Director, Jacqui Lieberman. Literary agent Anne Edelstein, who saw early on the value of this work, helped bring the book into being. I'd also like to thank Nion McEvoy, Charlotte Stone and everyone else at Chronicle Books, as well as the book's designers, John Sullivan and Dennis Gallagher of Visual Strategies.

Other special people we want to thank are our program coordinator Marie Moll; attorney Amy Bowerman; Penelope Saltzman and Tom Olsen, legal counsel from Wilmer, Cutler and Pickering; photographers Paul Hosefros of *The New York Times*, Fred Sweets of *The Washington Post*; former *Newsweek* photographer Arthur Grace, and JB Pictures' Mark Peterson; Eliot Liebow; Steve Barrett; Reuter's Ralph Alswang; Peter Howe and Jay Lovinger of *Life* magazine.

Our energetic board of directors continues to guide and inspire Shooting Back: Lisa Mihaly, Roberta Ain, Roberta Youmans, Jim Whittaker, and Pat Hanrahan.

Several foundations, corporations, individuals, and institutions generously contributed time, resources, and talent to Shooting Back: Philip Brookman and other staff at the Washington Project for the Arts hosted our first Shooting Back exhibit; Alby Segall and Loren Behr of The Children's Museum of Denver; Exodus Youth Services; Ilford Photo Corporation; Chrome, Inc.; Asman Photographic Services; Garrett Lab; Image, Inc.; Community of Hope; The Carpenter's Shelter; National Coalition for the Homeless; WLTT Radio; The Enterprise Foundation; and Suzy Farren and the Catholic Health Association. Several foundations generously support Shooting Back: the Morris and Gwendolyn Cafritz Foundation, the Public Welfare Foundation, the Eugene and Agnes Meyer Foundation, the W.K. Kellogg Foundation, and the Community Foundation of Greater Washington.

DEDICATION

To all homeless children

"Tragically, many of our precious little ones live in extremely distressful environments reminiscent of war-torn landscapes in other lands. The suffering of children is cruelly democratic, without regard for background. Native American children, African American, Hispanic, and Caucasian youngsters—all are growing up in a culture that hypocritically denounces violence while also extolling it as a virtue, shielded in moralistic language. These children, deprived of opportunities, suffer both an official and even sometimes a familial neglect as heinous as during any period in human history . . ."

JIM HUBBARD, 1991

"I want to take a picture with my camera. With a bunch of people in it, and show the President the picture."

Nick, 9, *1989*

"If I wasn't here [at Shooting Back, Inc.] right now, I could be back on the corner or somewhere selling drugs, shooting somebody, or killing somebody for some money."

Dion Johnson, 13, *1991*

INTRODUCTION / ROBERT COLES

A few years ago, when talking with homeless children in the greater Boston area, I was brought up short by a girl of ten, living in a shelter with her mother and two sisters. As I watched her draw a picture of herself, and of a school building nearby, she suddenly picked up a black crayon, hitherto unused, and put a large X over the entire piece of paper she had been using. I was surprised, saddened. I thought I knew, right away, what had informed her abrupt decision — a conviction that life had little to offer her, and that, accordingly, there was no point in trying to portray either herself or any part of the world that happened to be familiar to her. But she had another psychological and moral agenda in mind, as I soon enough learned when she rather earnestly tried to explain herself, her sense of things: "That," she told me, pointing directly to her X, "is what people think of us, but they are wrong, and I know they are, and if I could, I'd tell them!"

I immediately wanted to hear what she would say to the "people" she had mentioned. She was not forthcoming, however. She stared glumly at the crayon she had just used, then looked beyond me to a window, which offered her a view of an old inner-city church. I prodded her — told her it mattered that she and others in her situation let the rest of us know what she had to say. But she seemed deaf to my entreaties. She did glance at me once or twice, but with a look, I thought, of skepticism, if not outright suspicion. Finally, I pressed her through a question: "Have you ever felt people looking at you as if they were ready to put an X on you in their minds?" She responded quickly to that question — even seemed to surprise herself with her vigorous manner of commentary, not to mention her deft, sharp words: "They don't look at us folks at all. They have bad words for us, or they can't say a thing — they ignore us. If they looked, they might be finding themselves upset, so they don't." A pause — and I assumed she'd had her say, made her powerful point, stated a critique: the indifference of others as a child had taken its measure. But she was not finished, I was to learn: "You see that church?" With that question addressed to me, I was left both to answer and to wonder about my respondent's intent. "Yes," I said, and emphasized my willingness to converse with several nods of my head. "Well," she declared — and a spell of silence, which I decided not to interrupt. After about five seconds — wherein she stared unremittingly at the church — she broke into a sustained narrative: "They can go into their church, but they don't come out any different. A minister told us Jesus lived poor, and people, a lot of people, didn't like Him, and they thought He was a big bother to them. He kept moving from place to place — so maybe *He* was homeless, too, you know."

Now she was looking right at me, and not at all inclined to let up doing so. Now I was silent, and I began to wonder both what to say, and what she expected me to say. Now I felt inadequate, ill at ease — until, at last, I broke eye contact with her, and with my eyes moved my field of vision to the church she had earlier been scrutinizing. Her vision, I began to realize, had given shape to mine — supplanted a sense of things I carried to that room without consulting her. In a sense, then, to draw upon this book's title, and its purpose as well, she had "shot back" with her eyes, her mind, her spirit, in such a way that I was able to learn a few things about not only her, but myself — her thoughts a prod to a bit of enlightenment on my part.

This book will, I suspect, offer its readers what that girl offered me — a glimpse of what others, poor and vulnerable and exceedingly hard-pressed, nevertheless manage to make of the world around them as they give it careful, shrewd, knowing scrutiny. This is a book of visual statements that have their own vigorous moral energy at work — reminders to us that so-called homeless children are, in fact, all too sensitive and alert to this world we all share, and all too ready, given a chance, to nudge us, even collar us, with the realizations and conclusions they have reached: the nature of their fate, with its grim prospects — "shot back," perhaps, in the hope that we who have so much more (including more money, more social and political influence) will be given proper notice, proper moral pause. One can only hope that such will be the case — that the world this book so honestly and insistently and penetratingly evokes and renders will be made part of our consciousness, our ethical lives, our activities as citizens.

JIM HUBBARD ON SHOOTING BACK

In the early 1980s, while a staff photographer at UPI in Washington, D.C., I began documenting the life of the homeless. After a few years, I focused on the homeless families. Increasing numbers were forced to live in cars, parks, and hotels and motels for temporary shelter, and among these shelters was the Capitol City Inn, a Washington welfare motel and a hell-hole in the power center of the world. Whenever I took pictures of the families there, the children wanted to hold and look through my camera.

Many of my visits to the motel included Dion Johnson's family. In their room, I was struck by the drawings and colorings and other art forms that had been created by the four Johnson children and hung by their mother, Vanessa. This musty and crowded space, not any different from a space in a refugee camp, had become a miniature gallery, with the show being the children's art. Besides the bright spirit coming from within each child, the art was the brightest light in the room.

On one particular afternoon, as I sat with Dion and his mother in their room, he showed me some snapshots he had taken of his family and friends. Both he and his mother were proud of the photos. I offered Dion an opportunity to take pictures and learn more about photography. He accepted and his powerful smile stretched from ear to ear.

I looked at Vanessa, as she said, smiling, "That's my Dion." I was struck by the pride that Vanessa Johnson had for her children and for the work that they created. In large part, this was what moved me to help Dion. This same energy and interest in tapping the creativity of the kids is the common thread running through Shooting Back.

Once the idea was born, Dion and I spent several hours each week strolling through the shelter, working to discover and train this child's creative side. As Dion and I walked around looking for pictures, several hundred others who lived at the Capitol City Inn ran up and asked to take pictures with the big professional camera Dion was using.

Dion and I looked at each other as the little hands grabbed for the camera, and knew we needed help. The next week I started a campaign of recruiting staff and freelance photographers stationed in Washington, D.C. Each week volunteer photographers joined me, and we made many visits to Dion's shelter and other shelters in the Washington, D.C., area. Chil-

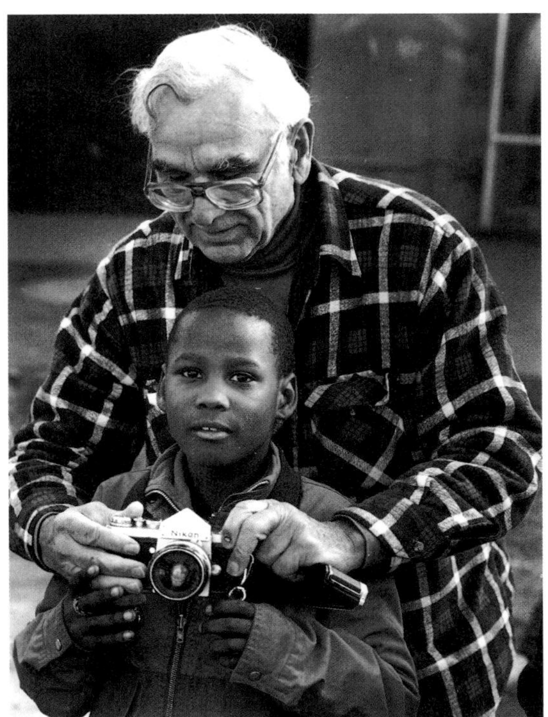

TOP: **Retired *Washington Post* photographer Douglas Chevalier teaches youngster at Capitol City Inn in Washington, D.C., 1989.**
BELOW: **Stephanie Gross works with children at The Carpenter's Shelter in Alexandria, VA, 1990.** *Photos by Jim Hubbard*

dren waited anxiously for us to arrive so that they could go out and take pictures of their world. Some of the photographers who worked with us included notables like Paul Hosefros of the *New York Times*, Fred Sweets of the *Washington Post*, Larry Downing of *Newsweek*, and freelancers including Steve Barrett, Mark Peterson, and Leslie Close.

Shelter life is a journey into despair. It is life on the edge. Many of the shelters I visited were the scenes of round-the-clock violence, drug dealing, abuse and cases of parental neglect, and widespread chaos. They were places not fit for a child. At the Capitol City Inn these horrors to children occurred on a regular basis. This dingy and dilapidated two-story former tourist motel, situated on a major six-lane road, became home for nearly seven hundred children and their parents. Between 1987 and 1989, five children died there. Two were stabbed to death by their overburdened father. One was hit by a train behind the shelter while playing the shelter children's favorite game of tag with the train. There wasn't even a playground for these children except on worn-out mattresses that they pulled from the trash. Another child died from a mysterious illness, and yet another burned to death when the mother left the room to find food.

Tragedy and violence become a regular part of life for the children living in the shelters. As I encountered these children, I realized that they are deprived at many levels. Though they do not have the protruding bellies from starvation and disease that I witnessed along the Thai-Cambodian border in 1979, these children without permanent homes are victims of profound injustice. Myriad factors place them at a risk level comparable to that for children in the slums of Calcutta and the children of war in Northern Ireland and Lebanon: violence, substance abuse, domestic violence, and a systemic indifference.

This reality prompts me to seek ways to alleviate the suffering. My methodology is to herald the struggle of the poor and, in particular, the homeless. Publicizing the plight of the homeless through the visual media is important and affirms the reality of the situation, the need for change, and the cry for help of the dispossessed. Ironically, we block the anguish of literally walking over the homeless, and then for visceral sensitization, we visit a gallery.

These deprived children were hungry for attention and someone who would help channel their powerful and creative energy. Even though they reside in the United States, these children had the same look of abandonment in their eyes that we have seen in the Romanian orphans and starving children in Asia and Africa. A collective social neglect has produced the stares that convey an urgency, an invitation to come into their lives. When I got to know Dion, there was no way I could resist the stares and the invitation any longer. I had to act in some attempt to save the children from this neglect.

Part of the intent in working with the children was to convey to them that they are important, as important as my own children. We wanted to let the children know that there were people out there who were willing to spend time and teach them. The children responded by being attentive and by showing us a love hard to find in other sectors of our society.

There were so many wonderful things that came out of our weekly photo sessions with the children. I felt a special relationship with Dion and his family. Relationships among other teachers and students surfaced and blossomed.

Fortunately, though some of the children disappeared precipitously from the shelter, we have maintained relationships with several of the children even since they have left shelter life. Many of the parents have been especially supportive of our work with their kids. Many parents, fearing the violence and chaos their children were subjected to on a daily basis, have pleaded with us to work with their kids as often as pos-sible. Many a time a young mother has approached me and asked if I could spend time with her child. I am always touched by this and would like to do more, but know of my limitations. All we can do is teach photography and other creative skills to the children. A fantasy of mine is to pluck the children from their environment and put them in a wonderful and safe situation. This remains a dream.

There were few rules in this photographic project. The idea was simple: the children would document their world inside the shelter or within one block of the shelter. They used the professional camera after a photographer taught them the basic use of it. The central theme was to allow the children to look through the viewfinder of the camera and take pictures of the world they perceive.

The results are in this book. The pictures are as diverse as the children who took them. They are both simple and elegant; they are honest beyond imagination. They capture moments impossible for an outsider to have ever perceived or experienced.

After seeing the children's work, a second agenda evolved: to have an exhibit of their work in an art space at some time in the future. An exhibit of the children's work would serve many purposes. They would become their own advocates. The pictures would show the ingenuity, the creativity, and the beauty of the children who authored them. The children's exhibit would also educate the American people about the injustices our children endure.

We worked with the children for more than a year and a half, teaching camera mechanics, while we built a body of work for the show. Many profound moments occurred during our photographic sessions. The photographers who came to work with the children in this period were given the opportunity not only to teach but to learn from their young students.

We have all been enriched by our experiences together, and we have seen firsthand the toll taken by the harsh environment in which these children live. One sad day we arrived at Capitol City Inn to work with the children just as the fire department was extinguishing a fire in one of the rooms. The fire claimed the life of a child, and some of our children took pictures of this grim scene. Dion took several.

A few months later, after Dion had moved into subsidized housing, he and his family were driven from their row house by a fire. This grisly reality has had a profound impact on Dion's life. The children we work with often see accidental death, as well as murder. The resident of Capitol City who stabbed his two disabled sons to death did so just the day after Dion's mother had fixed the mother's hair.

We learned firsthand also not only of the violence the children must cope with but the enormous strengths used to keep families together under some of the most adverse con ditions possible. Many of the parents of the children we work with are exhausted from the toils of making ends meet and keeping their families intact, while everything in the world is geared toward preventing success.

What has been enormously rewarding for me has been the continued interaction I have with some of the children. We decided that, after we finished photographing for our exhibit, we would have to set up some kind of permanent home so we could keep working with the kids. In 1989 I established the Shooting Back Education and Media Center in Washington, D.C. Our nonprofit center teaches not only photography and darkroom skills but also painting, drawing, and creative writing, with the help of many talented volunteers and enormous support from photographic laboratories and suppliers of photographic materials.

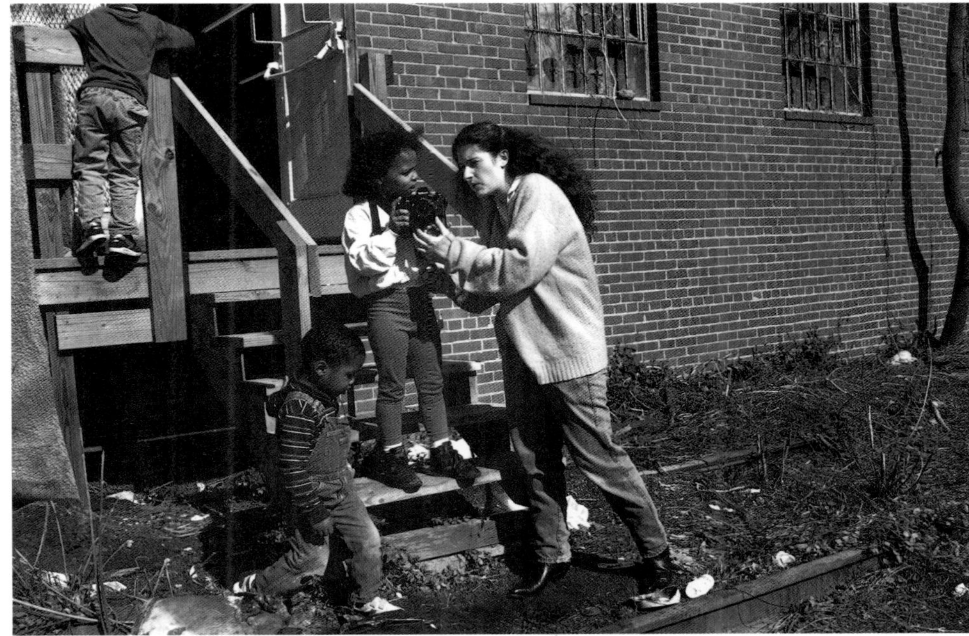

Kathleen Beall helps child in Washington, D.C., 1989
Photo by Jim Hubbard

Many cities across the country have asked us to replicate Shooting Back. We have established the first media center within a homeless shelter at The Carpenter's Shelter in Alexandria, Virginia. The Shooting Back Education and Media Center now works year-round with children in shelters, schools, and youth centers.

We had our exhibit, "Shooting Back," in a Washington, D.C., gallery; ten thousand people saw the exhibit, and millions of others saw stories about it on television and in the newspapers. *Life* magazine ran a seven-page layout of the children's photographs. Oprah Winfrey lauded our project and insisted we continue the work. A prestigious international photo show has invited us to France in 1991. Our exhibit is about to tour the nation.

The title of the project came from the lips of a nine-year-

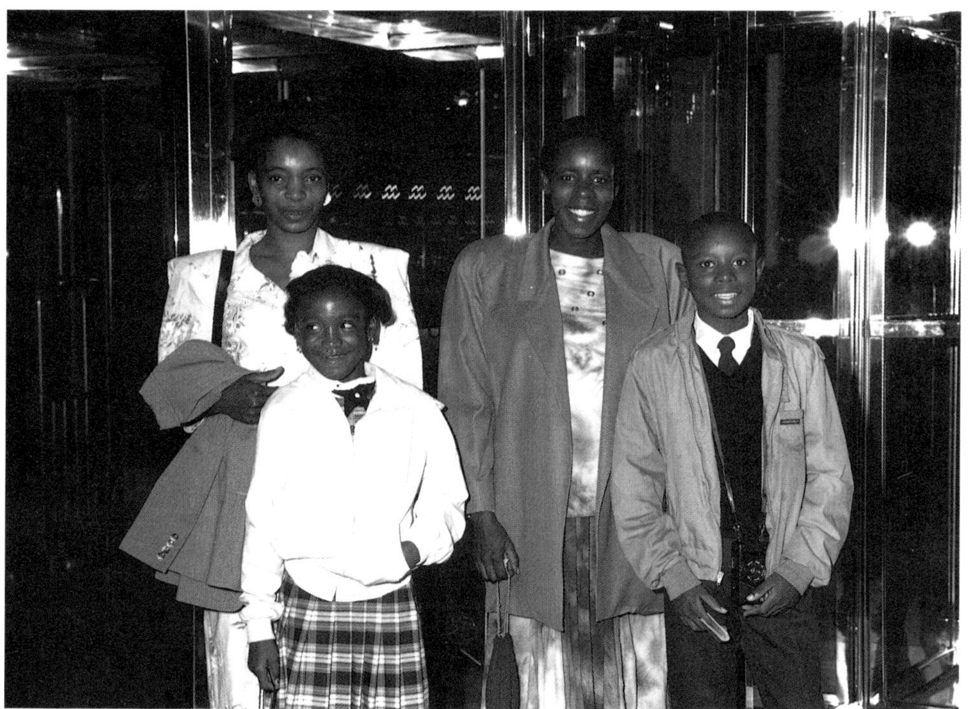

Patricia Williams with daughter Charlene and Vanessa Johnson with son Dion before the CBS Morning Show with Paula Zahn in Washington, D.C., 1990

Photo by Jim Hubbard

old boy, who, while holding a camera almost as big as himself, said, "We're shooting back." This young prophet made the remark while walking past used syringes along the curb in a neighborhood where shootings are a regular occurrence. I told him that he was a genius, and he had given us our name.

With our exhibit in Washington, D.C., and another in New York City, we have received enormous publicity both nationally and internationally. Our lives have been altered by this experience, and the children are continually having the limits of their world redefined. A recent trip to a television appearance illustrates this well.

The limo for the "Tim and Daphne Reid Show" picked us up in Washington for the one-hour drive to tape the talk show in Baltimore. Dion was on the trip, along with Charlene Williams, a school classmate whose family lived in the Capitol City Inn with Dion's and now lives in a project a short walk from the Johnsons'. The two were accustomed to a limo already, though their neighbors were startled as they looked through their kitchen curtains, registering disbelief as a chauffeur opened the door for the two happy youngsters in the middle of their less-than-regal neighborhood.

As soon as the kids were in the stretch, they flipped on the television. My daughter Hanna, along for the ride, smiled while the young threesome grew comfortable on the leather seats and entered into a fantasyland.

Hollywood's Jon Voight was about to be interviewed when we arrived on the set. Jon remembered us from some of the events he had attended in Washington in support of the homeless. He had testified on Capitol Hill with one of the other kids from Shooting Back, Calvin Stewart. They had talked about the struggle of homeless children. Now the kids were hungry, and one of the assistants on the show went to a nearby McDonald's to bring back their favorite cuisine.

Charlene laughed heartily as she watched Dion and me having our makeup applied by the show's makeup artist. Charlene pressed her index finger to the lines around the corners of my eyes and instructed the makeup artist to cover up "Jim's tree branches," the term she uses to describe the lines on my face. Charlene was next for makeup, and Dion almost fell over laughing at the sight of his friend having makeup applied for her television appearance.

We had been through this before when we traveled to New York City to appear on the CBS morning show. We were put up in an elegant hotel and were picked up in a stretch to arrive early at CBS. We had breakfast in the Green Room as the other guests entered and exited.

Then Paula Zahn interviewed us. She raved about our pictures, and as usual the kids became uncharacteristically quiet when America waited for their insights and commentary, as their photographs were shown on television sets around the country. Of course, before and after the interview, the kids chirped like sparrows and were full of antics. They were extremely excited about being on television, but intimidated to be on live.

Afterwards, Dion, Charlene, and their mothers went out with me to a Manhattan deli. An elderly man sitting at another table came over to us and congratulated us for our pictures. He said he was visiting New York from Massachusetts and had seen us in *Life* and on television. He told the youngsters how impressed he was with their work. As the mothers looked back in disbelief, Charlene and Dion slid under the table. Vanessa Johnson said, "Can you believe it, in New York, our kids are stars with all of the millions of people here?"

As we returned to Washington from the Baltimore taping, darkness fell and we were all very tired. In the big shiny car, Hanna was asleep in the rear seat. Charlene and Dion were sitting next to each other, shoulder to shoulder. Charlene's eyes closed, and her head fell on Dion's shoulder. Dion, as he did so often, sucked on two of his fingers as his eyes closed, too. It was such a touching scene, reflecting the sweetness of childhood.

Dion and Charlene often argue and bicker and verbally malign one another. They seem to be locked into a competitive relationship for the attention and affirmation of adults around them. Sometimes they smack each other with an open hand, or wrestle each other to the ground.

Sometimes, however, I sense a tenderness, a soft moment, between the two, and I realize they are quite fond of each other. As I watched them sleeping in the limo, I realized the love and protectiveness they had for each other. These children are so lovable and yet so vulnerable. They have witnessed and experienced so many horrors; they have been deprived of our society's riches. Yet despite deprivation and abandonment the children embody love, joy, strength, and beauty. They are priceless.

Our project, though originating humbly, has grown. In the two years since Dion and I started walking around the dark, dingy, and dangerous Capitol City Inn together, the photographs taken by the children have been seen by millions of people. They have become great teaching tools for other children and adults, who have learned about poverty and homelessness through the inquisitive eyes of the photographers. In essence, the photos have served as a rarely used pedagogy.

While the show has been enormously successful, its heart and soul lie within the brokenness and deprivation of marginalized children. Such photography and media luminaries as Robert Frank, James Brady, and Sam Donaldson visited the exhibit, and it comes as no surprise that they were moved by the images and by the creativity and genius of the children. Yet the other side to this project and the children who participate is even more arresting.

Dion is doing well in school now, but he is two years behind. His two years in the despair that pervaded the Capitol City Inn may be explanation enough for him to be behind grade level, as so few children there attended school regularly. Dion is the epitome of a child who can either become another victim of inner city violence or use his intelligence and talent to elude the temptations of street life, and to achieve what he aspires to accomplish. He says about himself immersed in photography, "If I wasn't here right now, I could be back on the corner or somewhere selling drugs, shooting somebody, or killing somebody for some money."

Over the past several years, I have come to know many homeless and formerly homeless families. My life has become enriched from being allowed into their lives, lives that—like so many others—have their moments of joy and pain. The families show all the marks of societal injustice, especially economic disparity and the callous lack of compassion society has shown them.

Their needs are great. They can live simply on so little, yet their strengths are mind boggling, not romantic. Many of these families live with enormous violence and deprivation. It takes discipline and perseverance for the parents to make sure their kids even get to school, let alone keep them engaged with their work there. In Dion and Charlene's school, a teacher was recently caught smoking crack in the building. One of the kids we work with was recently stabbed. Another child's mother attempted suicide. The children see the victims of drug and alcohol abuse each day. Most of the children have seen victims of shootings and knifings.

Many times under the stresses of managing to keep families intact, a parent will become ill. While it is wonderful that we are being invited to prestigious national and international events, that the children are literally being recognized as they walk down the streets, private wounds threaten to belie the success. One mother recently urged me to take her son if she should die, as she believes she will soon.

These parents and children alike are hungry for someone to care. Seeing the reality in which some of the kids grow up is heartbreaking and mandates a continued effort to help and teach the children. Daniel Hall, with the sweetest smile in his voice, calls me at the Shooting Back office on a regular basis, and asks, "When are you gonna come pick me up, Jim, so we can take pictures?"

Jim Hubbard
February 1991

Girls posing

Calvin Stewart, 17

Community of Hope, Washington, D.C.
1989
11" by 14", silver print

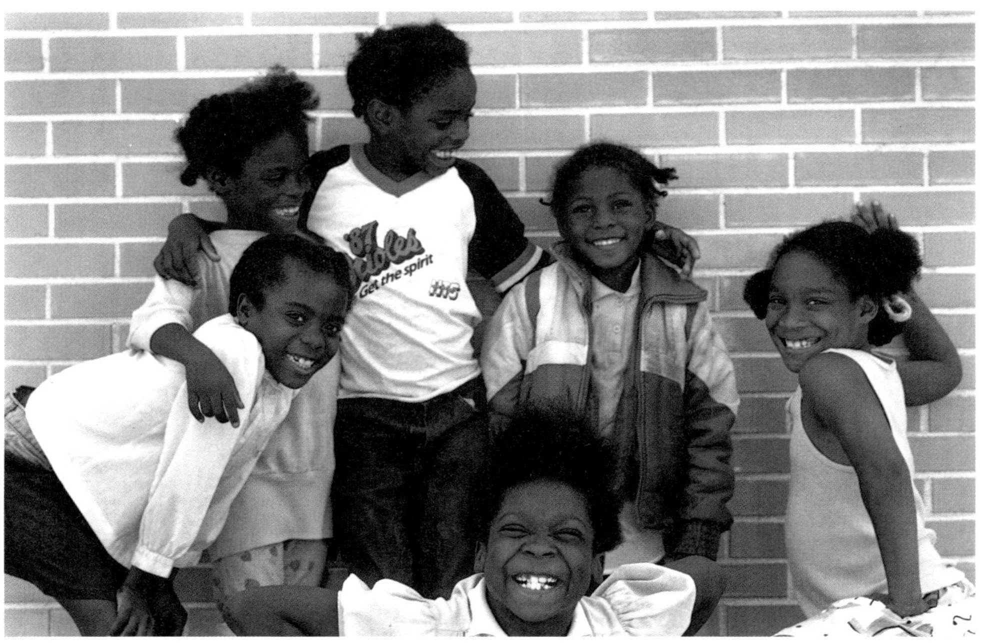

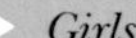 *Girls*

Dion Johnson, 11

Pitts Hotel, Washington, D.C.
1989
16" by 20", silver print

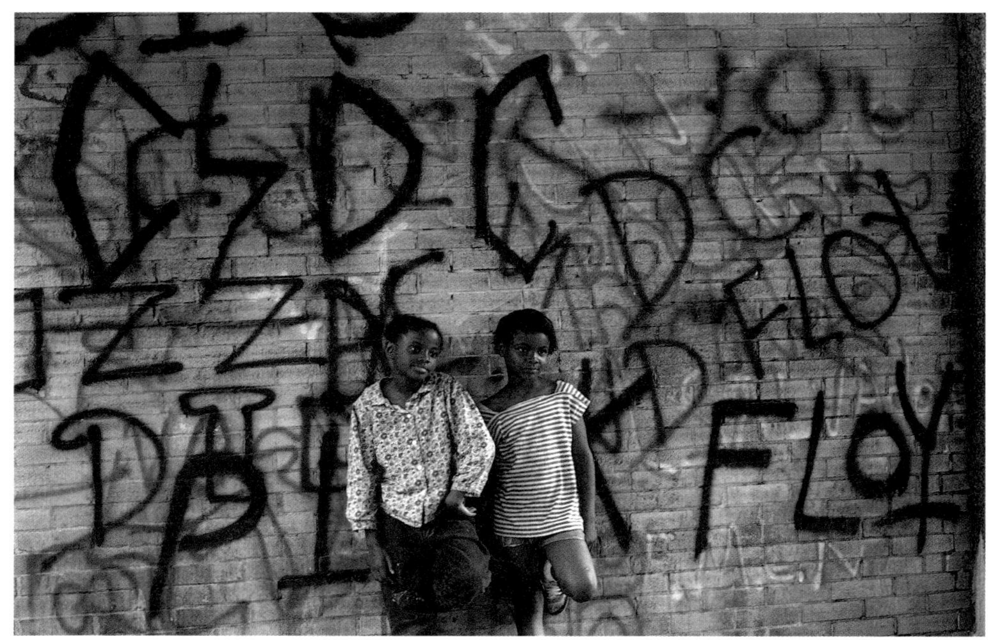

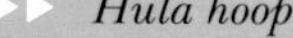 *Hula hoop*

Dion Johnson, 12

new residence, Southwest Washington, D.C.
1990
11" by 14", silver print

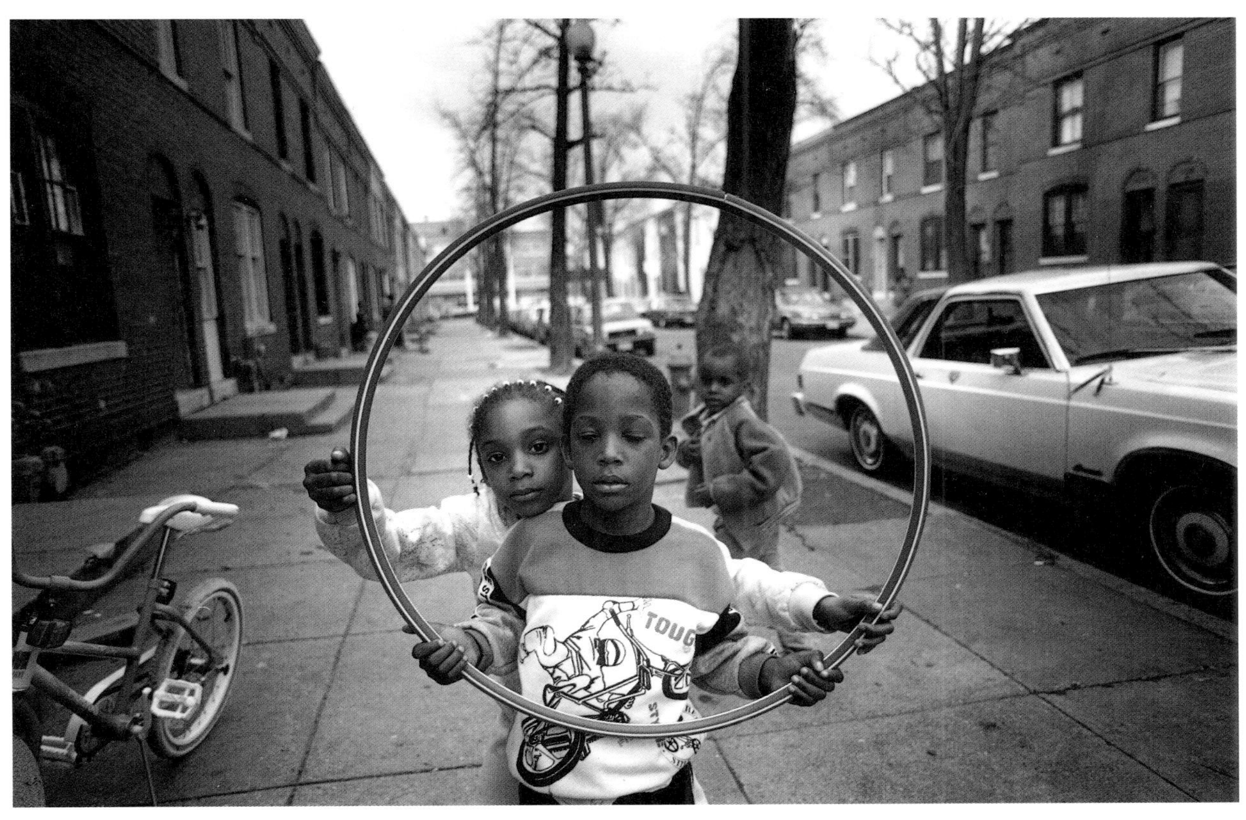

COMMENT FROM DION I want to teach photography to kids like you all taught me.

▶ *Trophy*

Dion Johnson, 11
Capitol City Inn,
Washington, D.C.
1989
11" by 14", silver print

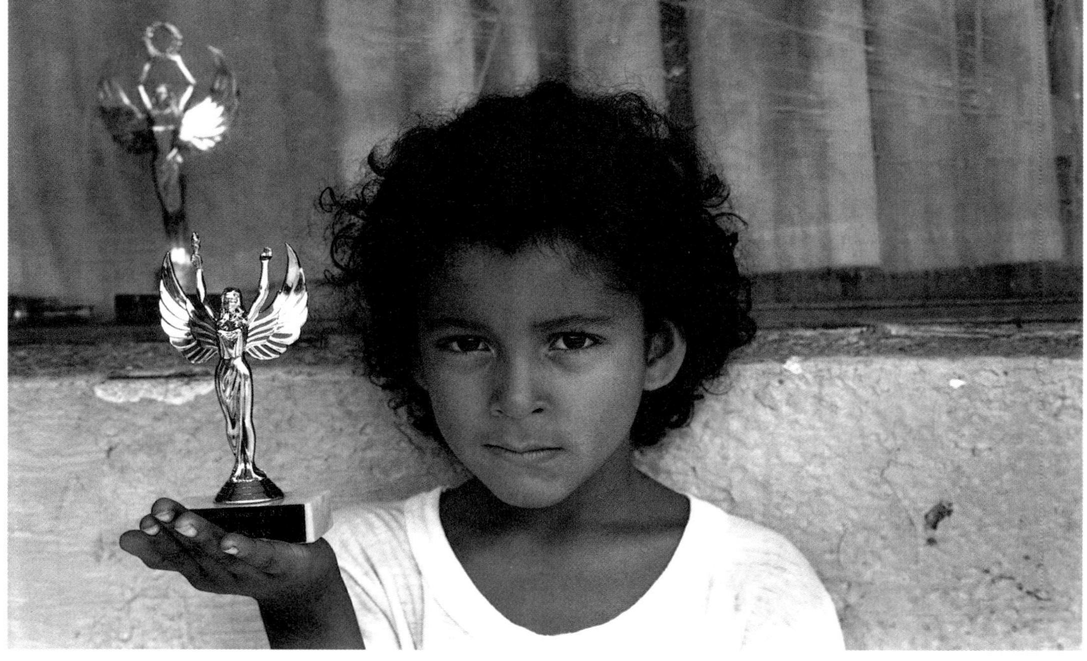

▶◀ *Girl*

David Burch, 12
Pitts Hotel,
Washington, D.C.
1989
11" by 14", silver print

▶▶ *Tears*

Danny Murray
Pitts Hotel,
Washington, D.C.
1989
11" by 14", silver print

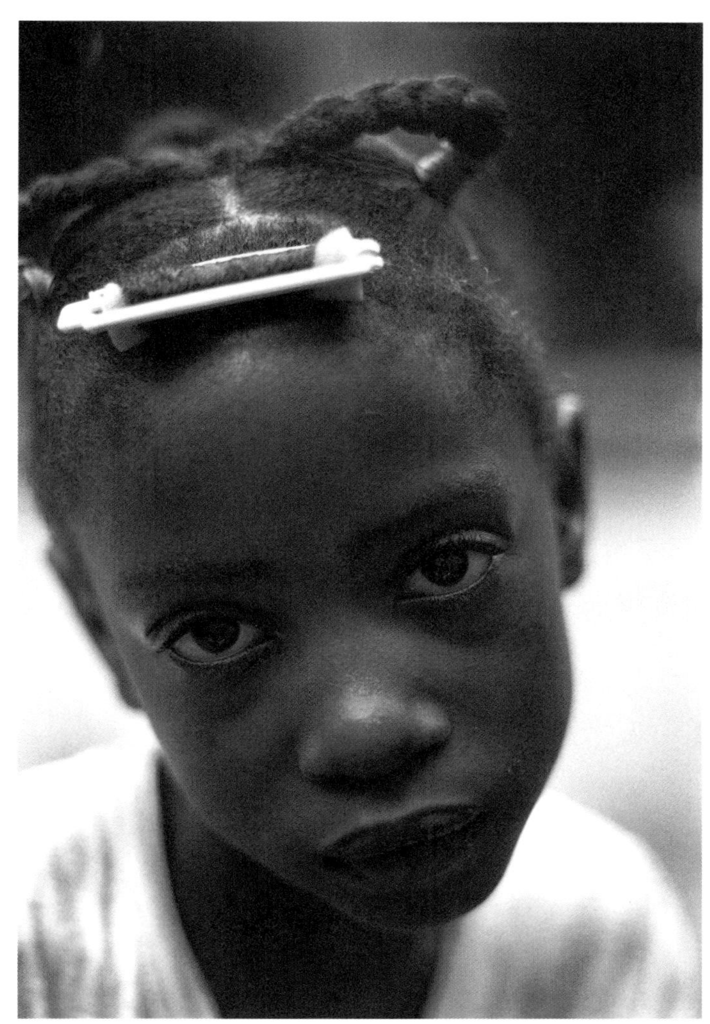

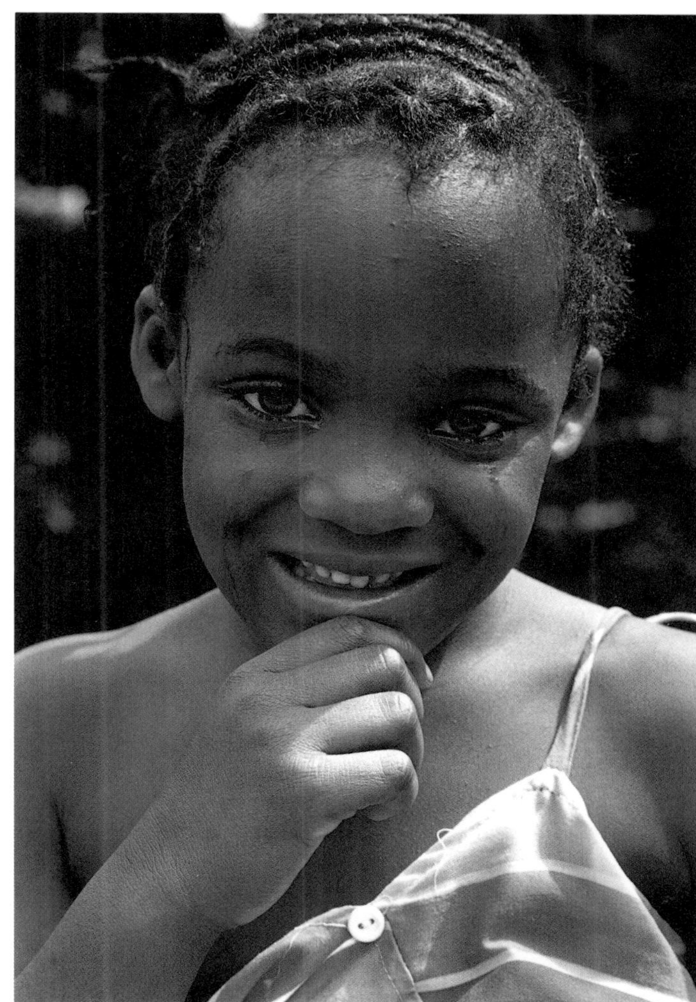

Pop gun

Arthur Taylor, 10
new residence, Southeast Washington, D.C.
1989
11" by 14", silver print

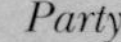

Party

Shawn Brooks, 11
The Carpenter's Shelter, Alexandria, Virginia
1990
11" by 14", silver print

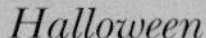

Halloween

Dion Johnson, 11
new residence, Southwest Washington, D.C.
1989
11" by 14", silver print

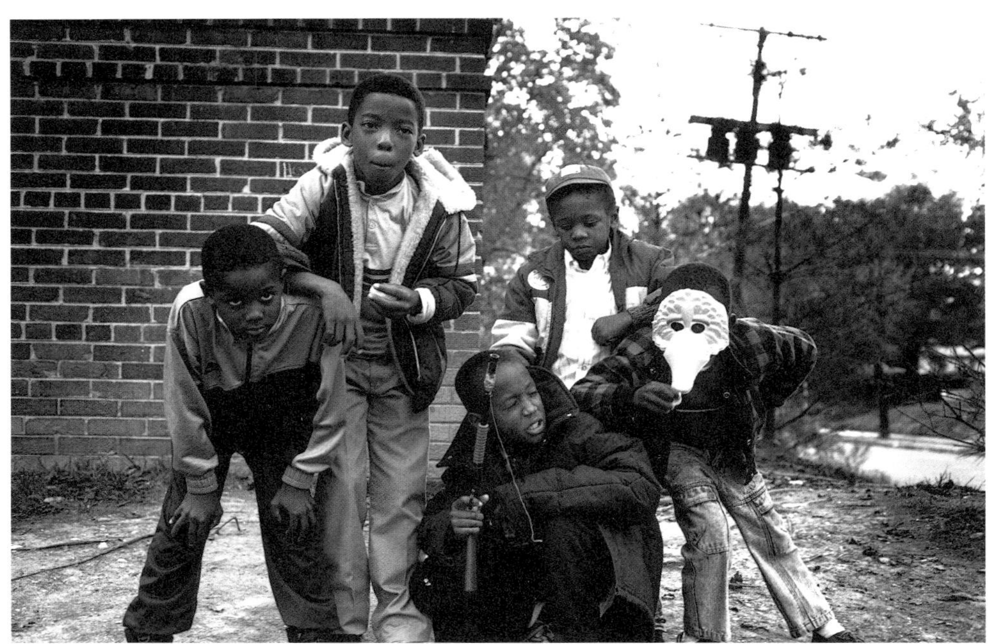

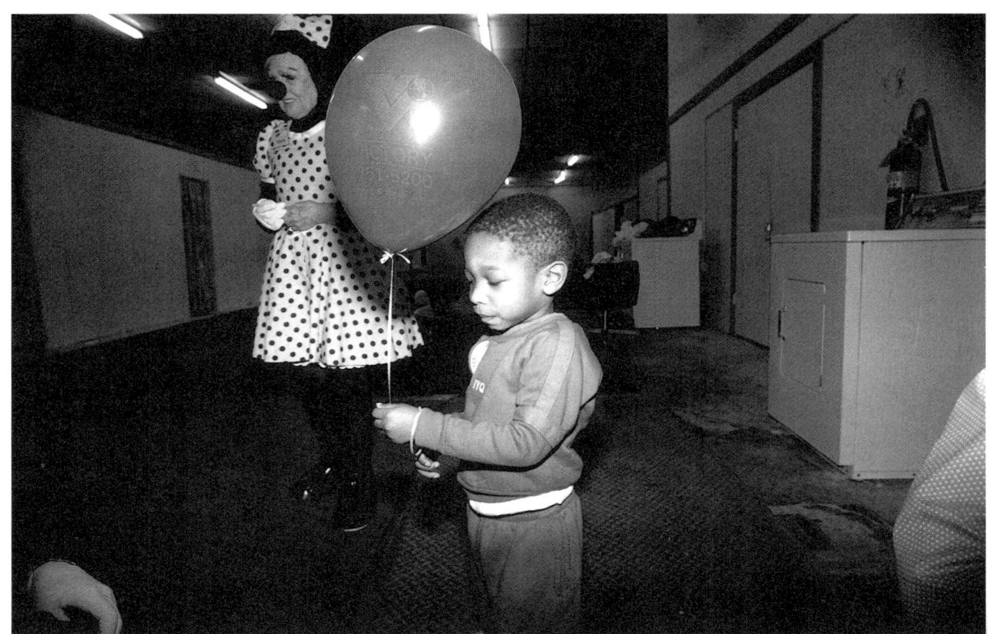

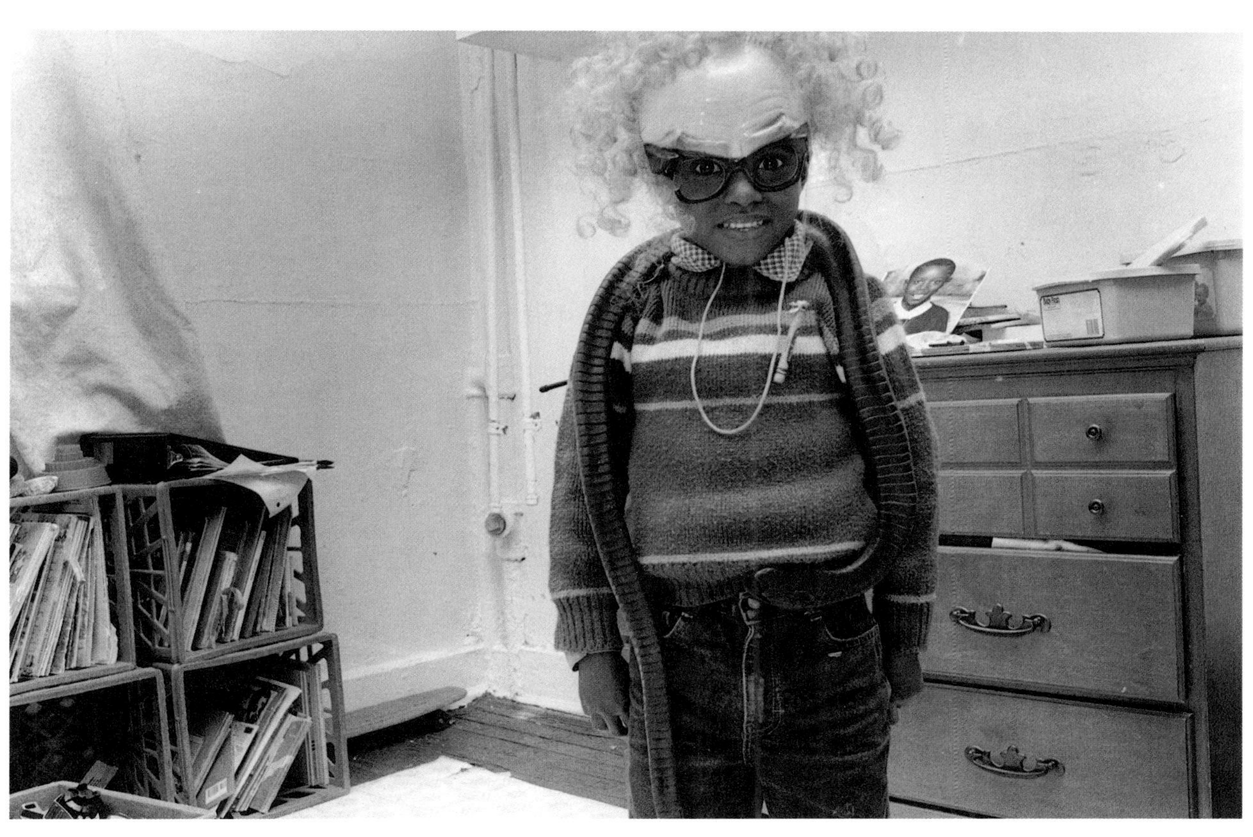

Girl on balcony

Daniel Hall, 9

Capitol City Inn,
Washington, D.C.
1989
11" by 14", silver print

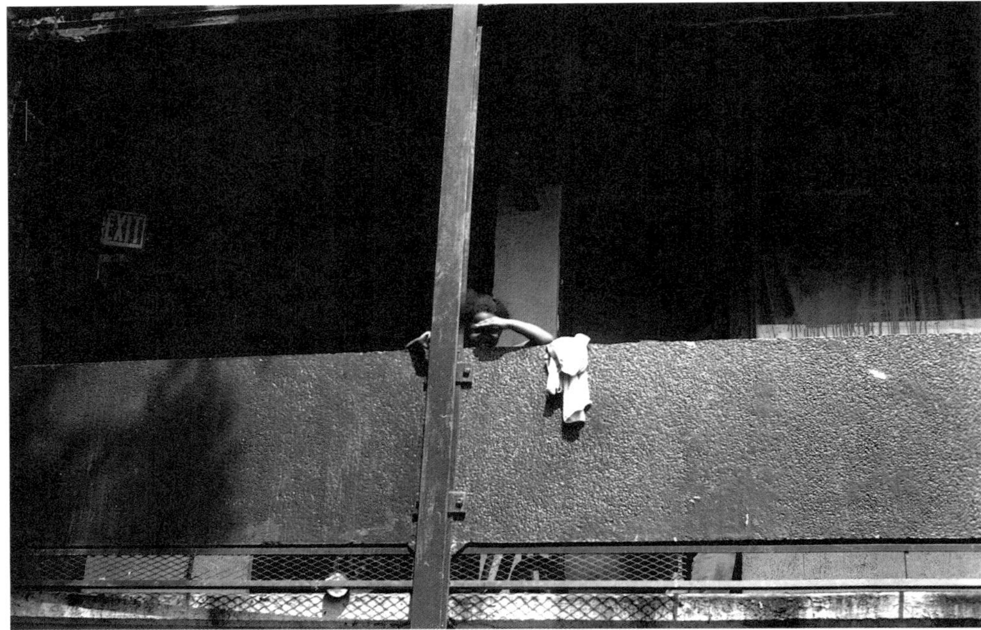

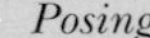

Posing

Alfred Cheadle, 14

Capitol City Inn,
Washington, D.C.
1989
11" by 14", silver print

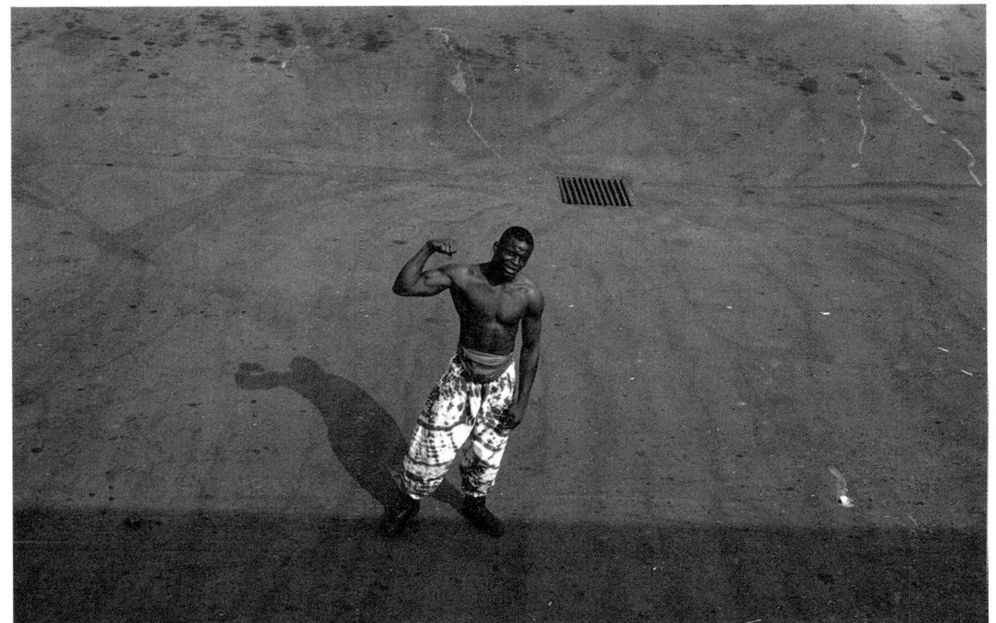

Girls

Daniel Hall, 9

Pitts Hotel,
Washington, D.C.
1989
11" by 14", silver print

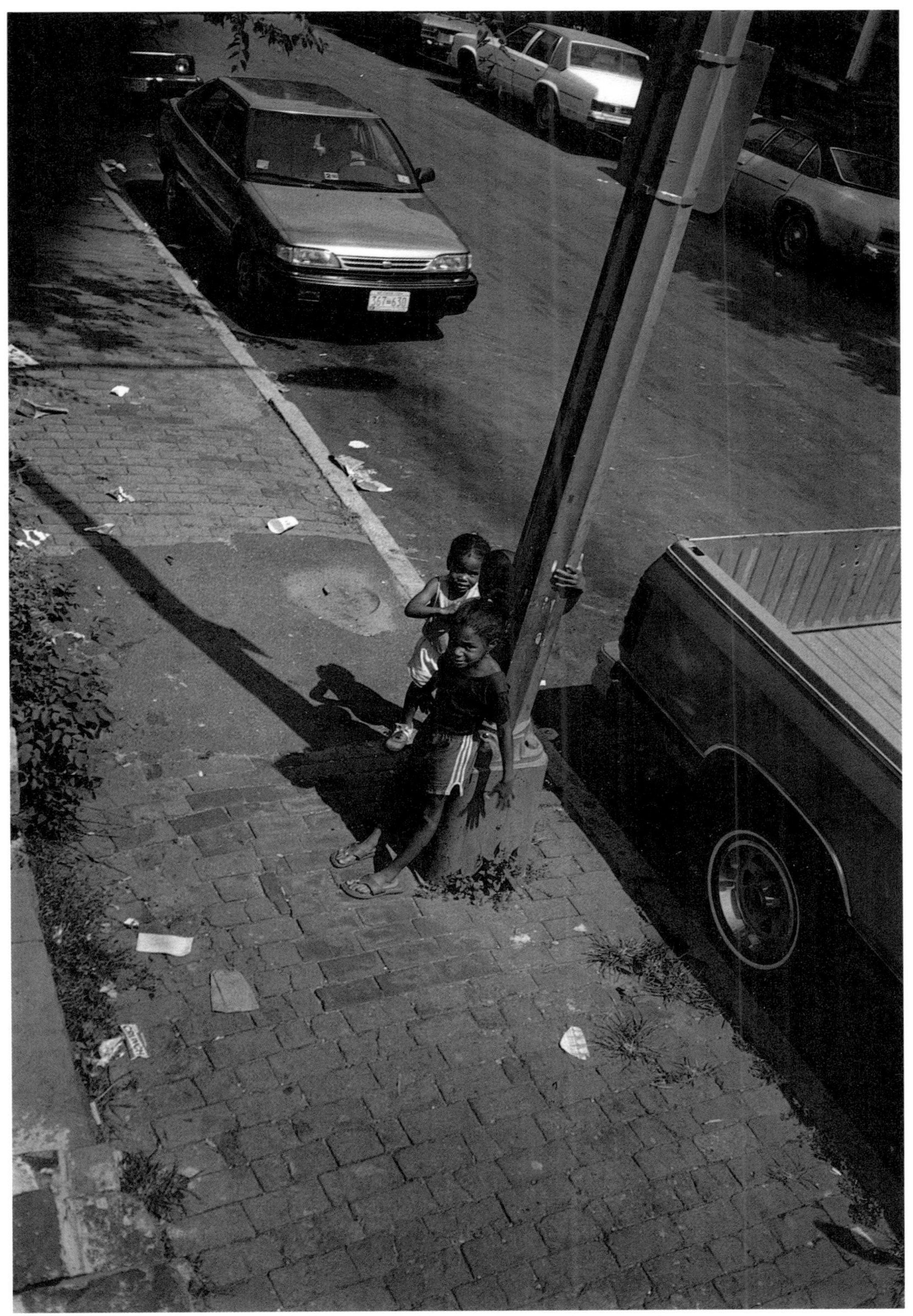

COMMENT FROM DANIEL

I like taking pictures. They make me proud of myself. My father said I did good; my mother said the same thing. My sister said I did OK.

▶ *Fred*

Calvin Steward, 17
General Scott Hotel
Washington, D.C.
1989
11" by 14", silver print

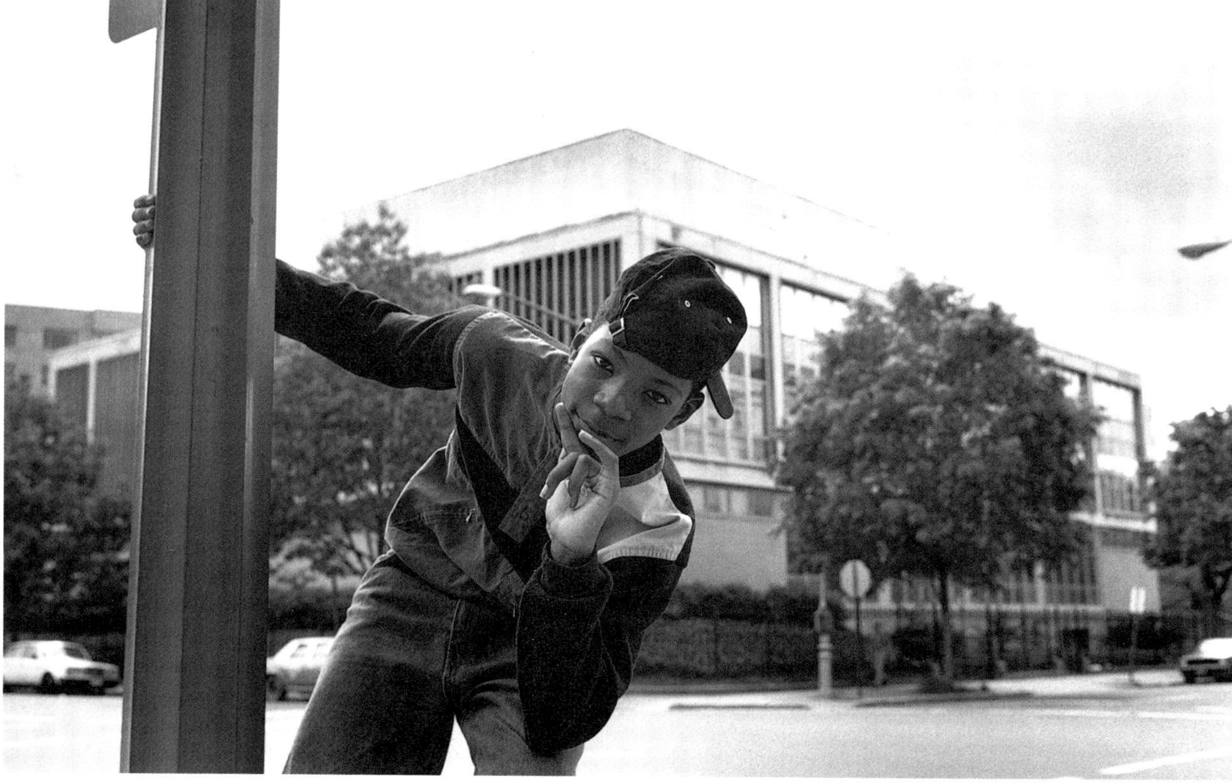

COMMENT FROM CALVIN **When I go back into the shelters, you know, I understand what they're feeling. I don't talk to them a lot about the environment because I know it's a low-life situation. They become your friends, so they open up to you more if you talk to them with the sense, like, I've been there before.**

▶▶ *Boxcar pose*

Shawn Nixon, 18
The Carpenter's Shelter,
Alexandria, Virginia
1990
16" by 20", silver print

COMMENT FROM SHAWN I was embarrassed when I first came here, 'cause when I'd talk to girls, they'd be like — where do you live — and I'd be, like, oh, no — I can't tell you that. I got here because of getting in trouble with the law. I took my mother's gun — a .357 — I didn't do nothing with it, I just had it in my possession. I left it at a girl's house, and when I was bringing it back, a cop stopped me, and they arrested me.

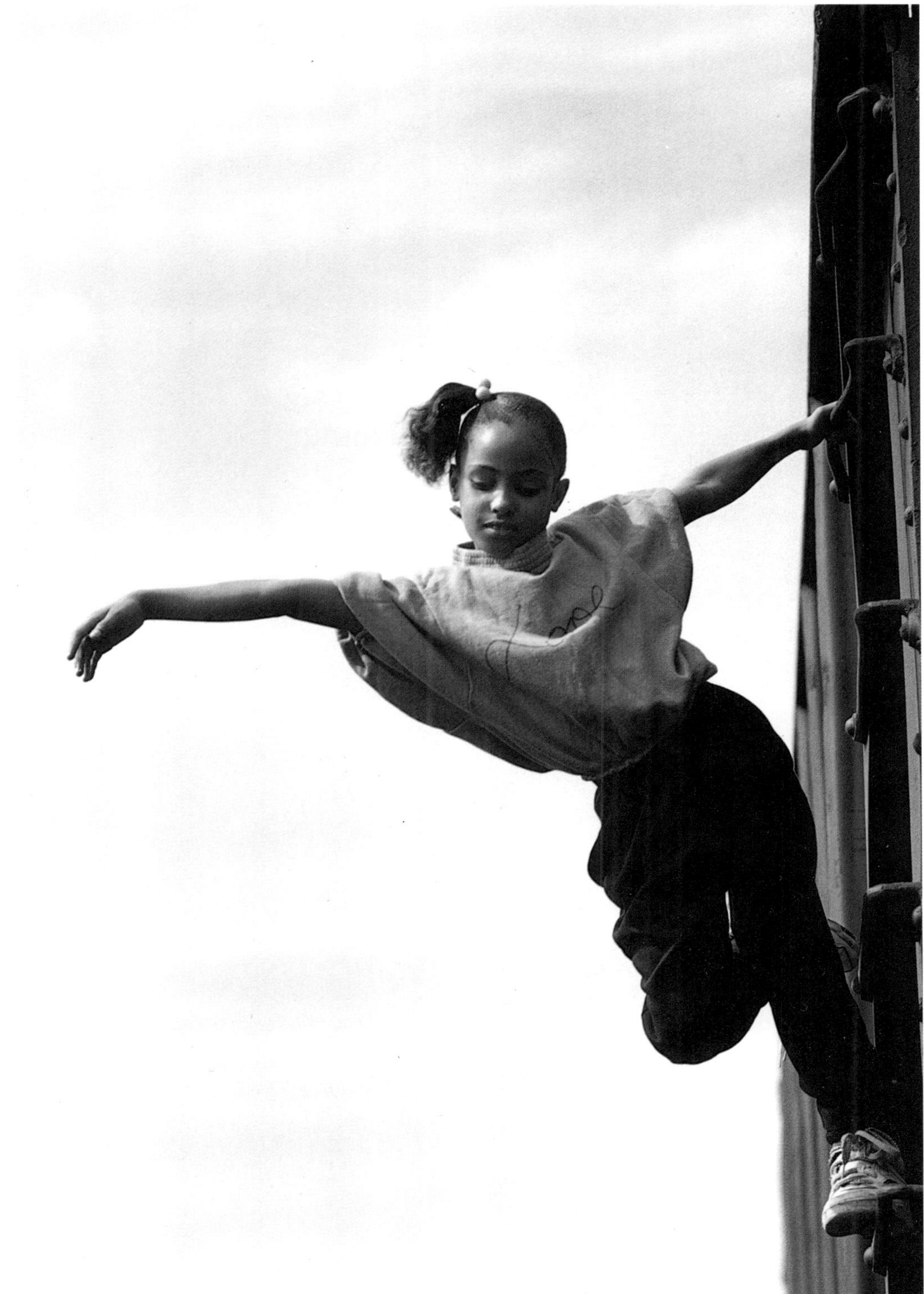

▶ *Kid on street*

Dion Johnson, 11
new residence,
Southwest
Washington, D.C.
1989
16" by 20", silver print

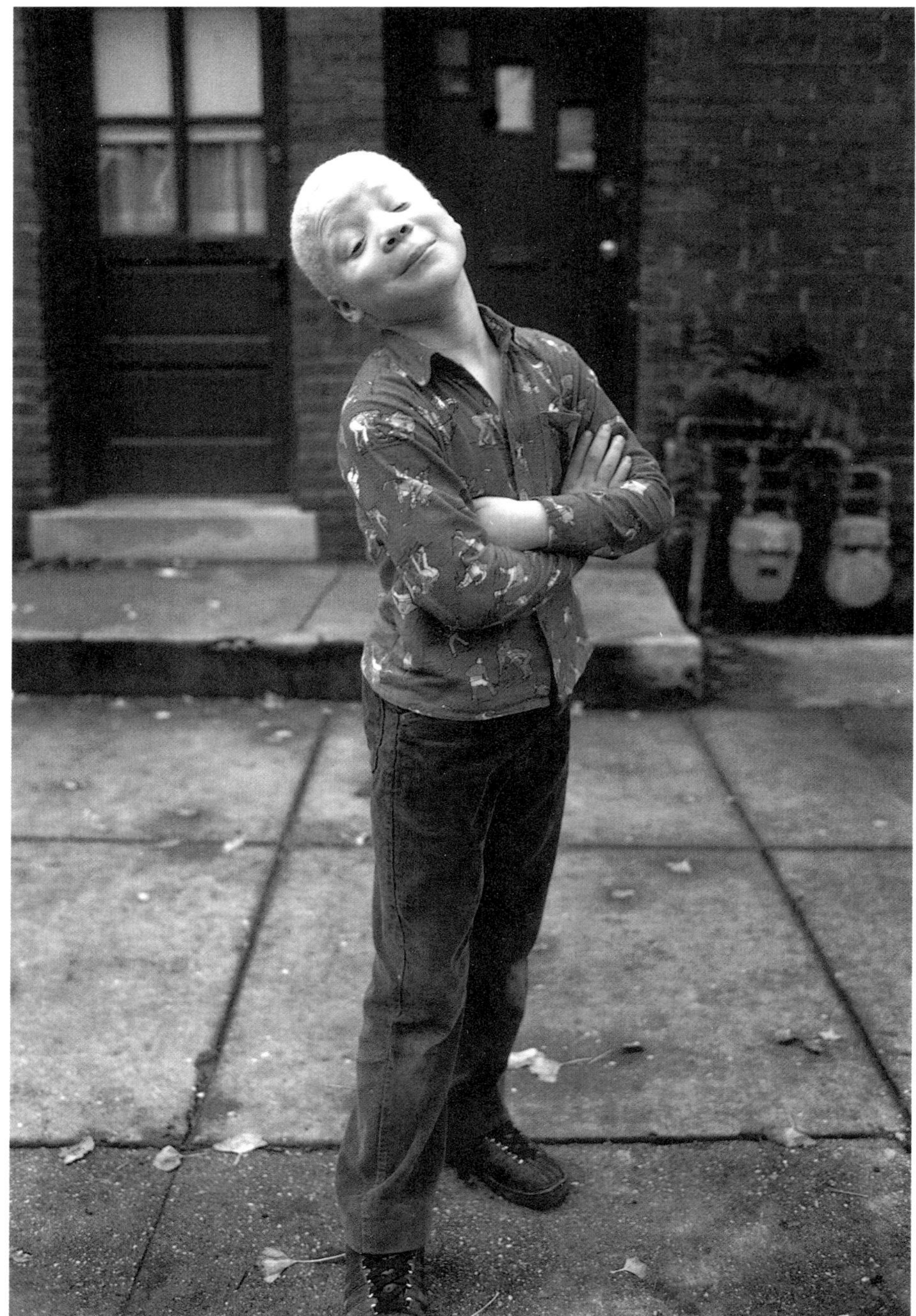

▶▲ *Girl on balcony*

Joseph Maxie, 9
Community of Hope,
Washington, D.C.
1989
11" by 14", silver print

▶▼ *Skateboard*

Tiffany Sewell, 11
Pitts Hotel,
Washington, D.C.
1989
16" by 20", silver print

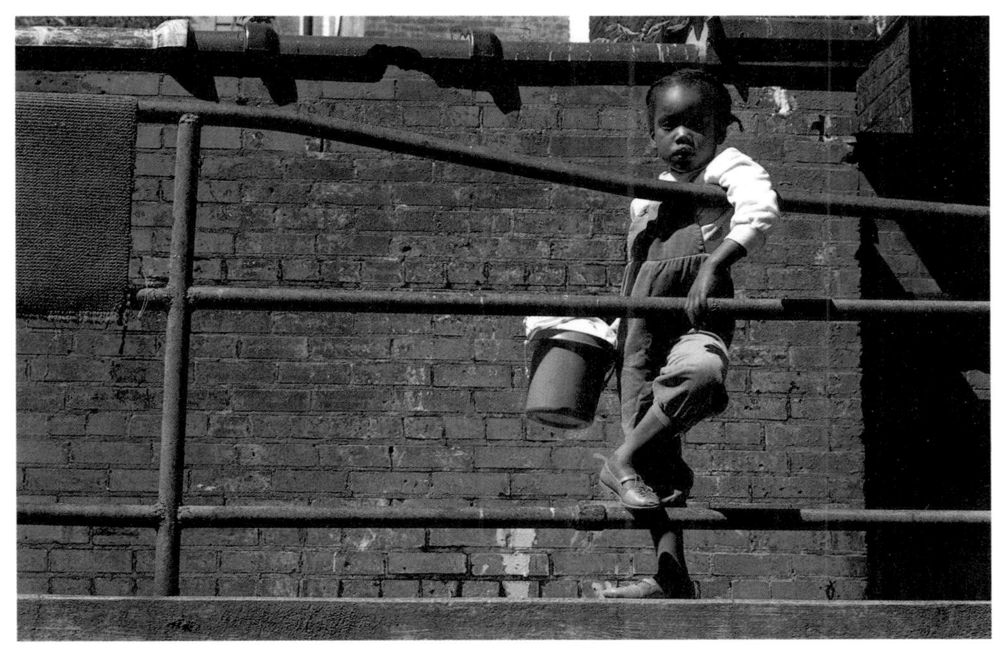

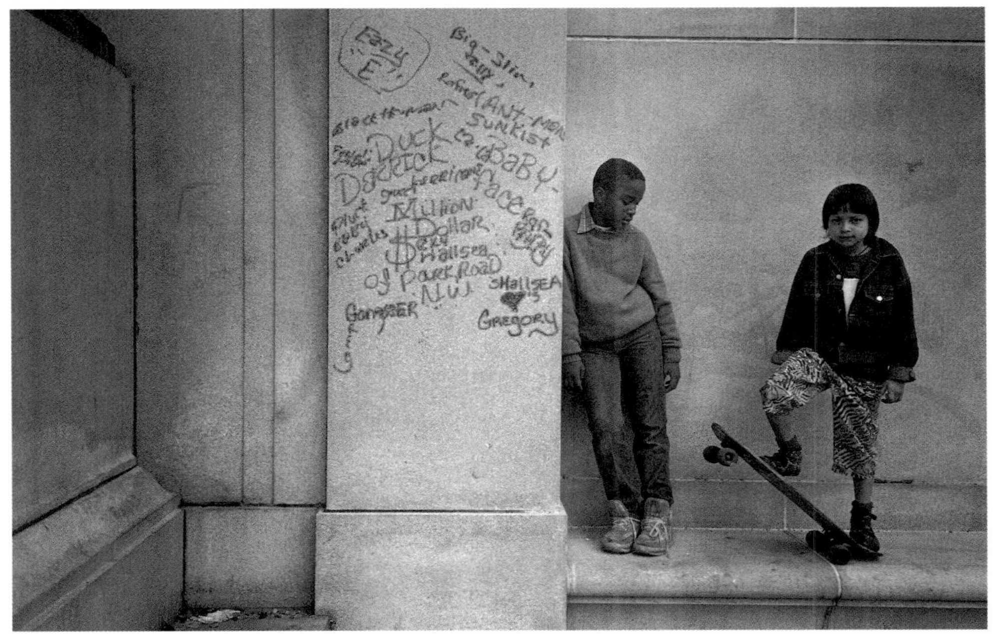
Eazy E
Big-Slim
SUNKIST
Duck
BABY-
face
Million
Dollar
Park Road
N.W.
SHallSEA
GREGORY

▶ *Girl in shelter*

Rasheeda, 10
Community of Hope,
Washington, D.C.
1989
11" by 14", silver print

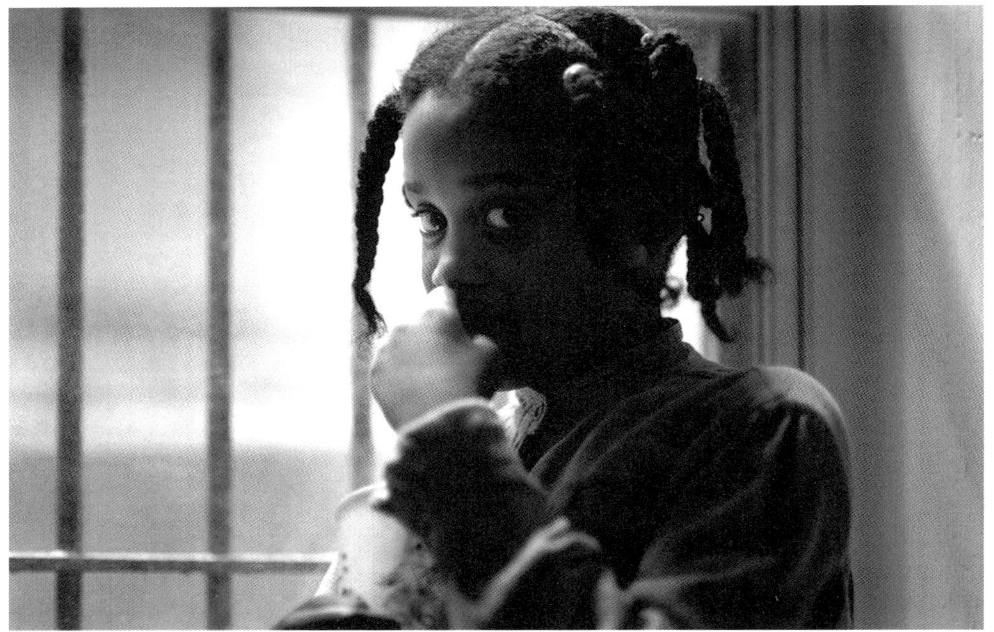

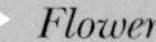 *Flower*

Arthur Taylor, 10
Community of Hope,
Washington, D.C.
1989
11" by 14", silver print

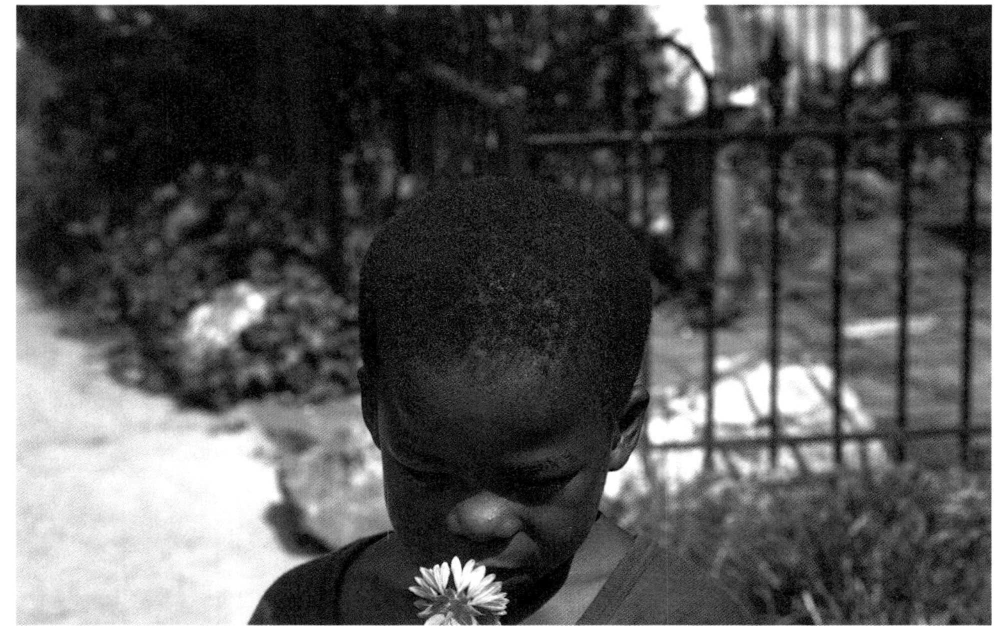

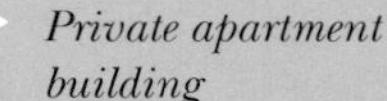 *Private apartment building*

Theresa Ann Taylor, 14
Community of Hope,
Washington, D.C.
1989
11" by 14", silver print

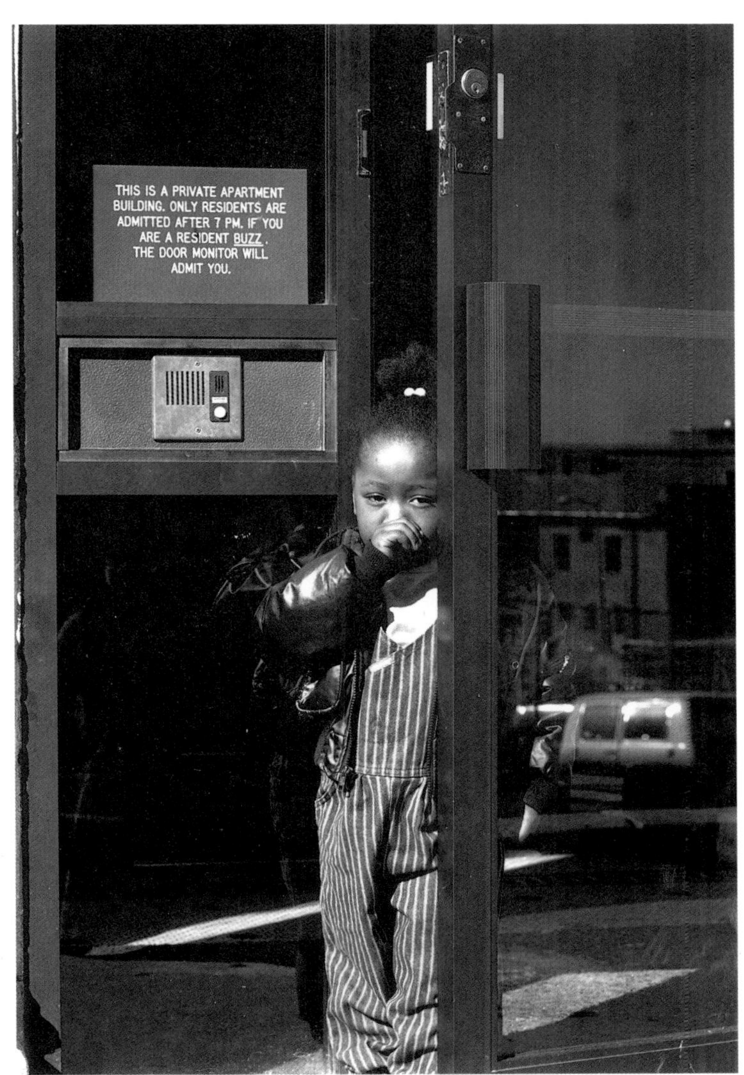
THIS IS A PRIVATE APARTMENT
BUILDING. ONLY RESIDENTS ARE
ADMITTED AFTER 7 PM. IF YOU
ARE A RESIDENT BUZZ.
THE DOOR MONITOR WILL
ADMIT YOU.

Girls

Wayne

Capitol City Inn,
Washington, D.C.
1989
16" by 20", silver print

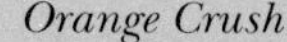 *Orange Crush*

Joseph Maxie, 9

Community of Hope,
Washington, D.C.
1989
11" by 14", silver print

Dion's little brother

Charlene Williams, 10

New residence,
Southwest
Washington, D.C.
1990
11" by 14", silver print

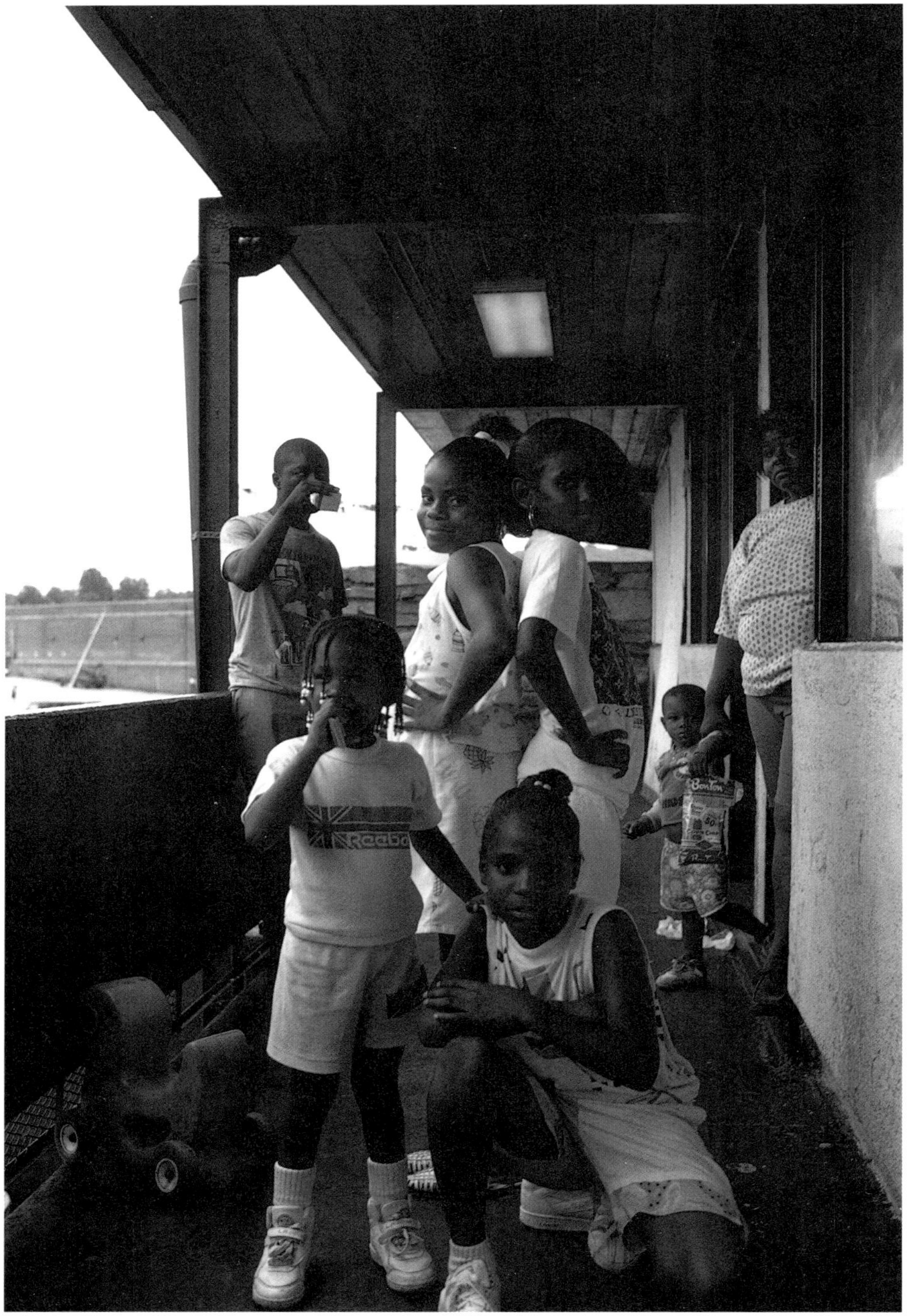

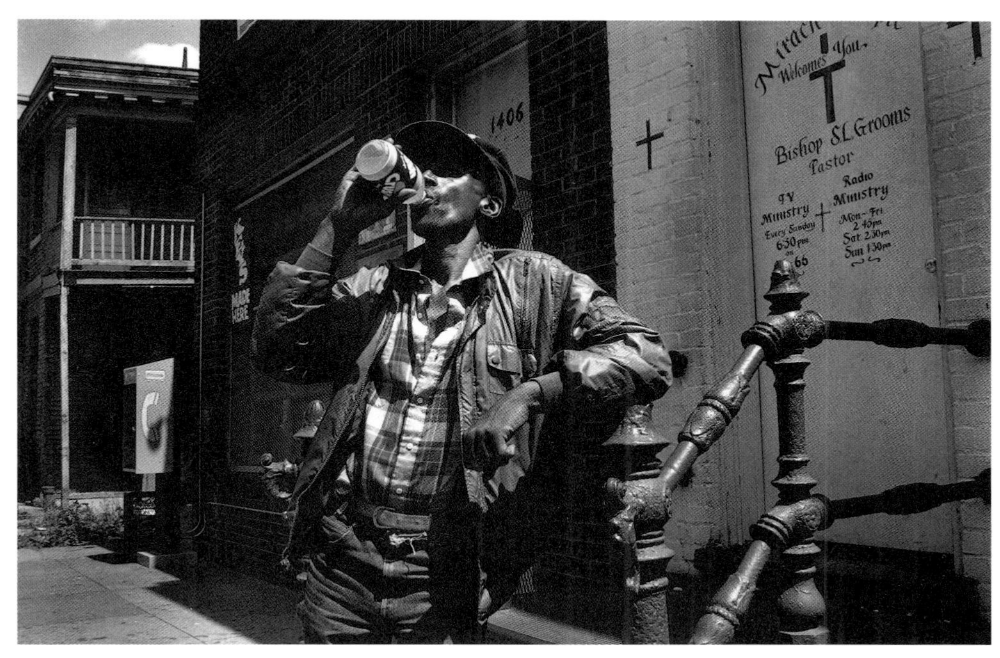
1406
Welcomes You
Bishop S.L. Grooms
Pastor
TV Ministry
Every Sunday
6:30pm
on
66
Radio Ministry
Mon-Fri
2:45pm
Sat 2:30pm
Sun 1:30pm

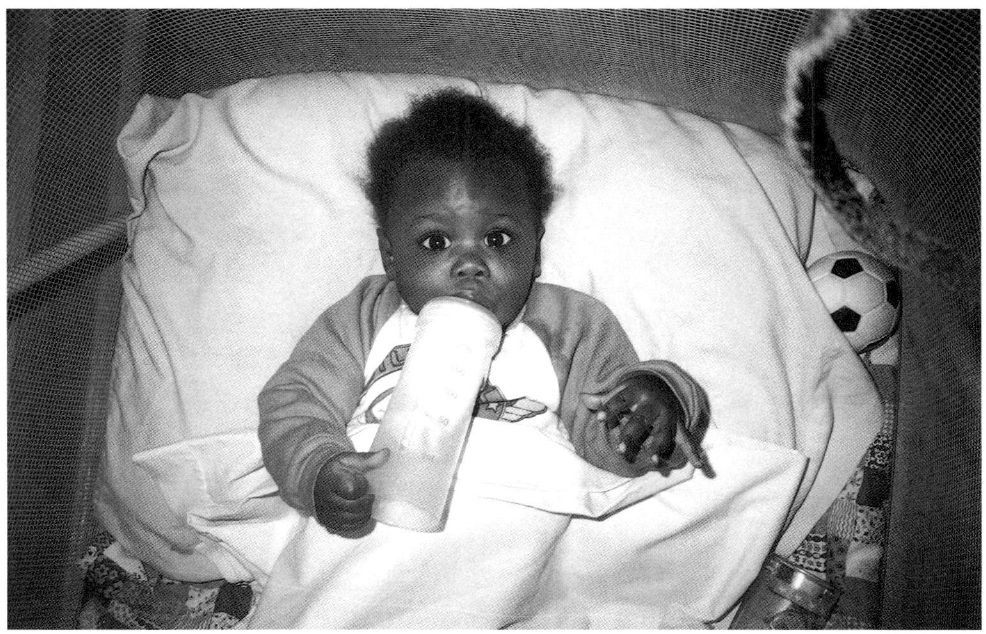

▶ *Girl on fire escape*

Tenisha Stephens, 9

Community of Hope,
Washington, D.C.
1989
16" by 20", silver print

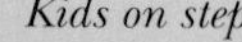 *Kids on step*

Shalinda

Capitol City Inn,
Washington, D.C.
1989
11" by 14", silver print

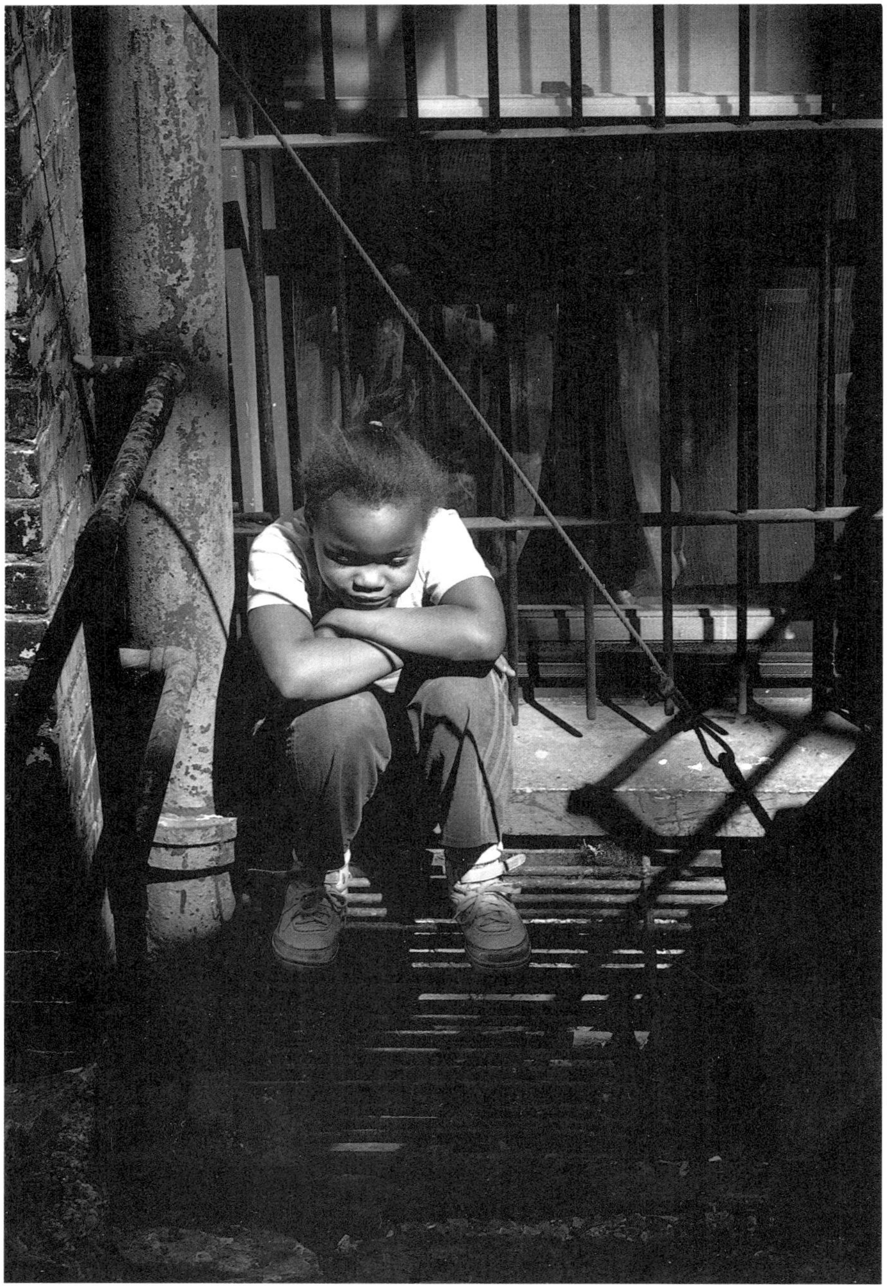

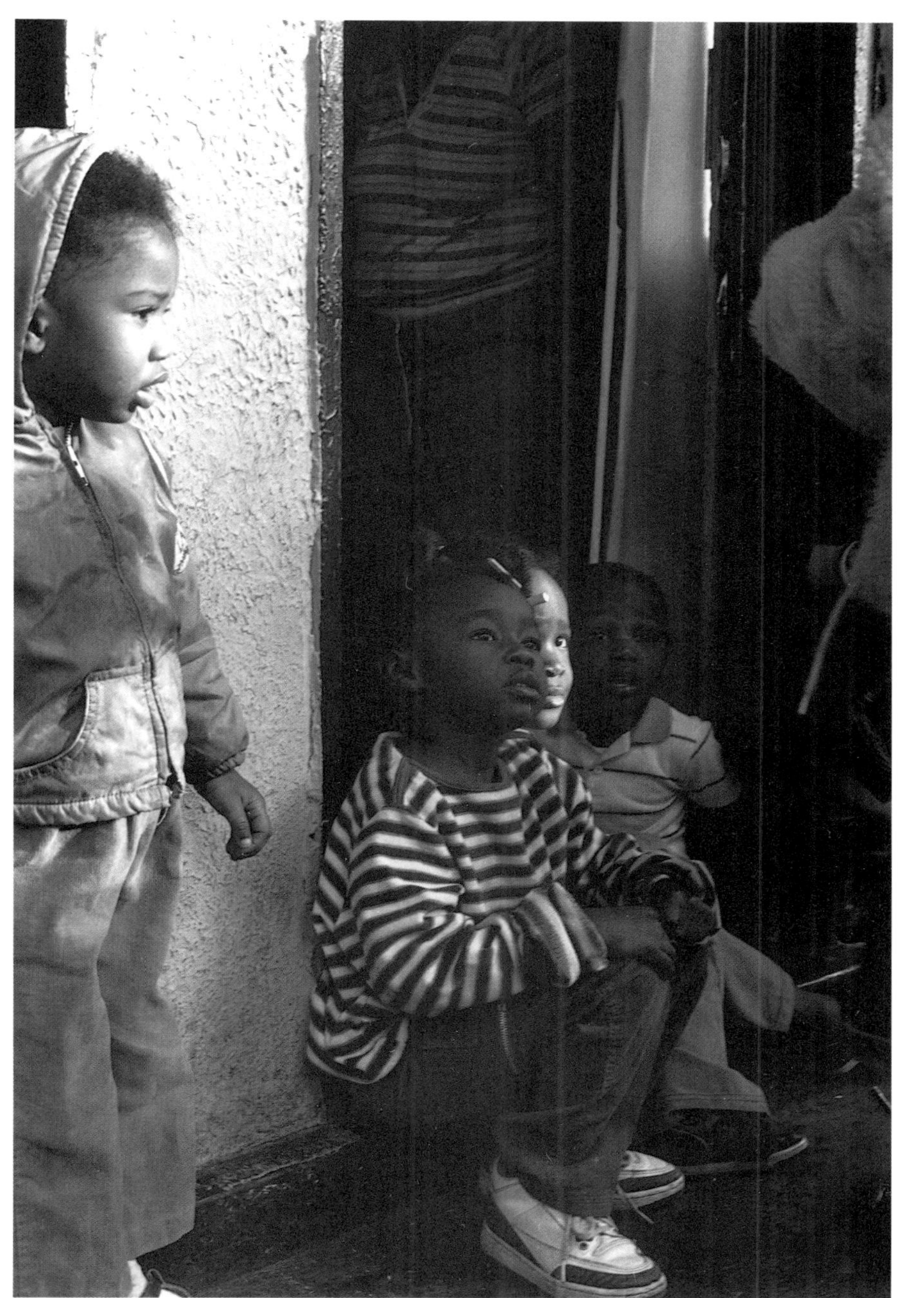

▶ *Boys in alley*

George Maxie, 10
Community of Hope,
Washington, D.C.
1989
11" by 14", silver print

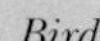 *Bird*

Charlene Williams, 11
new residence,
Southeast
Washington, D.C.
1990
16" by 20", silver print

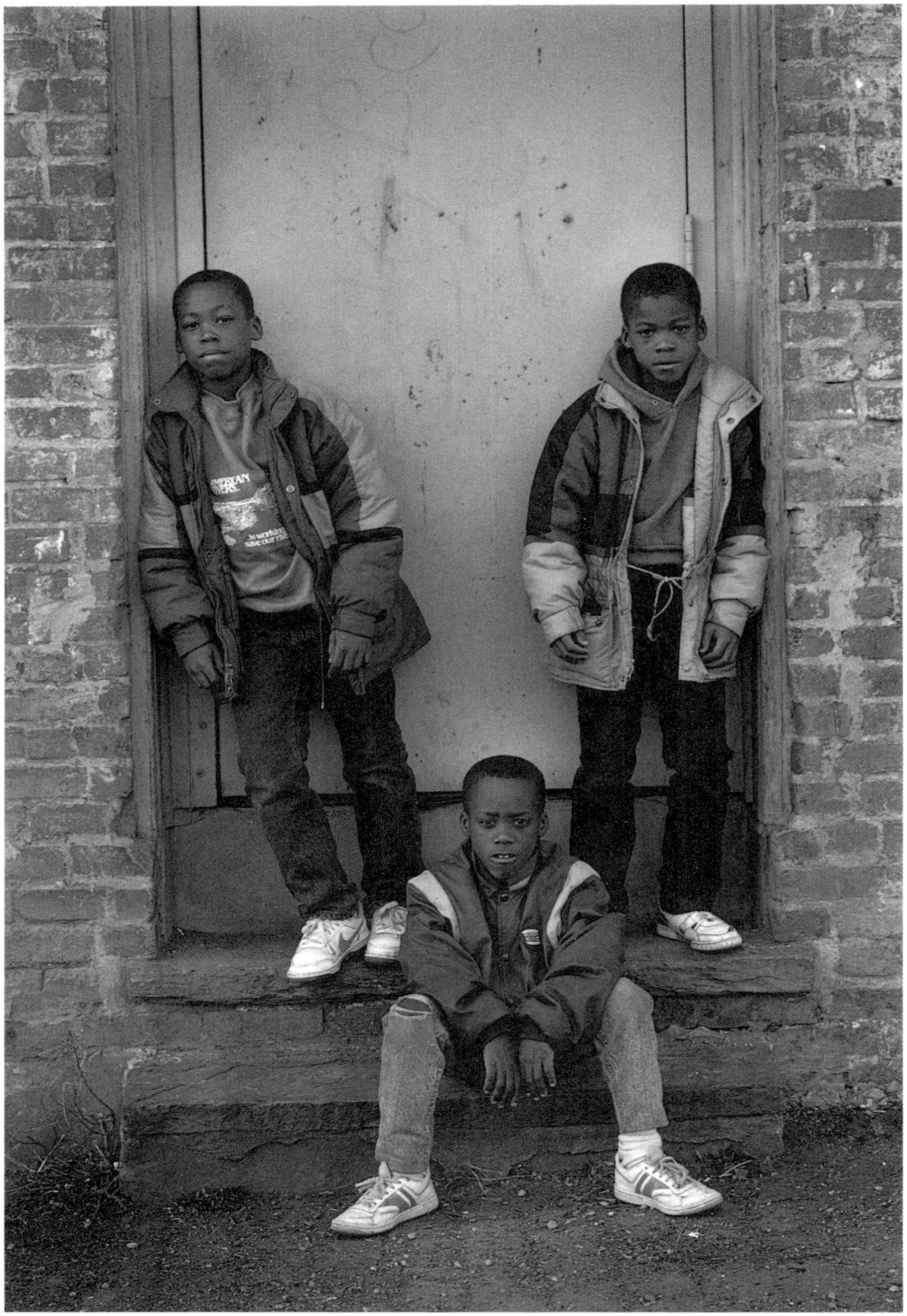

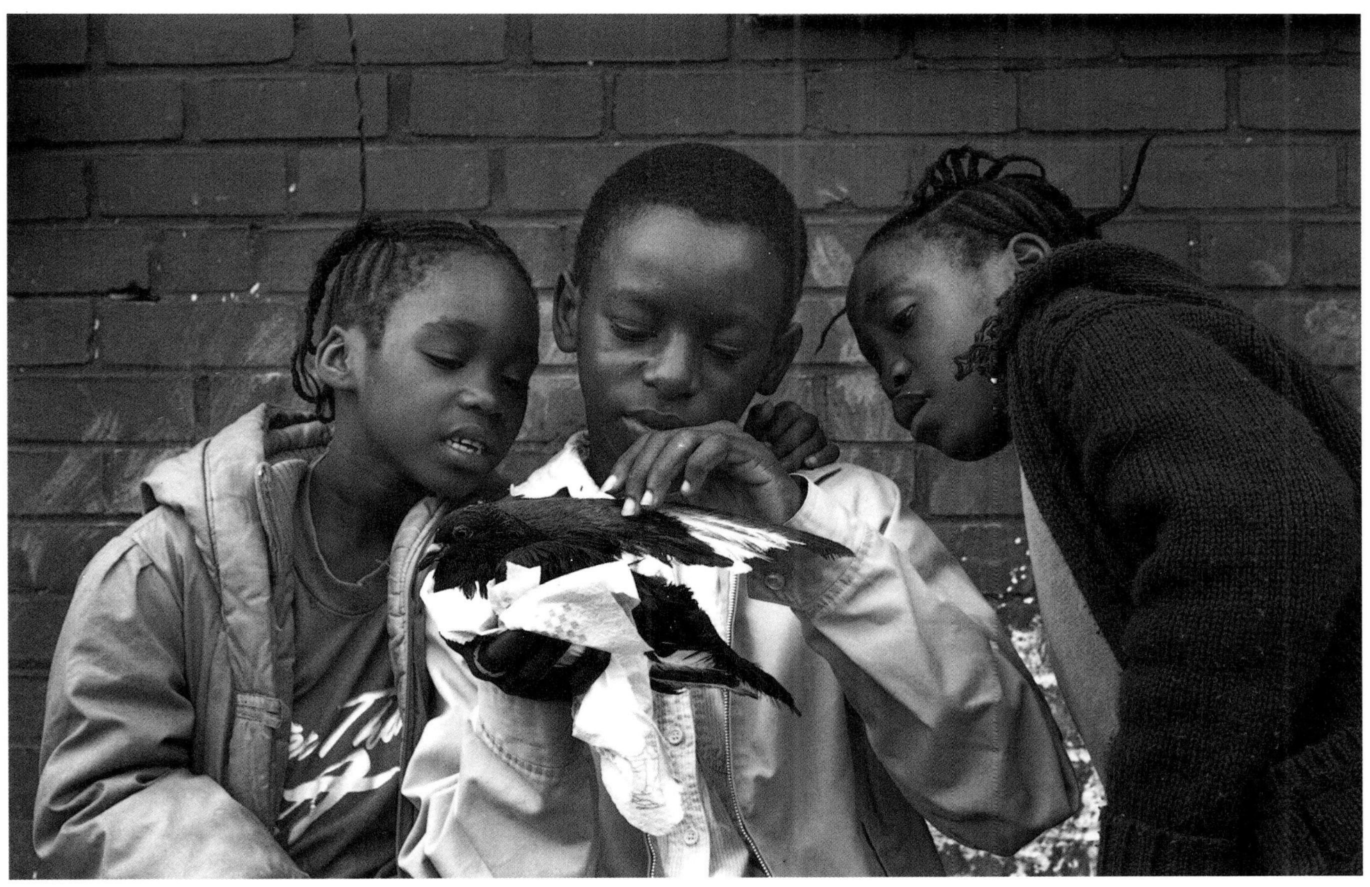

CHARLENE'S COMMENT My favorite picture that I took: that's me and my brother and my sister with a pigeon. My brother had found a pigeon, and the pigeon had been shot in the wing. My brother was trying to fix it, so I just told my brother to look at it, and I just put the timer on, focused it, and I ran over there to get into the picture. I want to be a photographer. COMMENT TO CHARLENE FROM SCHOOLCHILD I saw your picture, Birds, in the exhibit in New York. I saw it from way across the room and I felt drawn to it. . . . The girl on the left, her teeth show, like she understood pain and in that instant, experienced it for the bird.

▶ *Boy in shelter*

Carissa Etheridge, 15
Community of Hope,
Washington, D.C.
1989
16" by 20", silver print

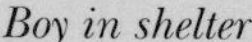

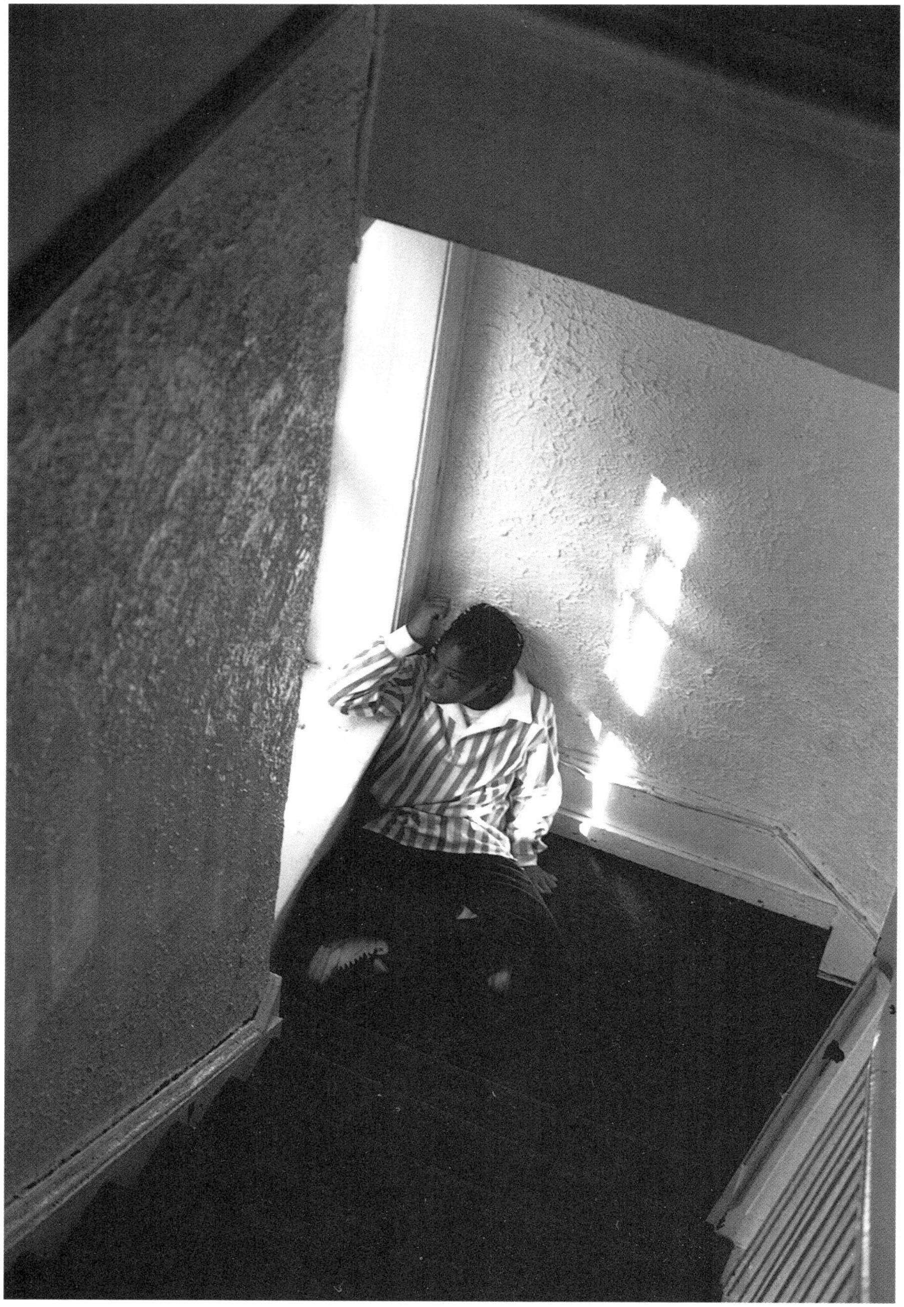

Boy in shelter

Tamicka Hodge, 12
Community of Hope,
Washington, D.C.
1989
11" by 14", silver print

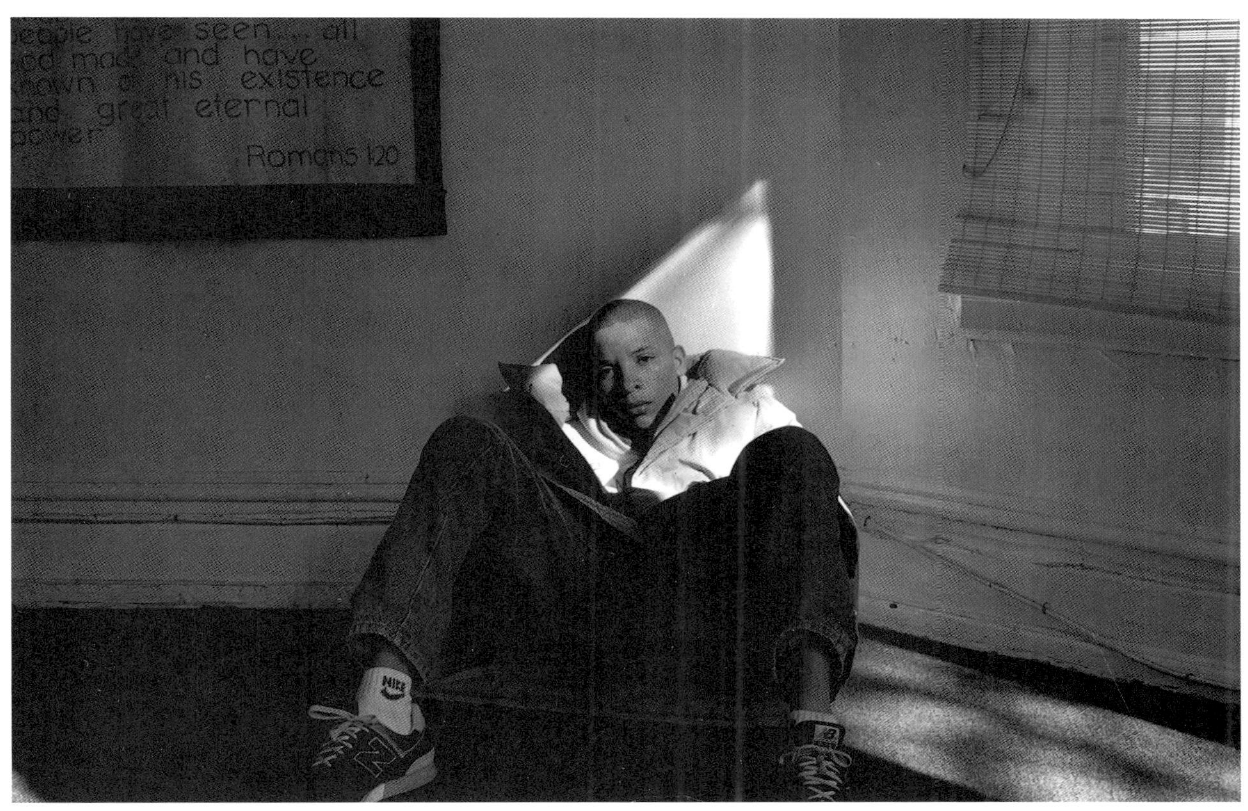
seen ... all
and have
his existence
eternal
Romans 1:20

▶ *Child in window*

David Burch, 12
Capitol City Inn,
Washington, D.C.
1989
11" by 14", silver print

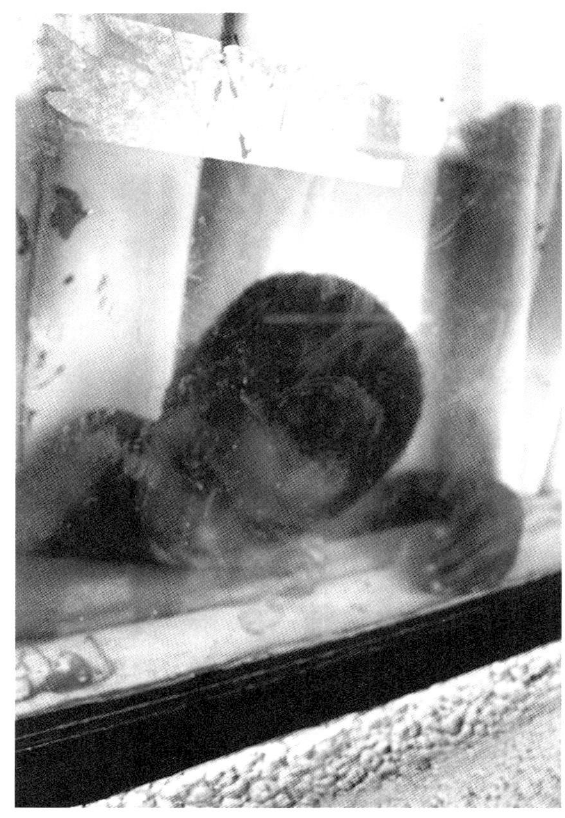

▶ *Looking in window*

Arthur Taylor, 10
new residence,
Southeast
Washington, D.C.
1989
11" by 14", silver print

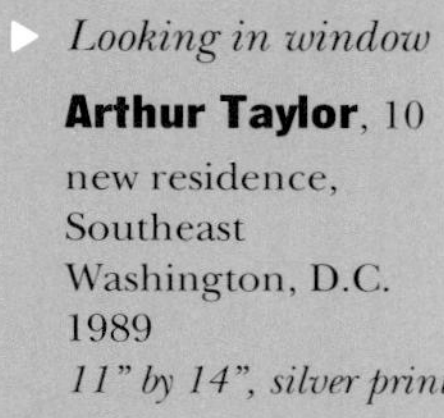

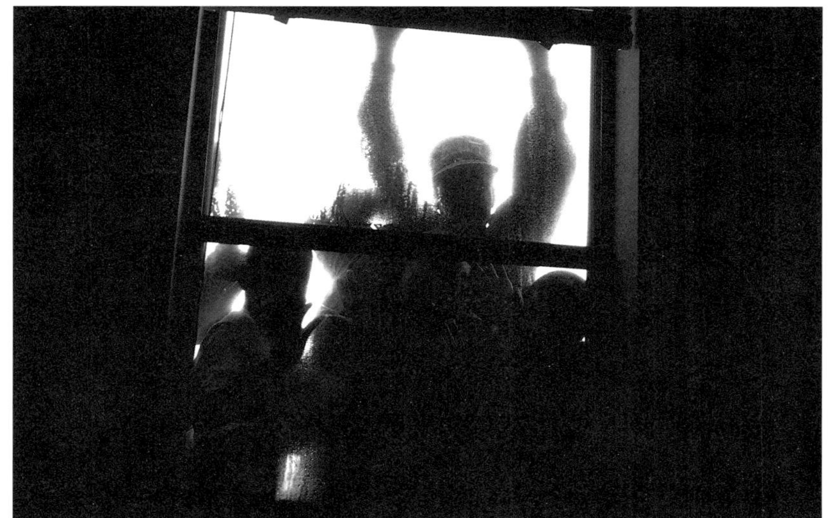

▶▶ *Back to the shelter*

Nicole Mitchell, 11
Community of Hope,
Washington, D.C.
1989
11" by 14", silver print

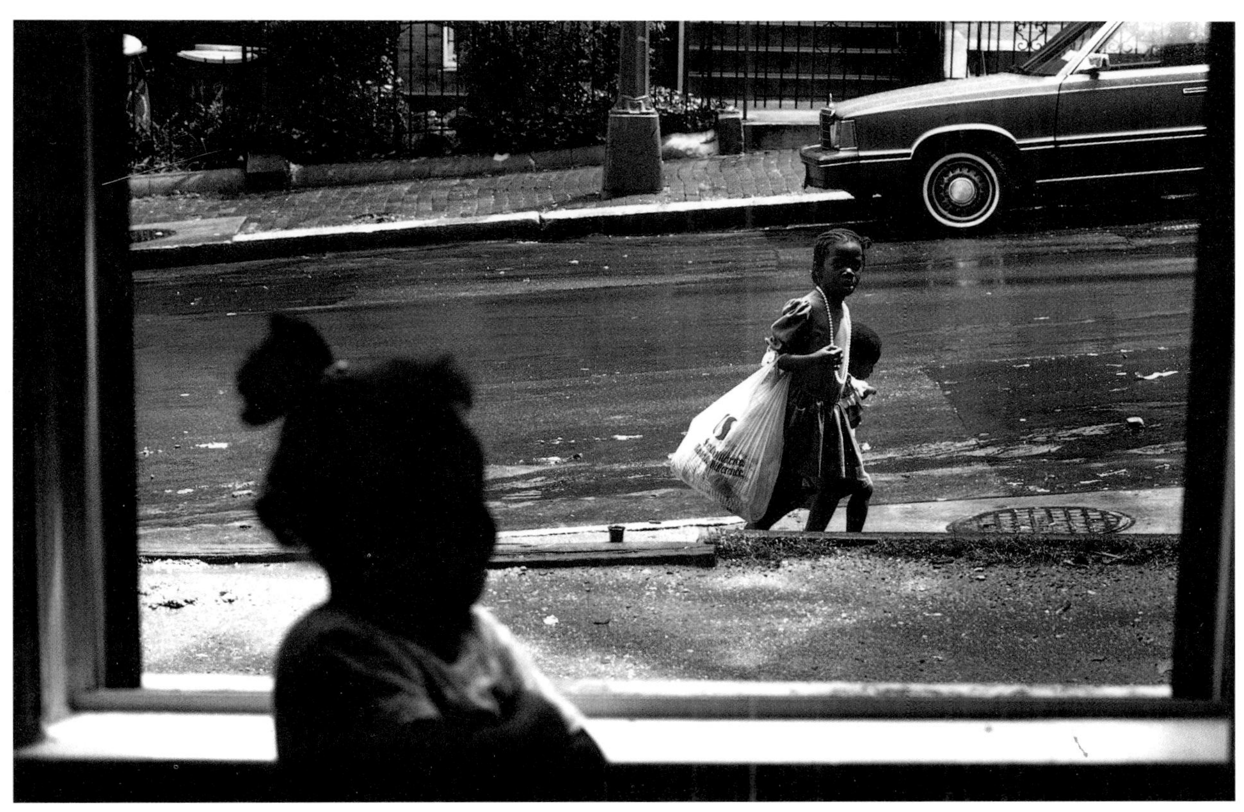

COMMENT FROM SCHOOLCHILD By looking at these pictures it makes me feel that I am happy for what I have in life.

▸ *Children*

Daniel Hall, 9

Capitol City Inn,
Washington, D.C.
1989
11" by 14", silver print

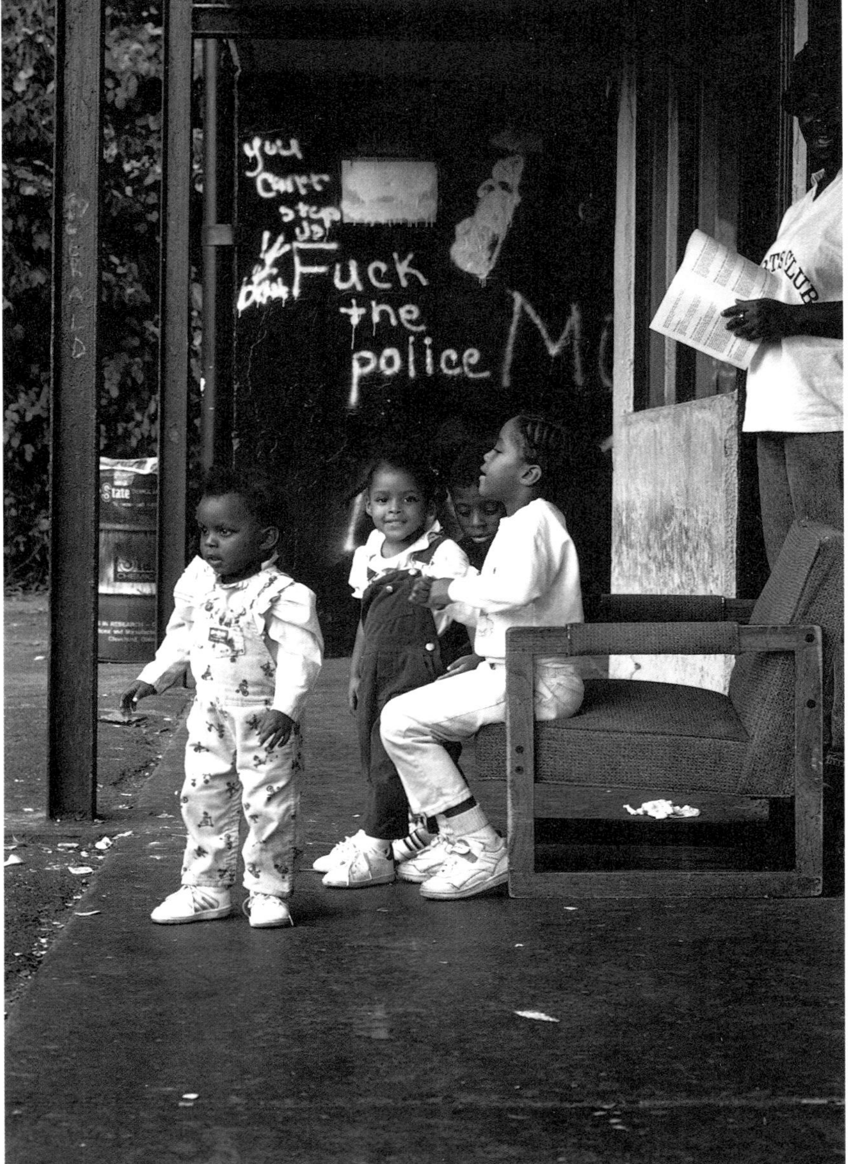

▸▸ *Boy*

Daniel Hall, 9

Pitts Hotel,
Washington, D.C.
1989
16" by 20", silver print

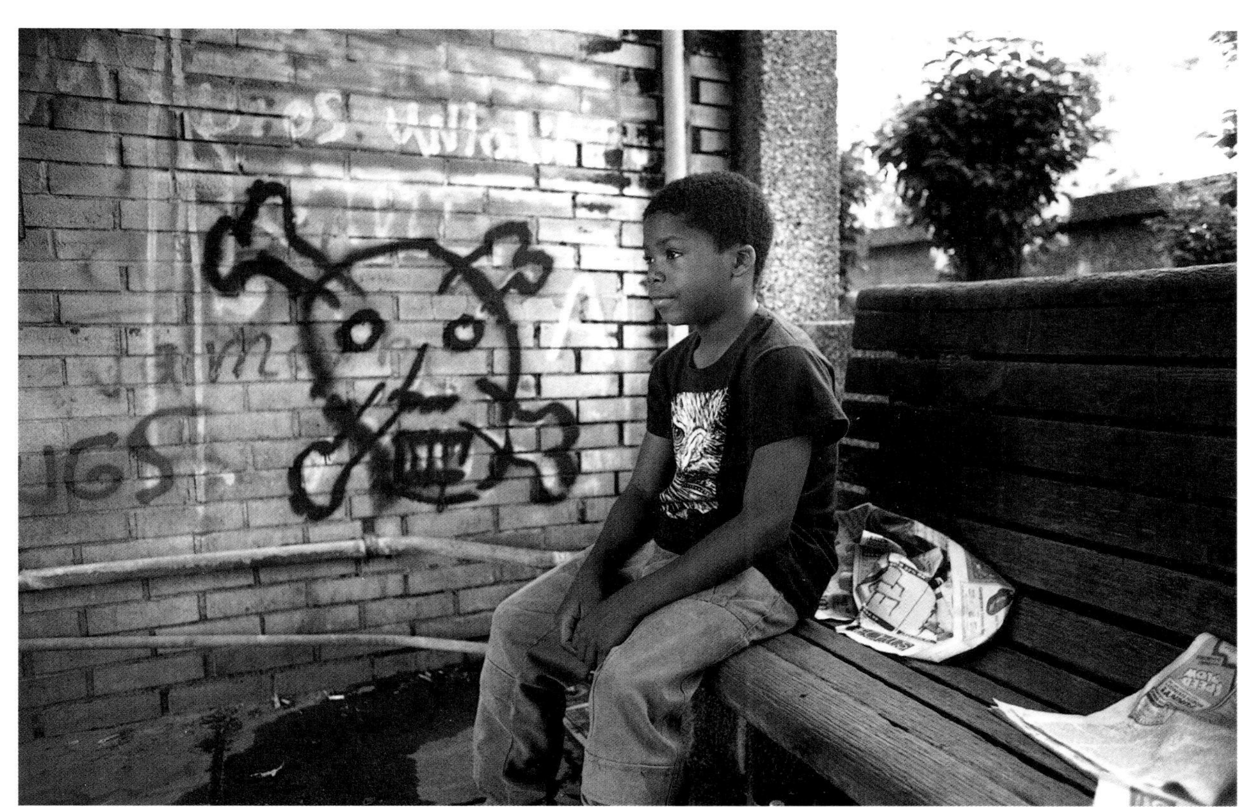

Play

Chris Heflin, 9
The Carpenter's Shelter,
Alexandria, Virginia
1990
11" by 14", silver print

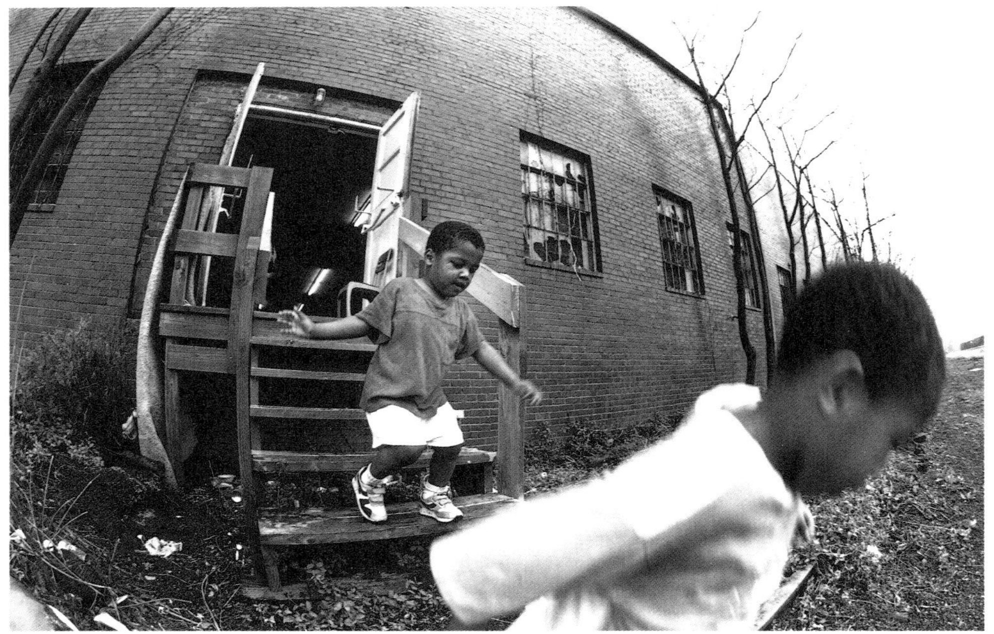

Playing behind shelter

Tikela Findley, 12
The Carpenter's Shelter,
Alexandria, Virginia
1990
11" by 14", silver print

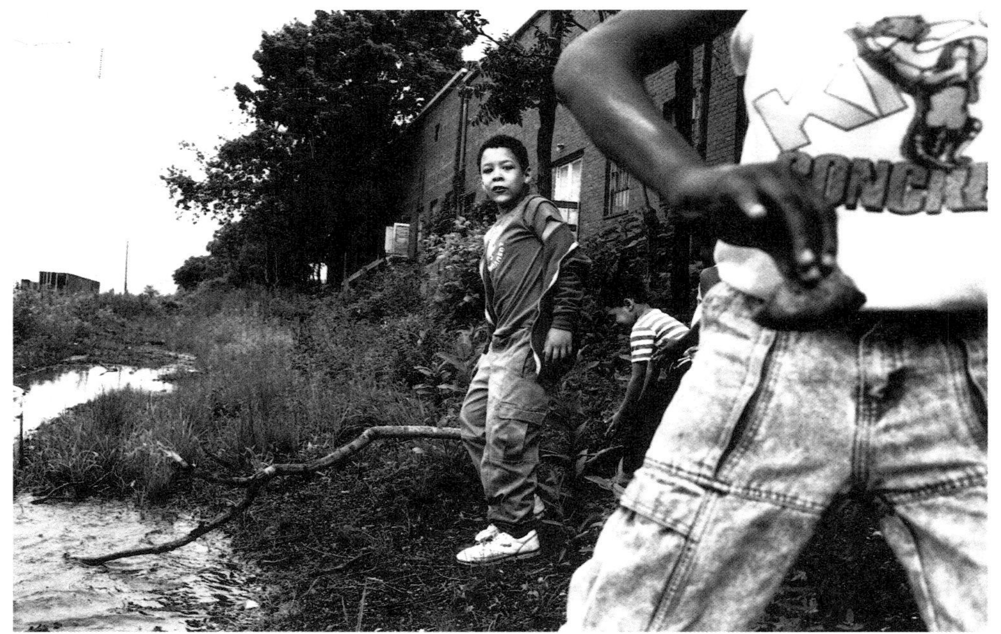

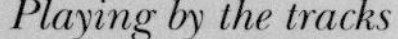

Playing by the tracks

Chris Heflin, 9
The Carpenter's Shelter,
Alexandria, Virginia
1990
16" by 20", silver print

CHRIS'S COMMENTS This is the kids on the train tracks, jumping. They are at the shelter. The best part of the shelter is the train track.

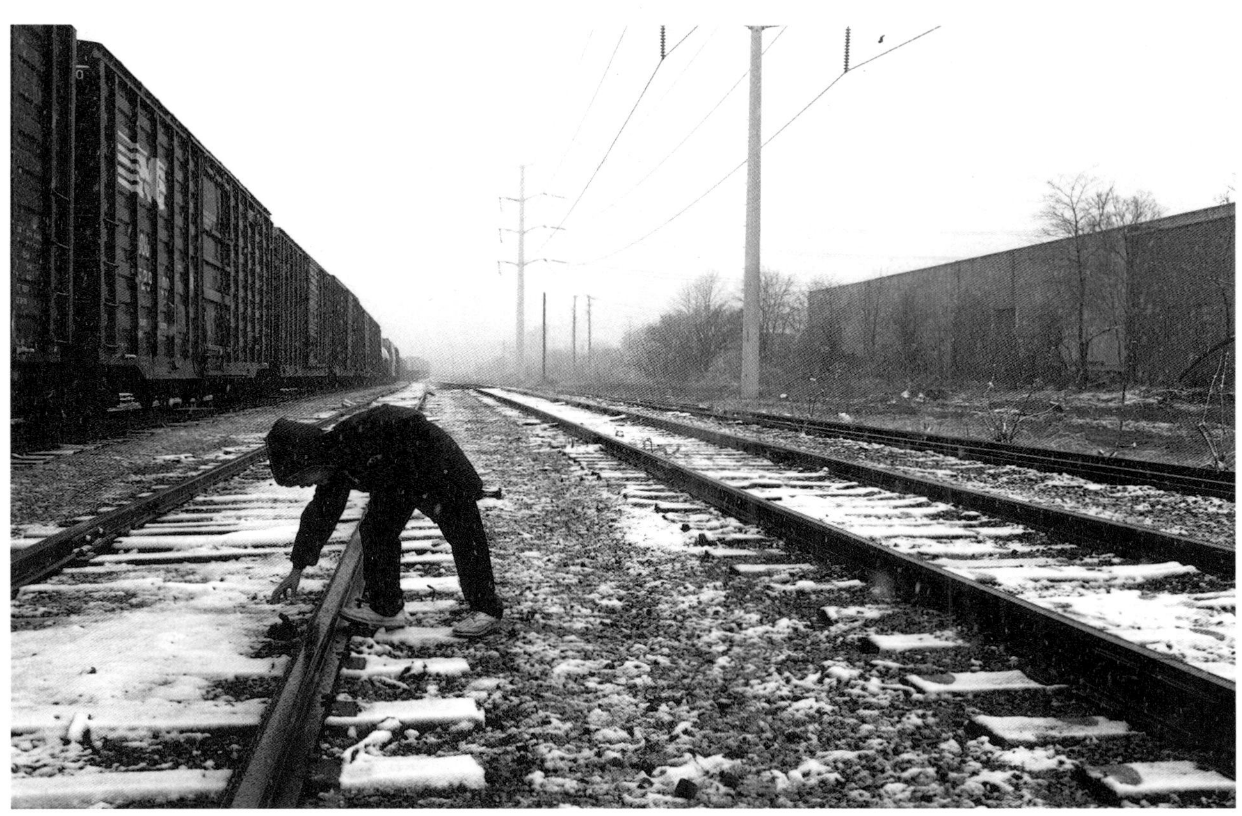

▶ *Pitts Hotel, Washington, D.C.; hotel used to house homeless families, closed 1990*

David Burch, 12
Pitts Hotel,
Washington, D.C.
1989
11" by 14", silver print

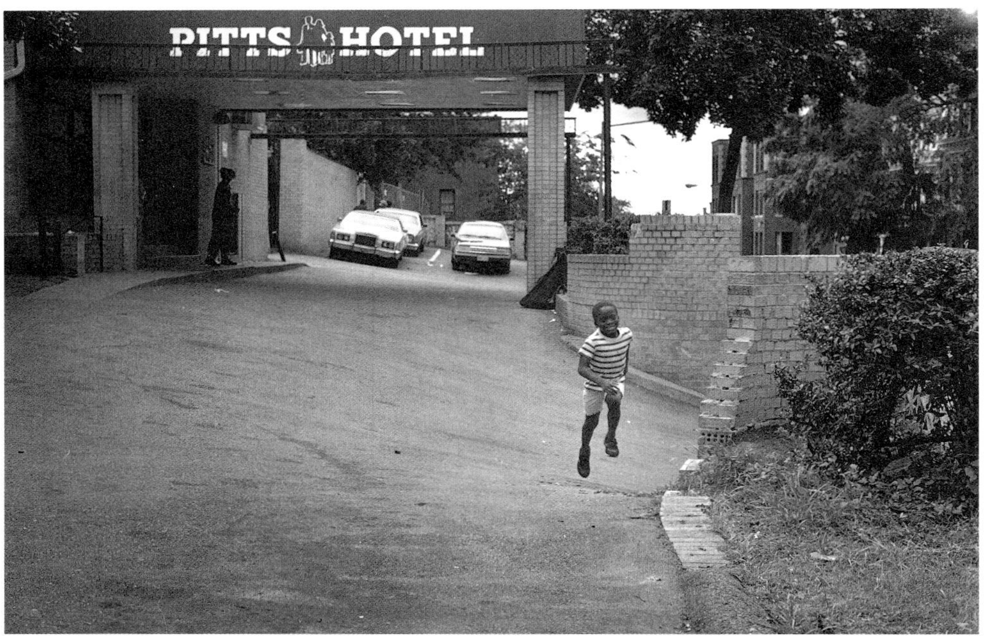

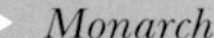 *Monarch*

Rasheeda, 10
Capitol City Inn,
Washington, D.C.
1989
11" by 14", silver print

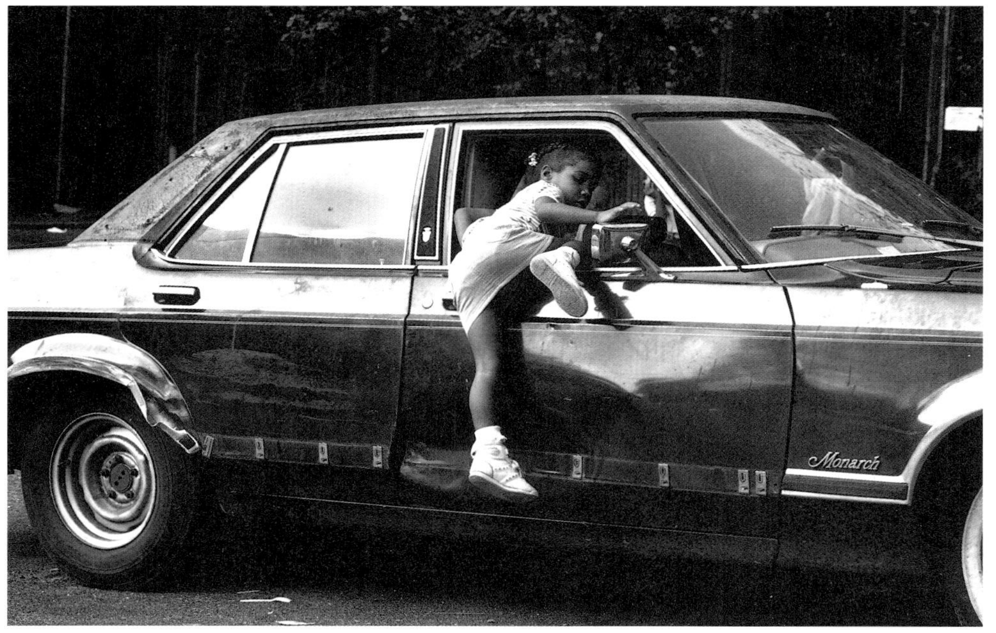

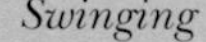 *Swinging*

Charlene Williams, 11
new residence,
Southeast
Washington, D.C.
1990
16" by 20", silver print

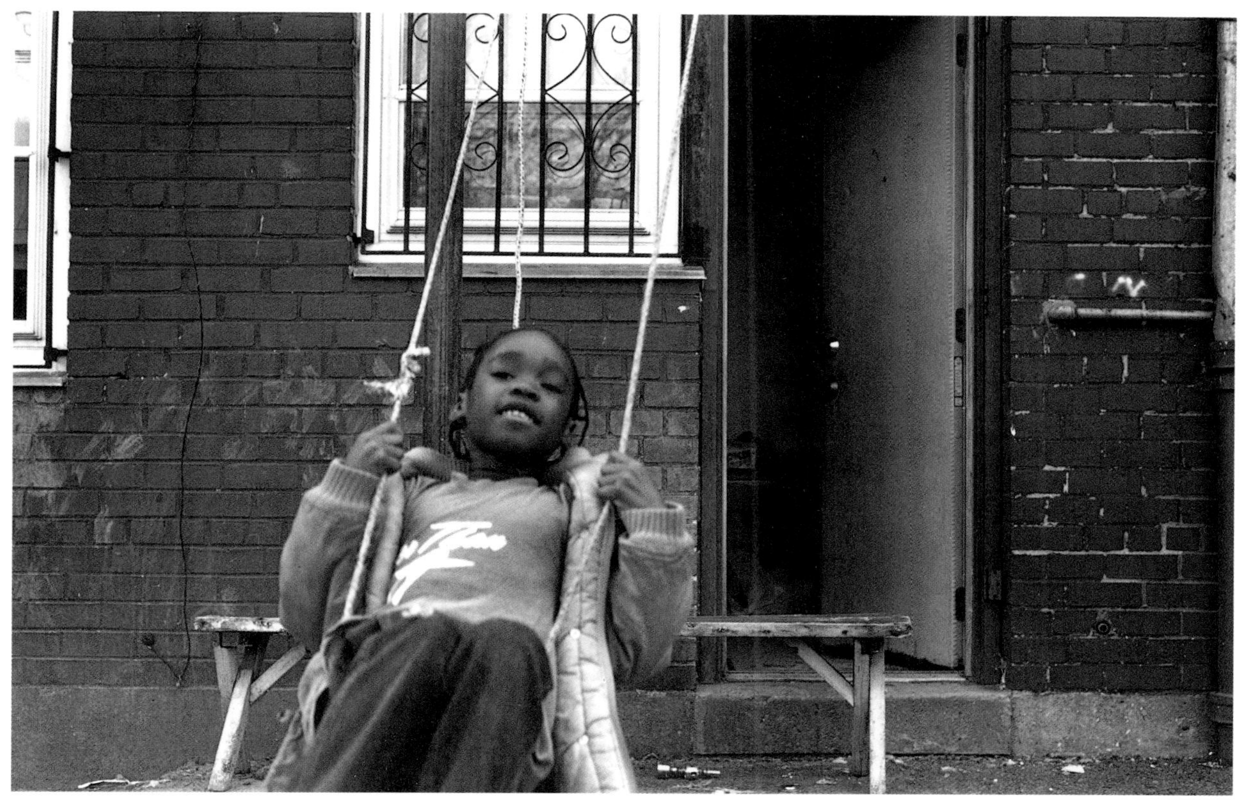

COMMENT FROM PEPPERTINA (CHARLENE'S SISTER, IN THE SWING) **I would like to leave earth to the planet Mars.**

▶ *Double-dutch jump rope*

Dion Johnson, 11
Capitol City Inn,
Washington, D.C.
1989
11" by 14", silver print

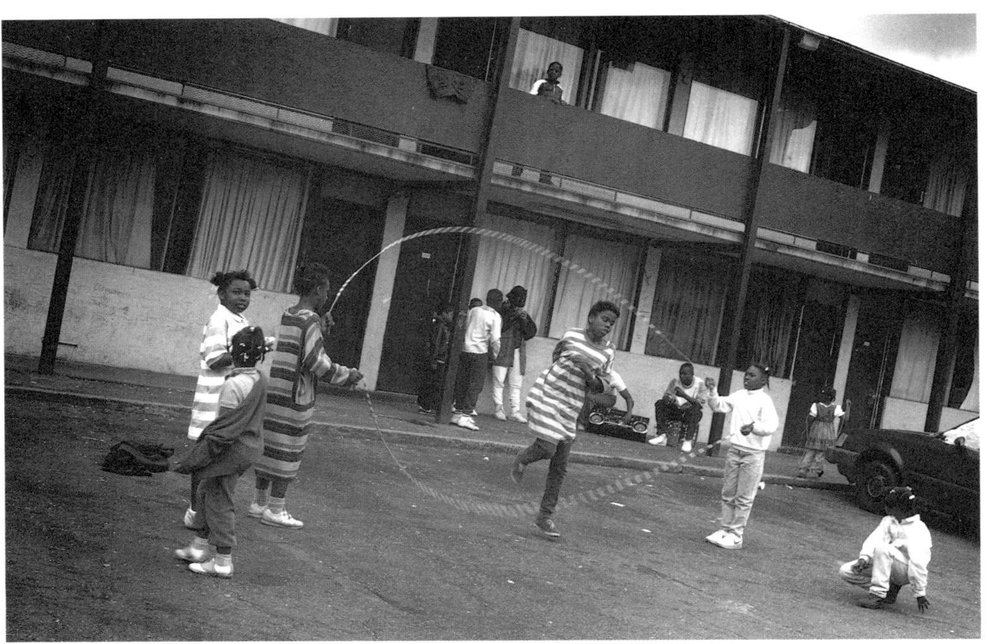

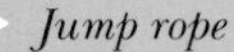 *Jump rope*

Calvin Stewart, 17
Clifton Terrace,
Community of Hope,
Washington, D.C.
1989
11" by 14", silver print

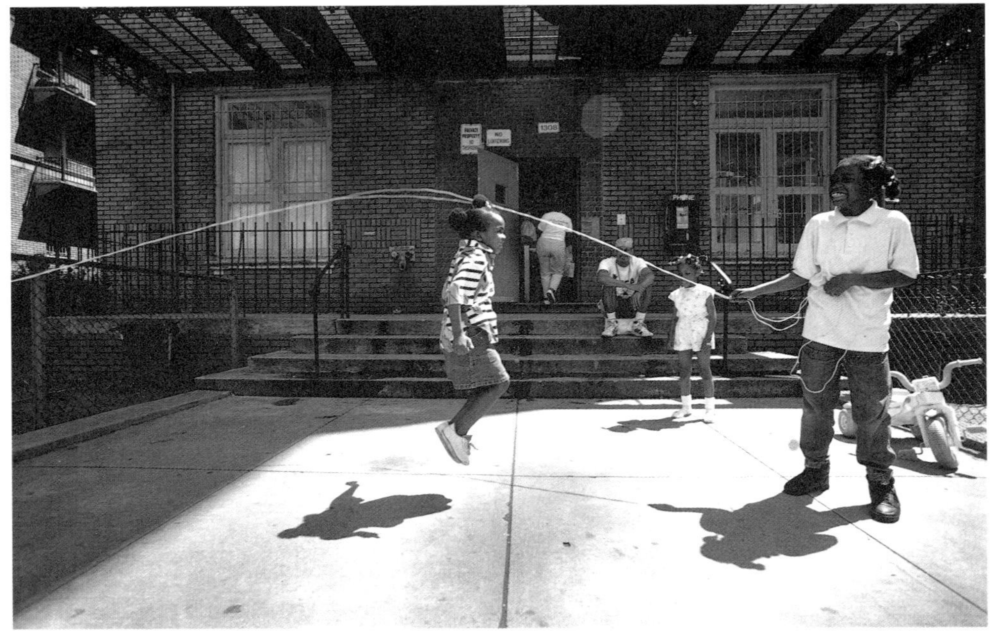

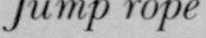 *Jump rope*

Tenisha Stephens, 9
Community of Hope,
Washington, D.C.
1989
11" by 14", silver print

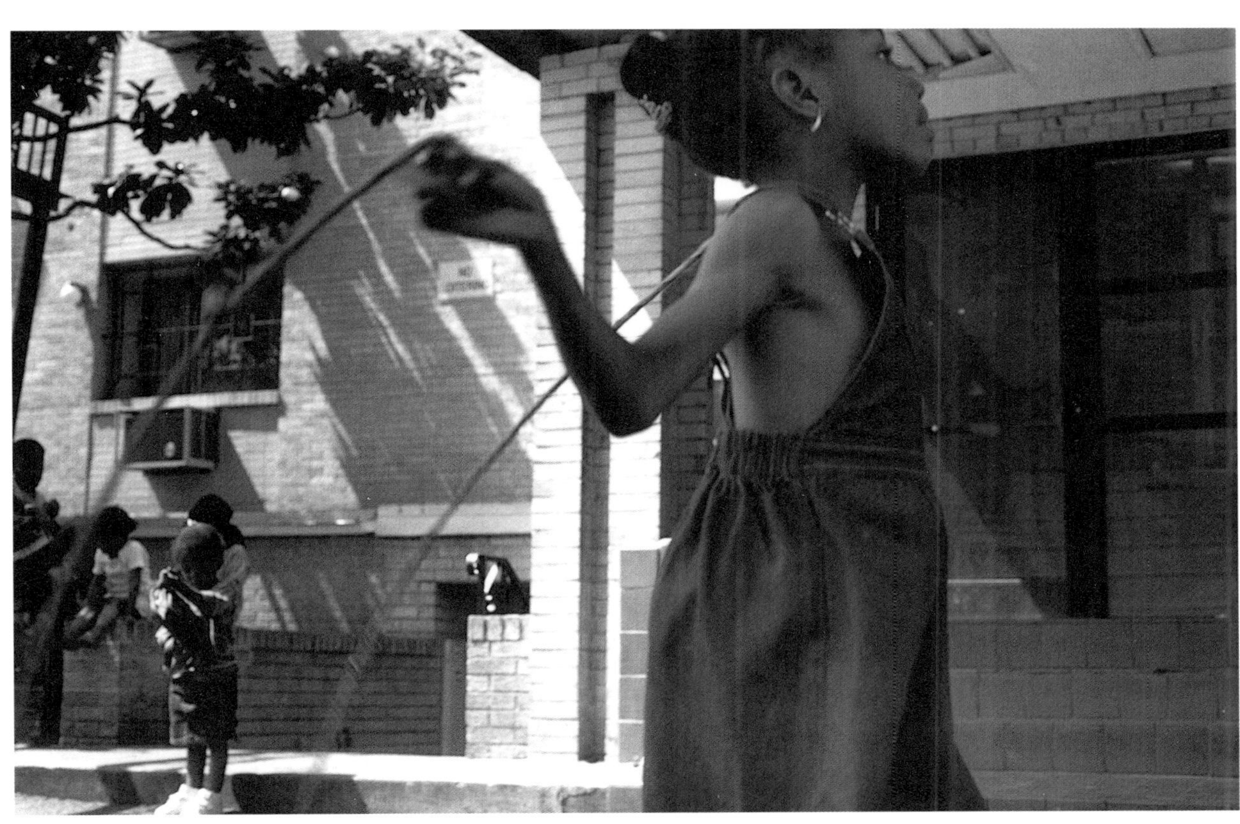

▶ *Swimming*
Alex Christian
Pitts Hotel,
Washington, D.C.
1989
11" by 14", silver print

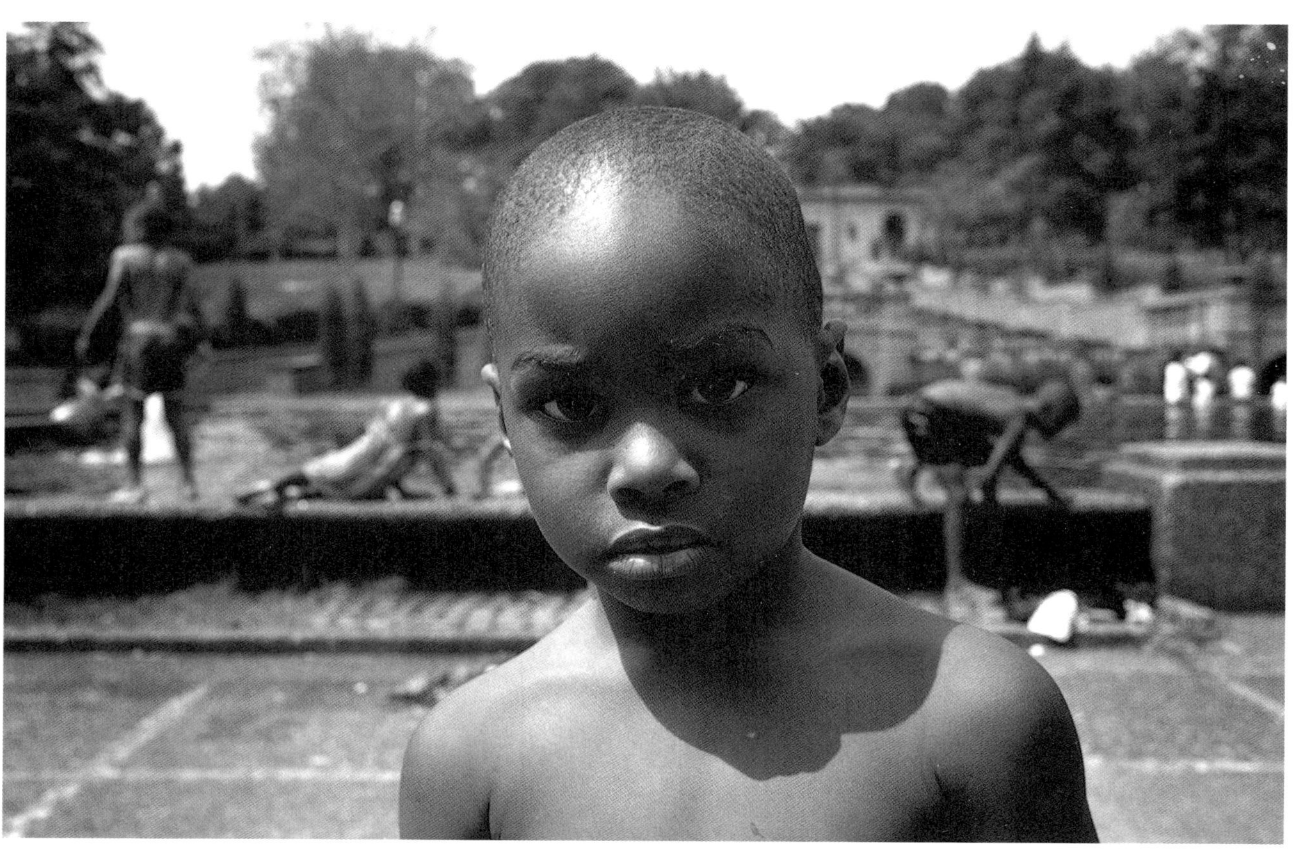

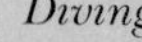 *Diving*

Columbia Thomas, 11
Malcolm X Park,
Pitts Hotel,
Washington, D.C.
1989
11" by 14", silver print

▶▼ *Showing off*
Columbia Thomas, 11
Malcolm X Park,
Pitts Hotel,
Washington, D.C.
1989
11" by 14", silver print

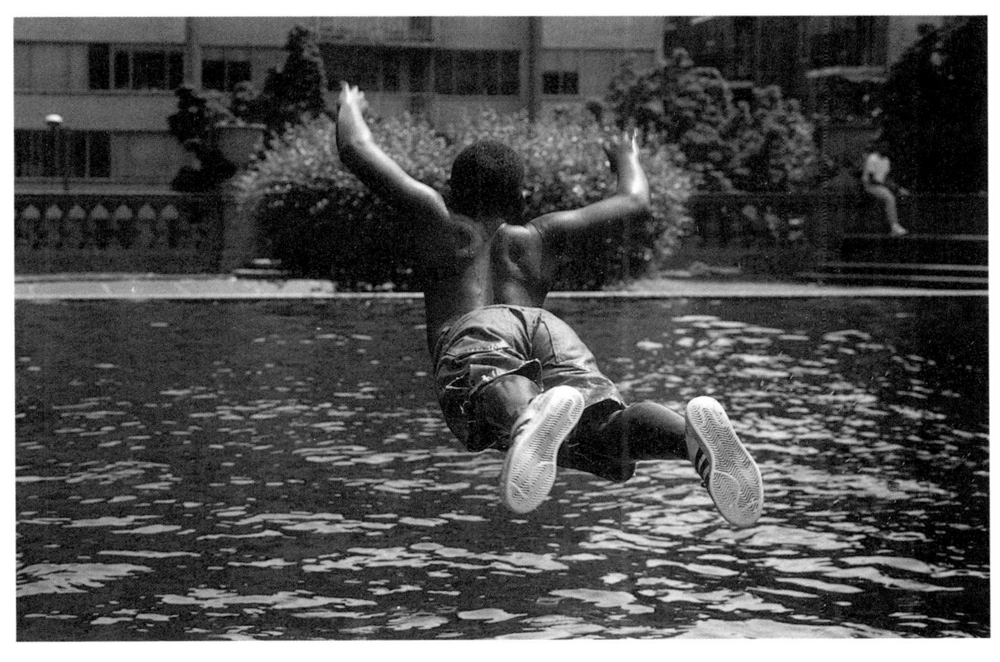

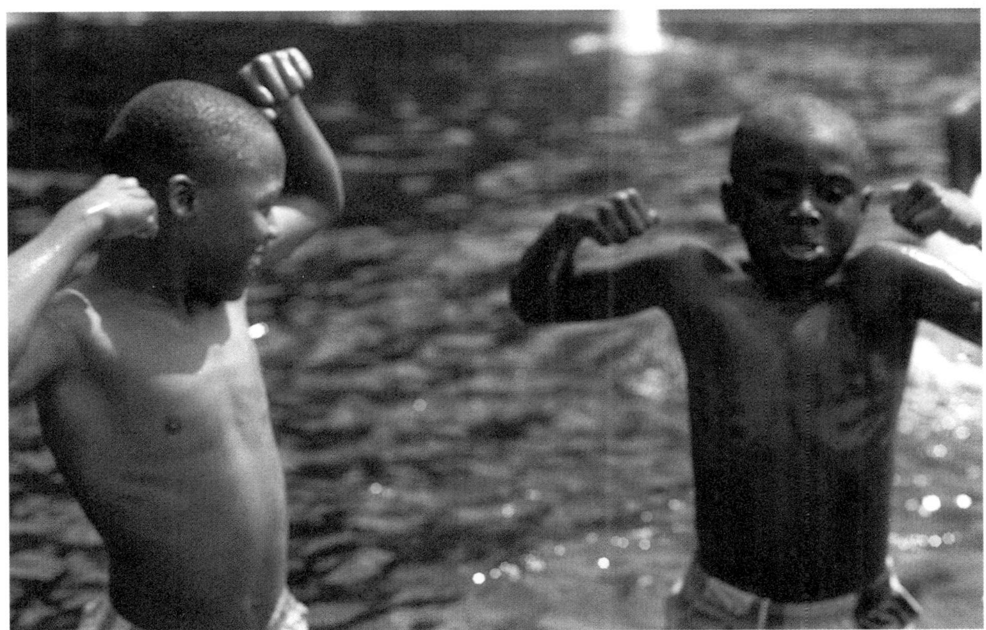

Cooling off

Dion Johnson, 11
Capitol City Inn,
Washington, D.C.
1989
11" by 14", silver print

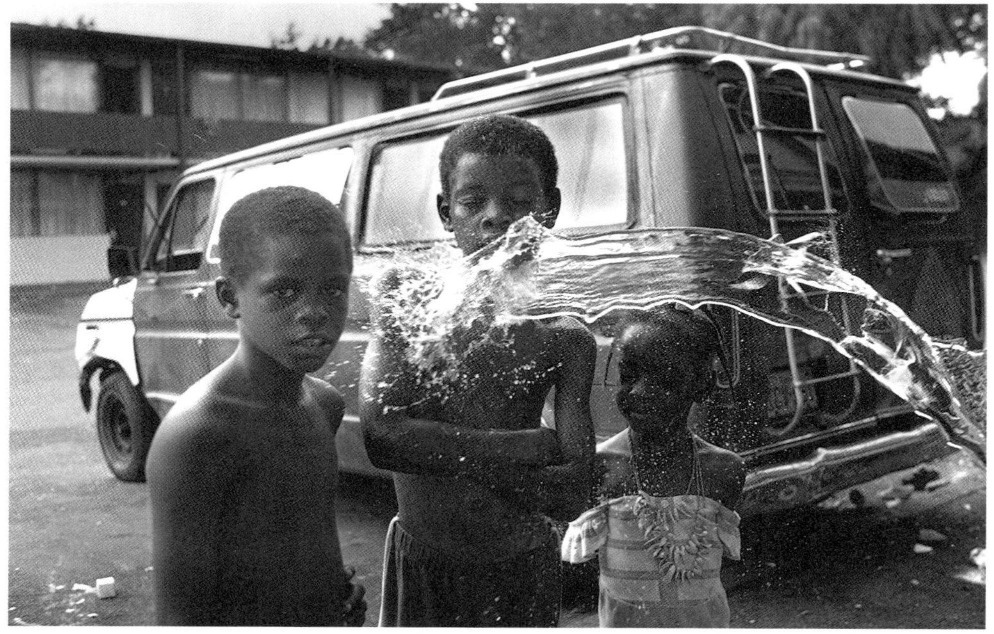

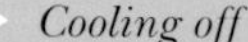 *Cooling off*

Dion Johnson, 11
Capitol City Inn,
Washington, D.C.
1989
11" by 14", silver print

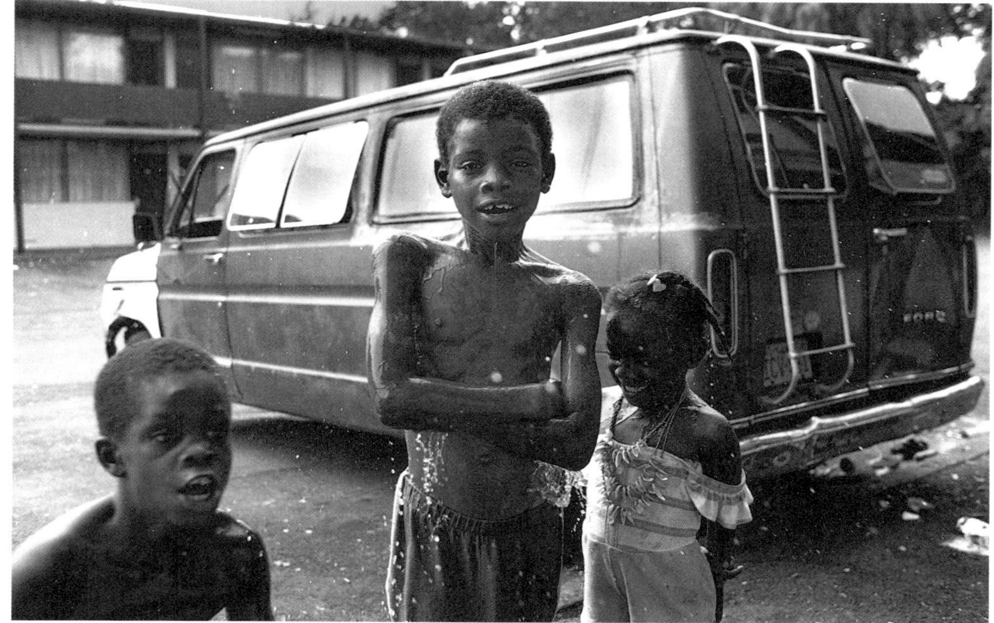

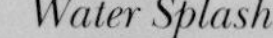 *Water Splash*

Dion Johnson, 11
Capitol City Inn,
Washington, D.C.
1989
11" by 14", silver print

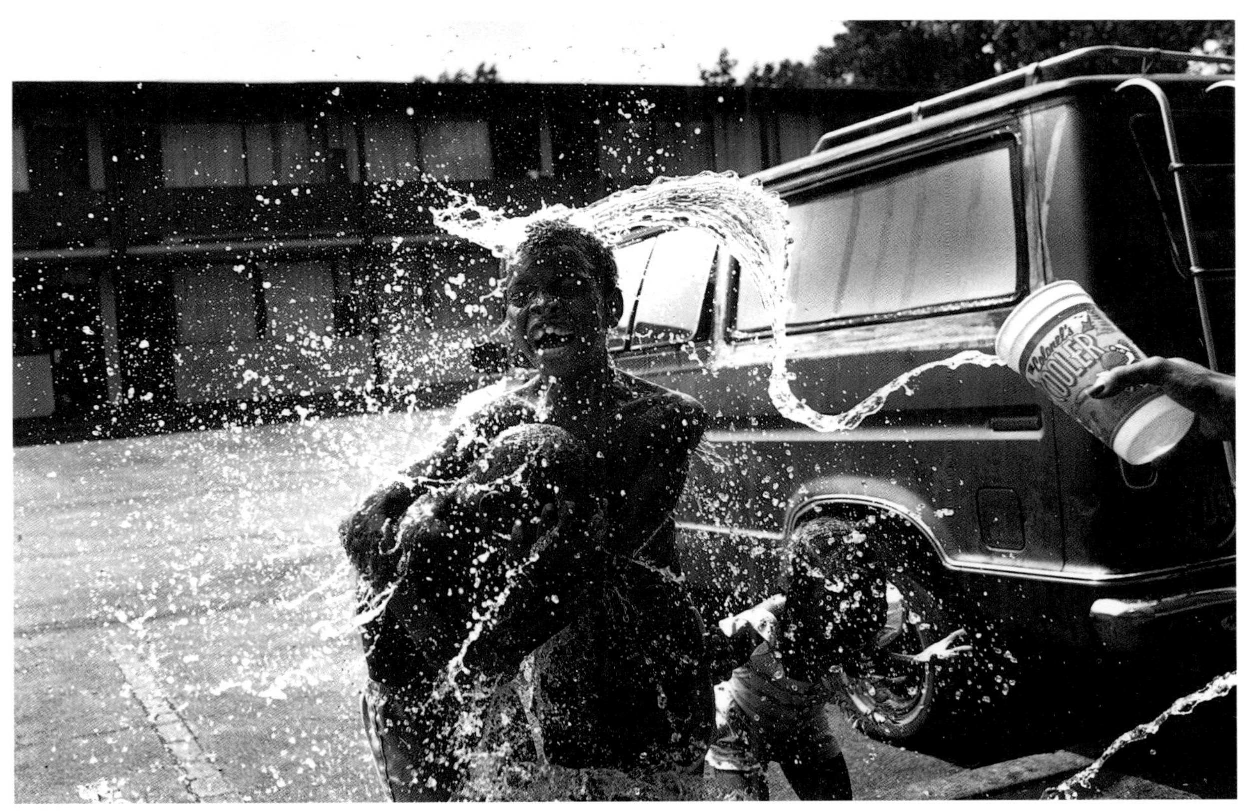

DION'S COMMENT One day at Capitol City Inn we had a water fight and I told my friend and his sister to pose so I could take their picture. His mother took a cup of water and threw it on them. **COMMENT TO DION FROM SCHOOLCHILD** I like the . . . picture of the kid getting splashed with water, I like how the kid sits there and barely notices the water.

▶ *Hopscotch*

Linda Christian

Community of Hope,
Washington, D.C.
1989
11" by 14", silver print

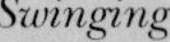

Swinging

Dion Johnson, 12

new residence,
Southwest
Washington, D.C.
1990
11" by 14", silver print

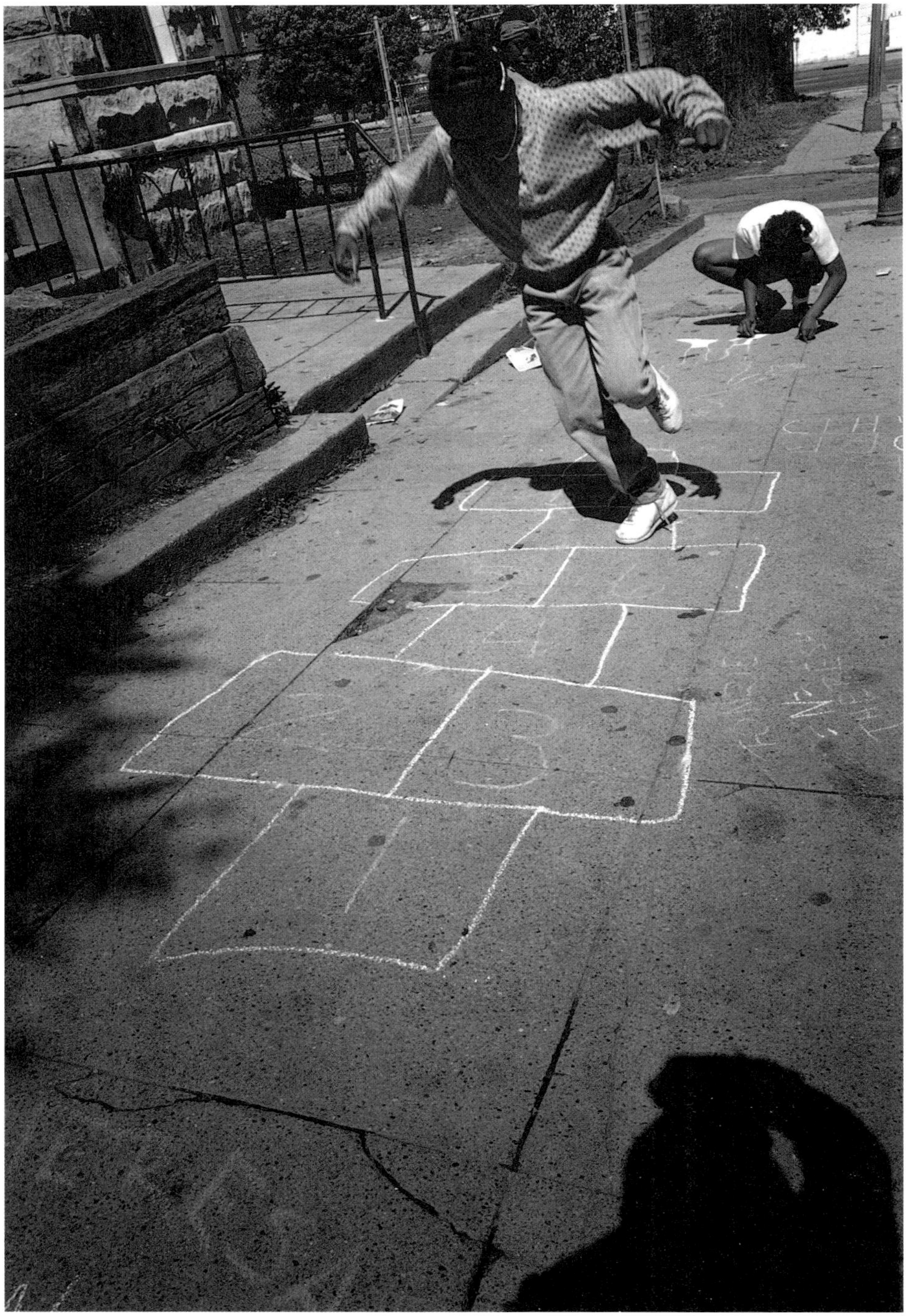

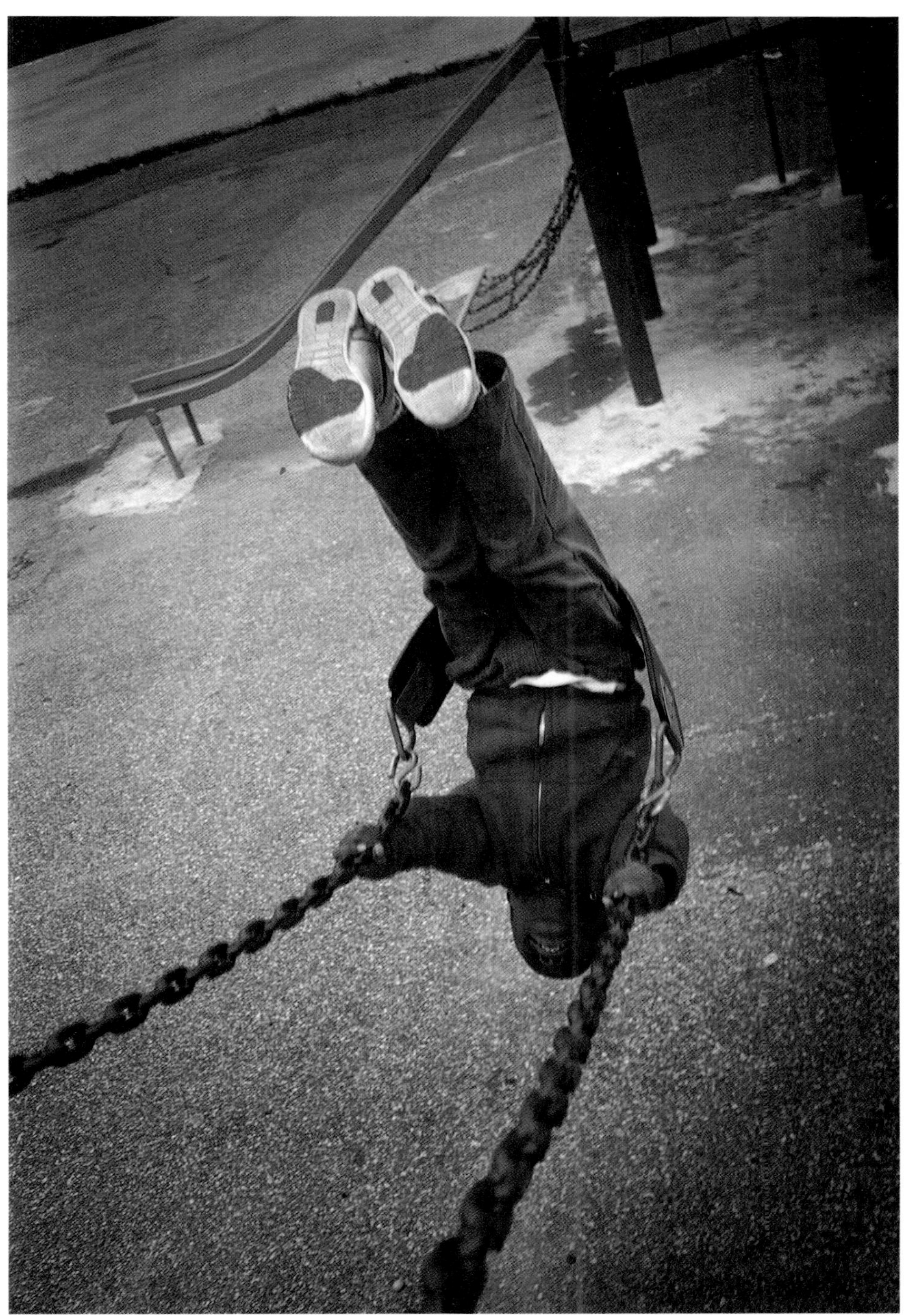

COMMENT FROM DION **When I come back home, I'm normal because I just go outside and play and do what I have to do. But when it's time to take pictures, I take pictures.**

Shopping cart

Daniel Hall, 9

Capitol City Inn,
Washington, D.C.
1989
11" by 14", silver print

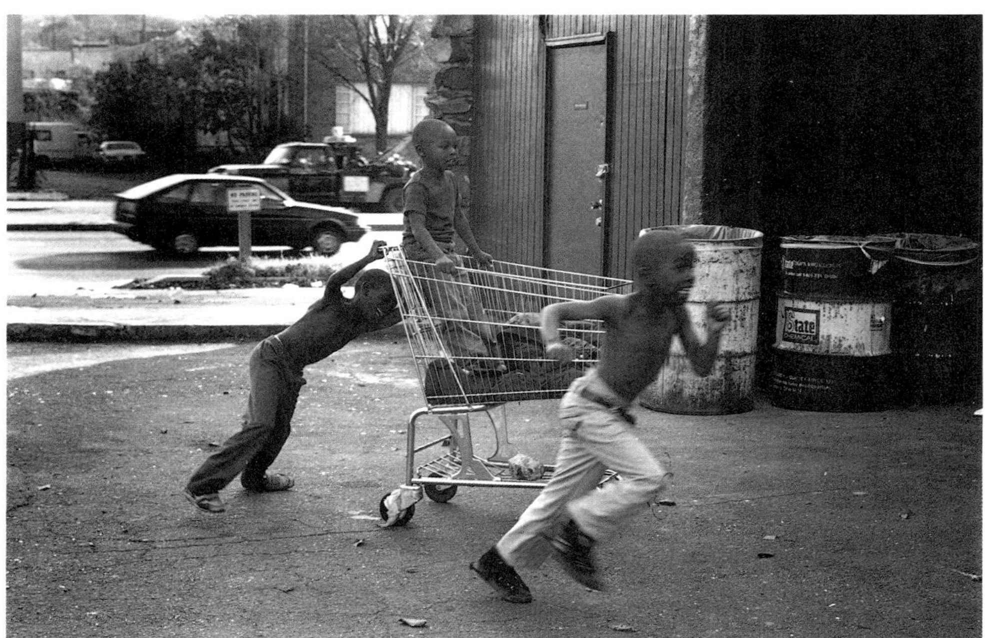

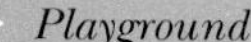 *Playground*

Jeffrey Turner, 9

Reston Shelter,
Reston, Virginia
1989
11" by 14", silver print

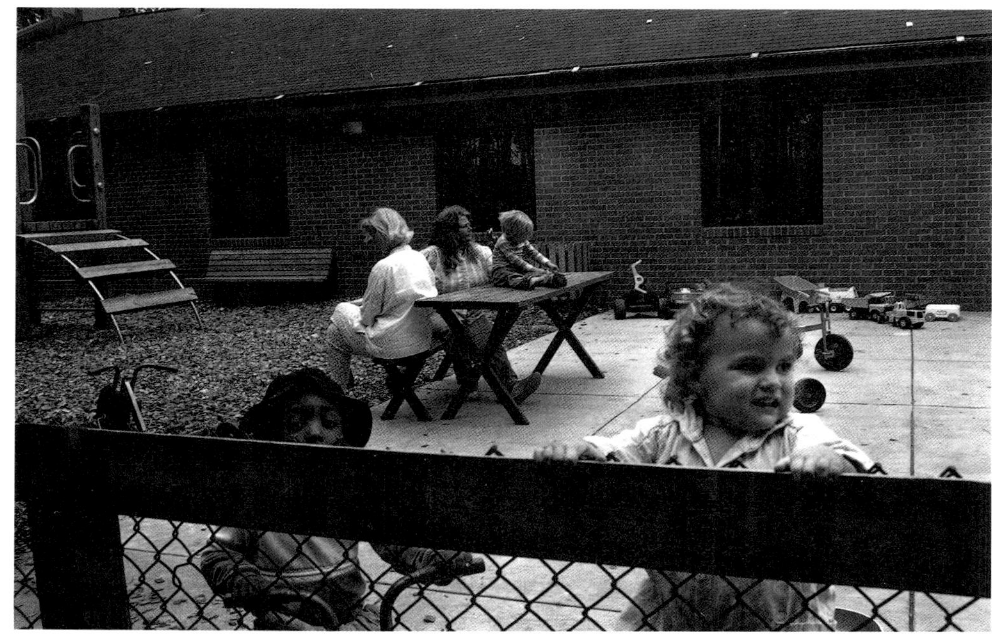

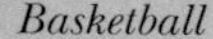 *Basketball*

Dion Johnson, 11

Capitol City Inn,
Washington, D.C.
1989
16" by 20", silver print

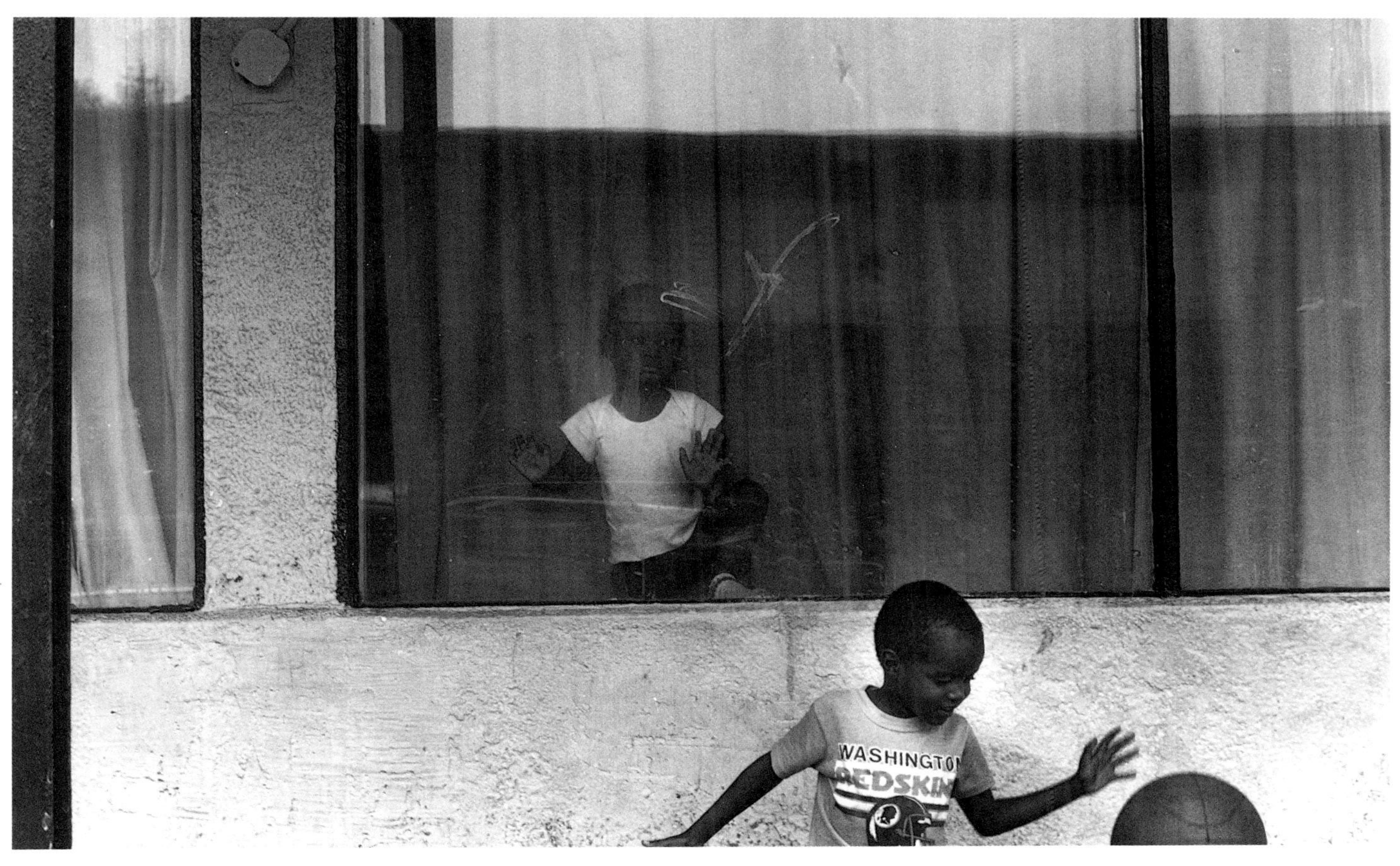

DION'S COMMENT That's my little brother, the boy with the basketball. I don't know who the baby is. My mother drew a picture with a little boy twirling a basketball on his finger. My little brother kept trying to do it, so I just told him he didn't know how to do it, but just bounce the ball so I could take a picture of him. The ball slipped out of his hand and hit the window and when the little baby crawled up in the window to see what hit it, I just snapped the picture. My mother thought it was funny.

Back bend

George Maxie, 10
Community of Hope,
Washington, D.C.
1989
11" by 14", silver print

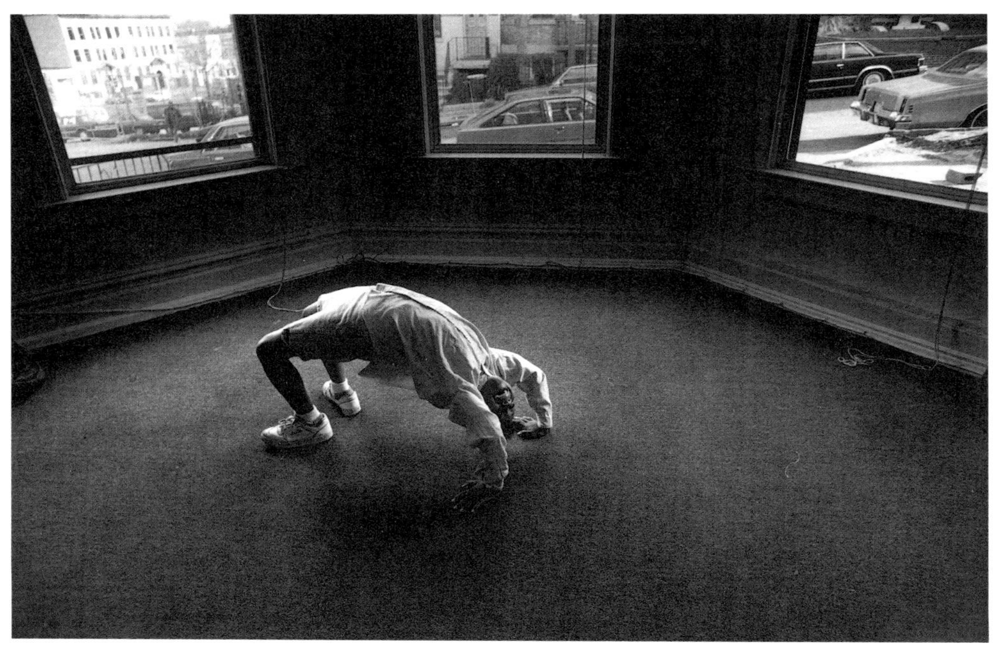

Playground

Kevin
Capitol City Inn,
Washington, D.C.
1989
11" by 14", silver print

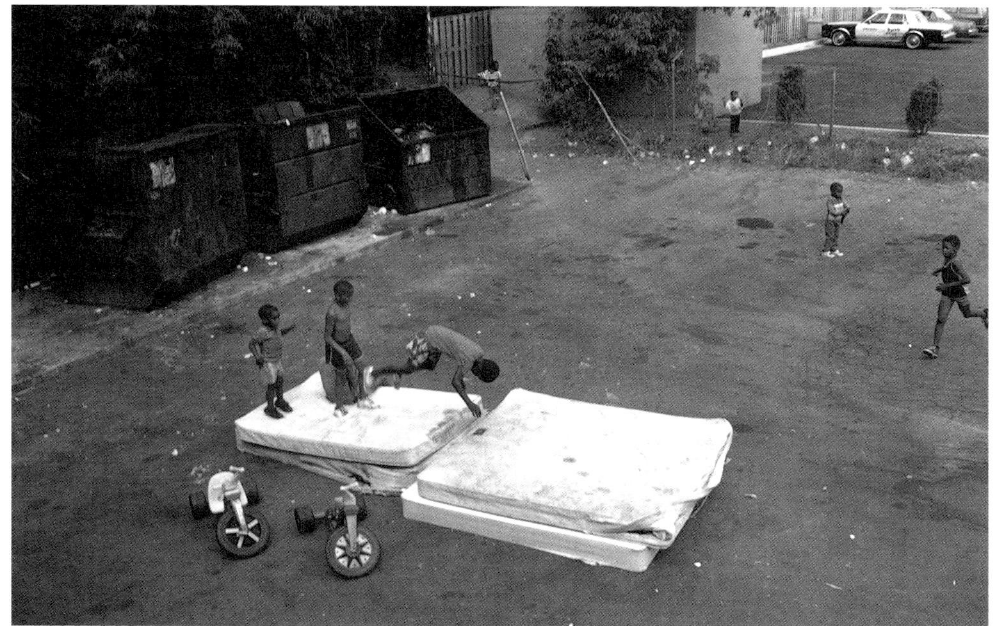

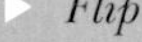

Flip

Daniel Hall, 9
Capitol City Inn,
Washington, D.C.
1989
20" by 24", silver print

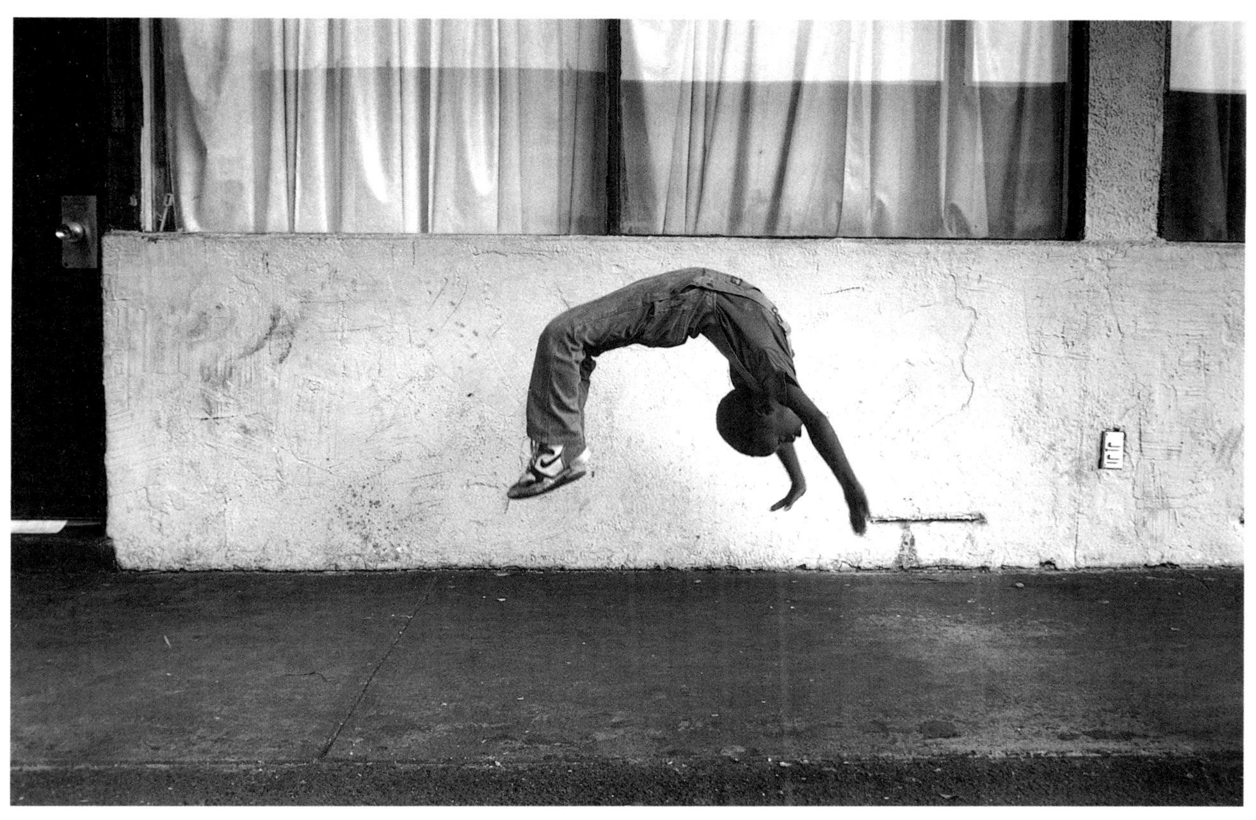

DANIEL'S COMMENT It took him a long time, 'cause he kept messing up.

Kissing in shelter

Jocelyn Robertson, 15

Community of Hope,
Washington, D.C.
1989
11" by 14", silver print

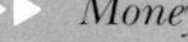

Money

Shadonna

Capitol City Inn,
Washington, D.C.
1989
11" by 14", silver print

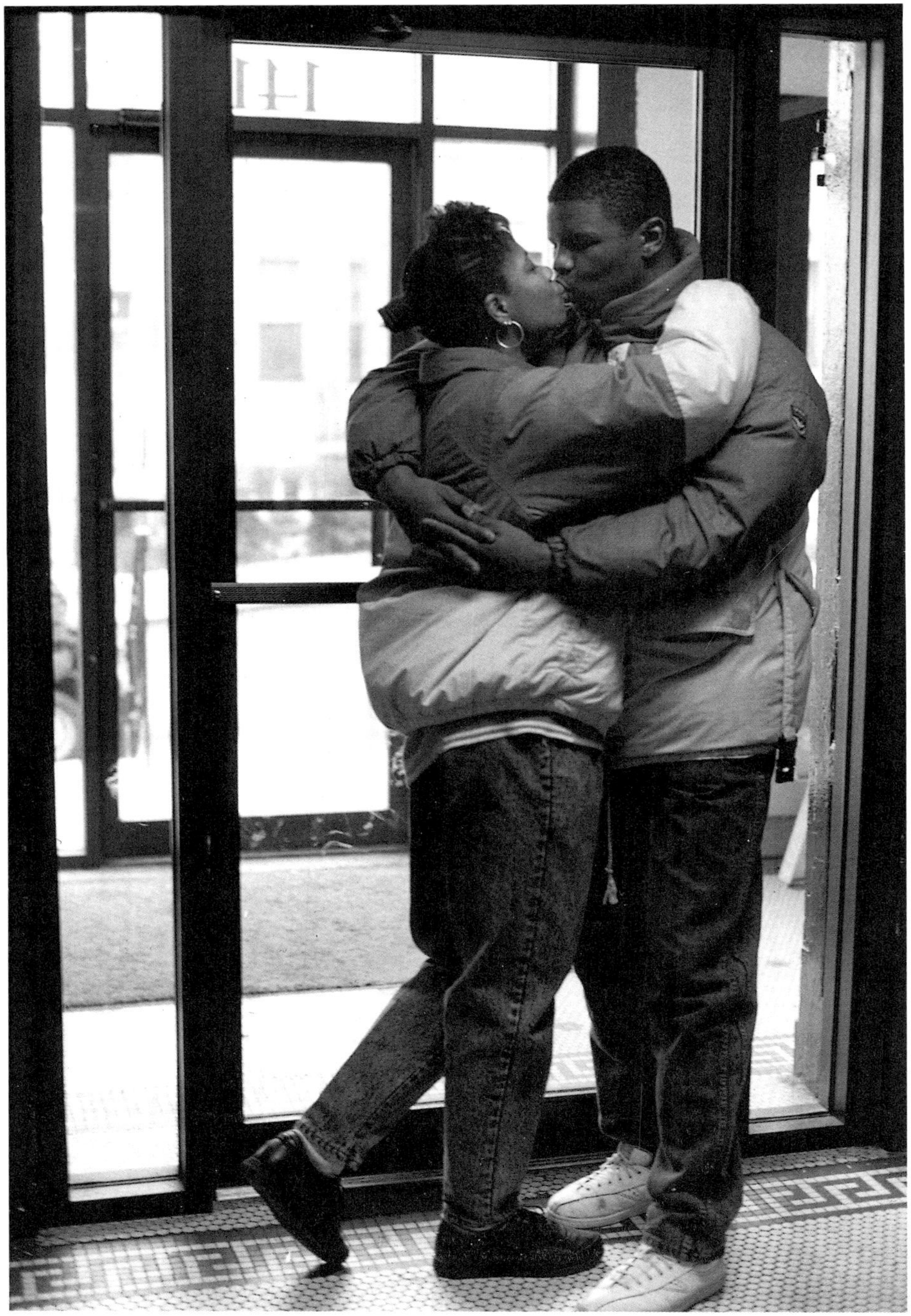

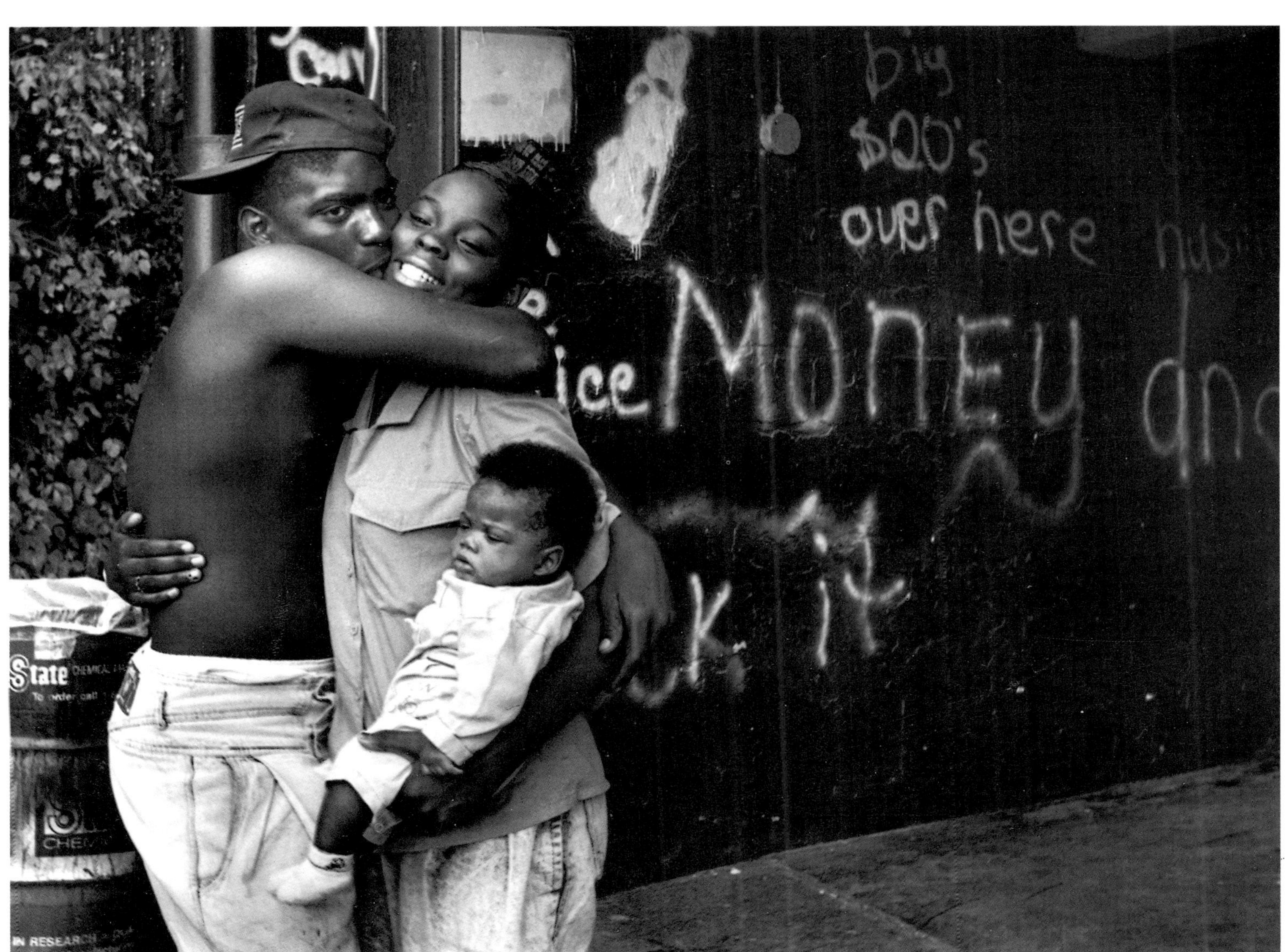
big
$20's
over here
MONEY
State

Mother and child

Berry Paul, 9

Capitol City Inn,
Washington, D.C.
1989
11" by 14", silver print

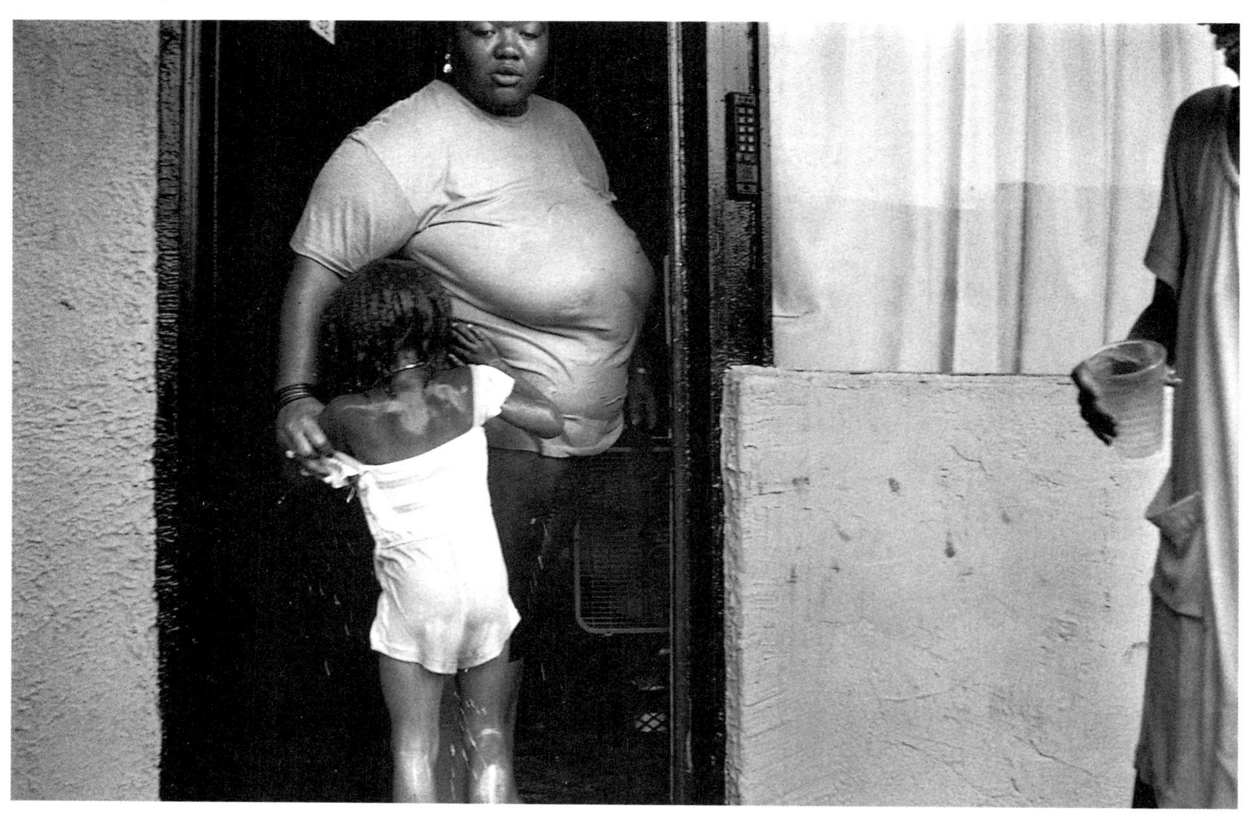

Angela Robertson

Keesha Carroll, 12

Community of Hope,
Washington, D.C.
1989
11" by 14", silver print

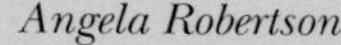

Hug

Nicole Mitchell, 11

Holiday Park Shelter,
Wheaton, Maryland
1989
11" by 14", silver print

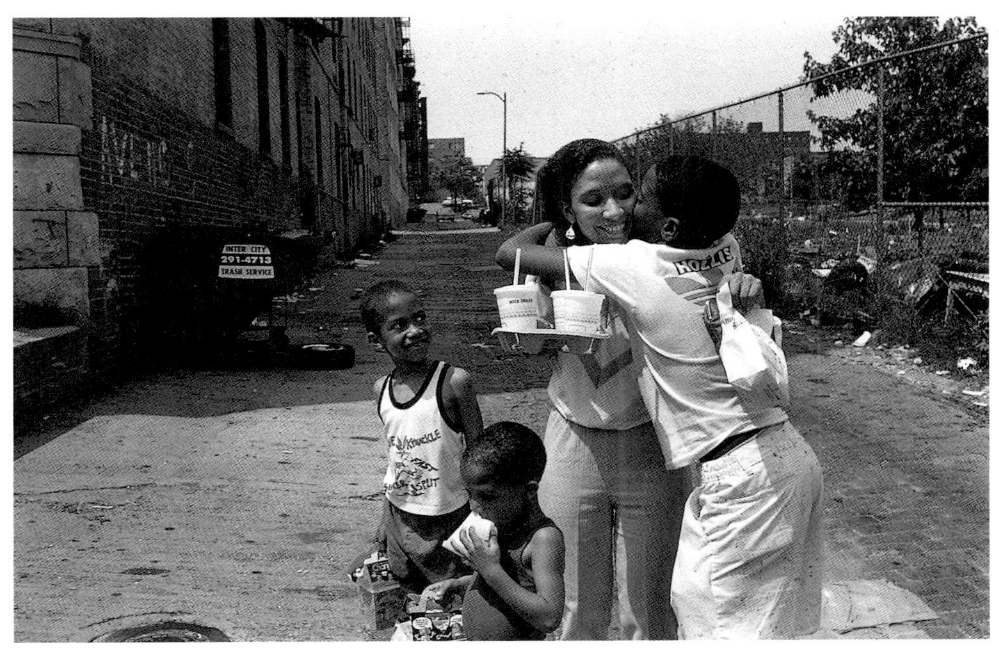
INTER CITY
291-4713
TRASH SERVICE

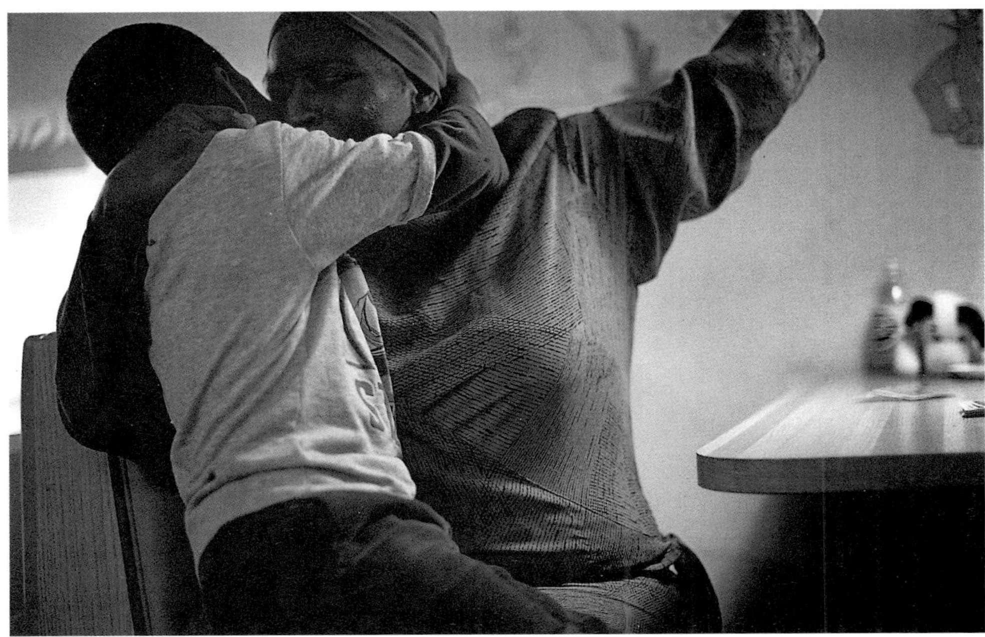

Homeless family

Tamicka Hodge, 12
Community of Hope,
Washington, D.C.
1989
11" by 14", silver print

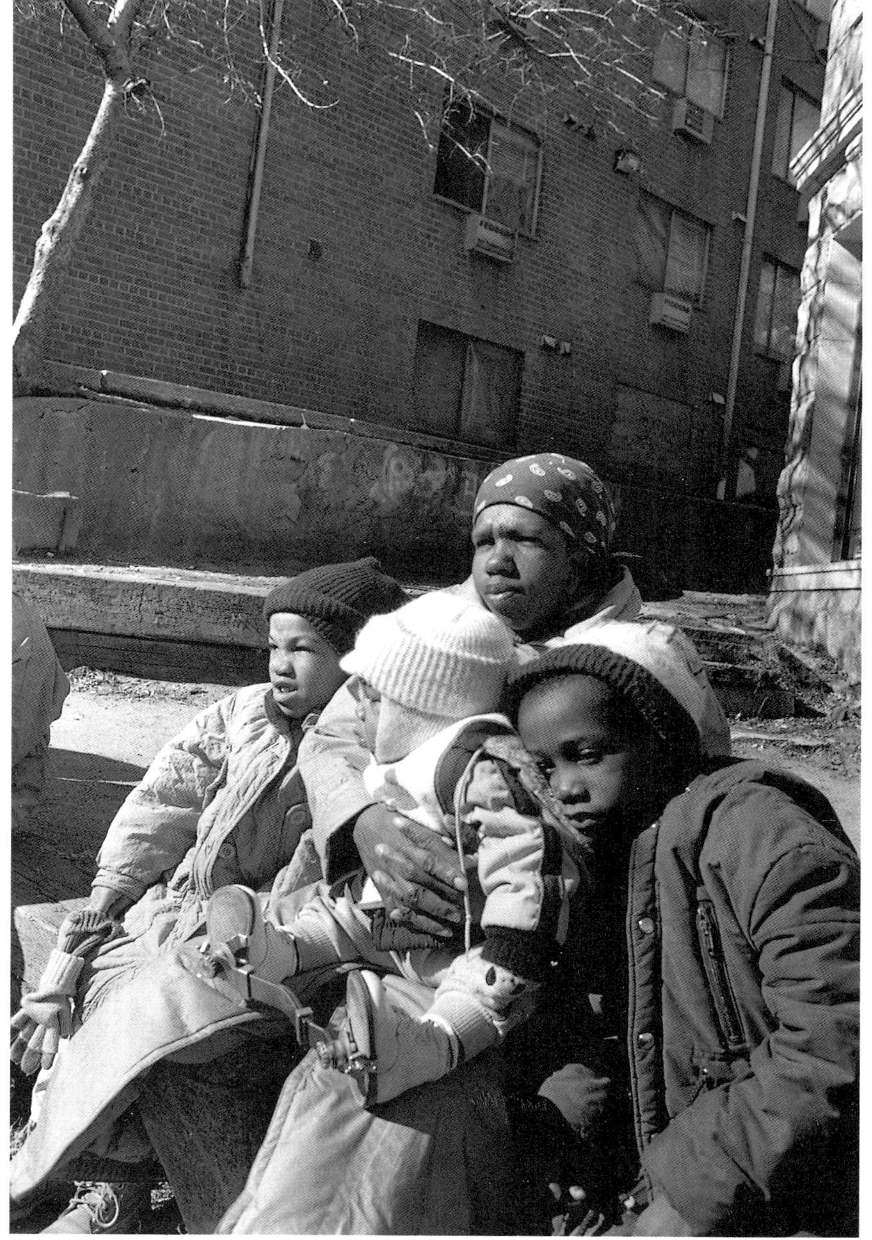

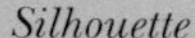

Silhouette

Carissa Etheridge, 15
Community of Hope,
Washington, D.C.
1989
11" by 14", silver print

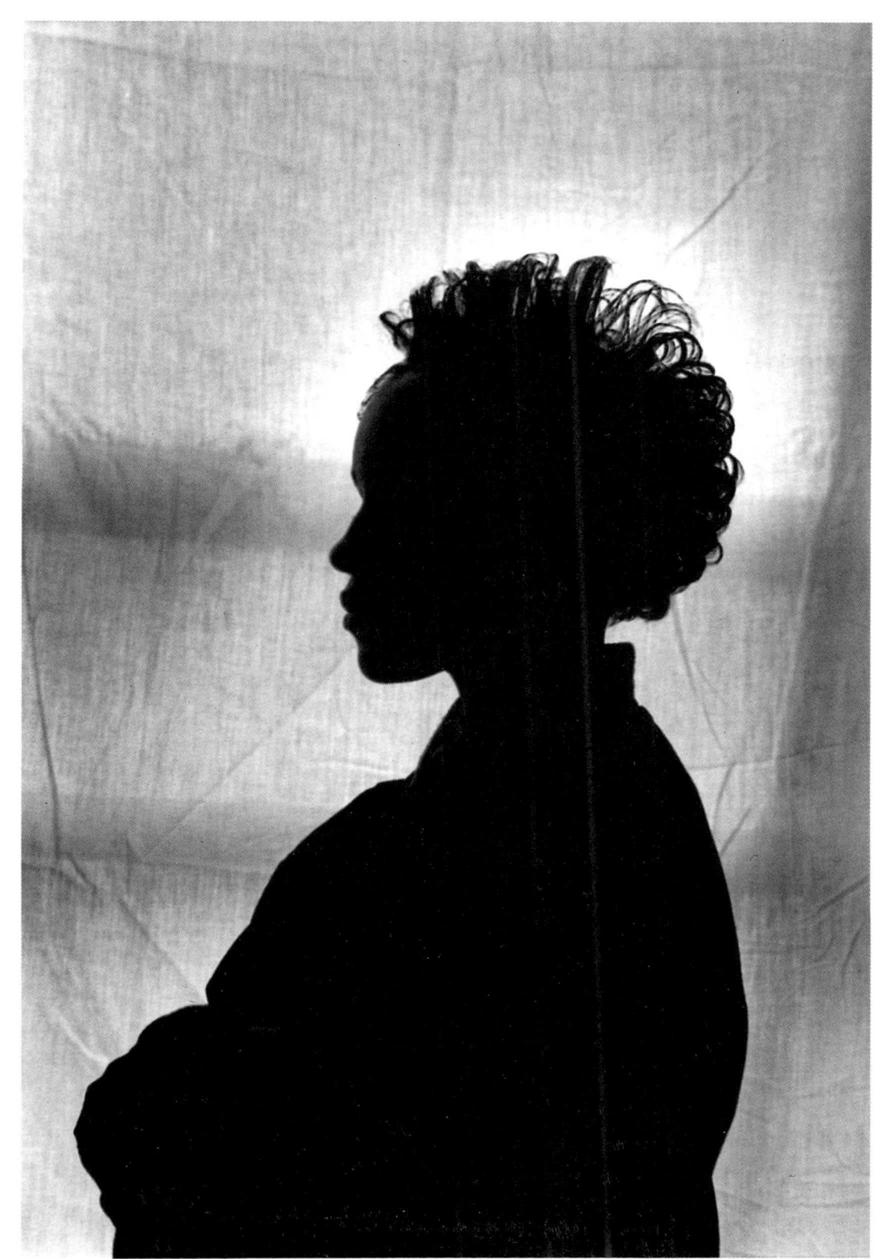

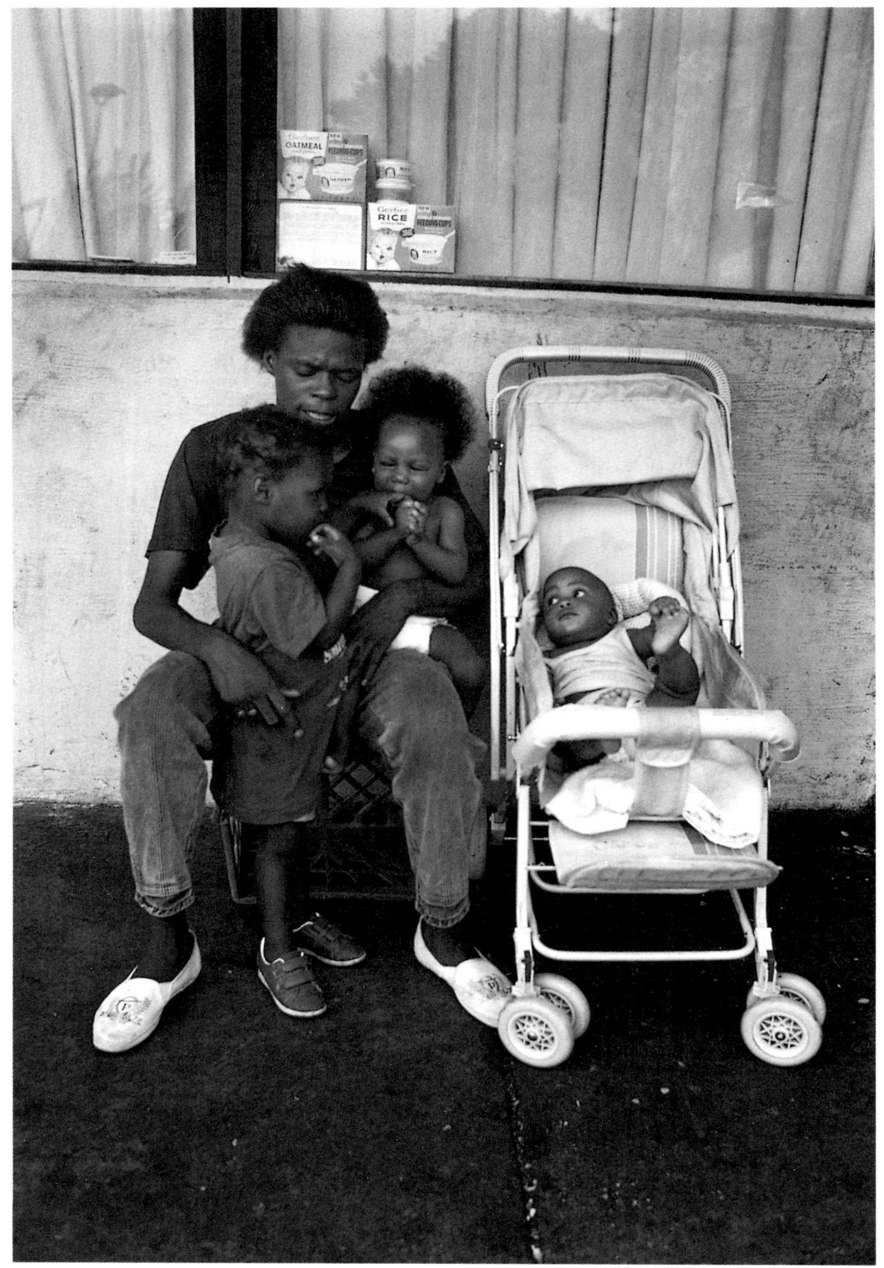

▶ *Family*

Alfred Cheadle, 14

Capitol City Inn,
Washington, D.C.
1989
11" by 14", silver print

▶▲ *Family on steps of shelter*

Daniel Hall, 9

Pitts Hotel,
Washington, D.C.
1989
11" by 14", silver print

▶▼ *Street vendors*

Calvin Stewart, 17

Malcolm X Park,
Community of Hope,
Washington, D.C.
1989
16" by 20", silver print

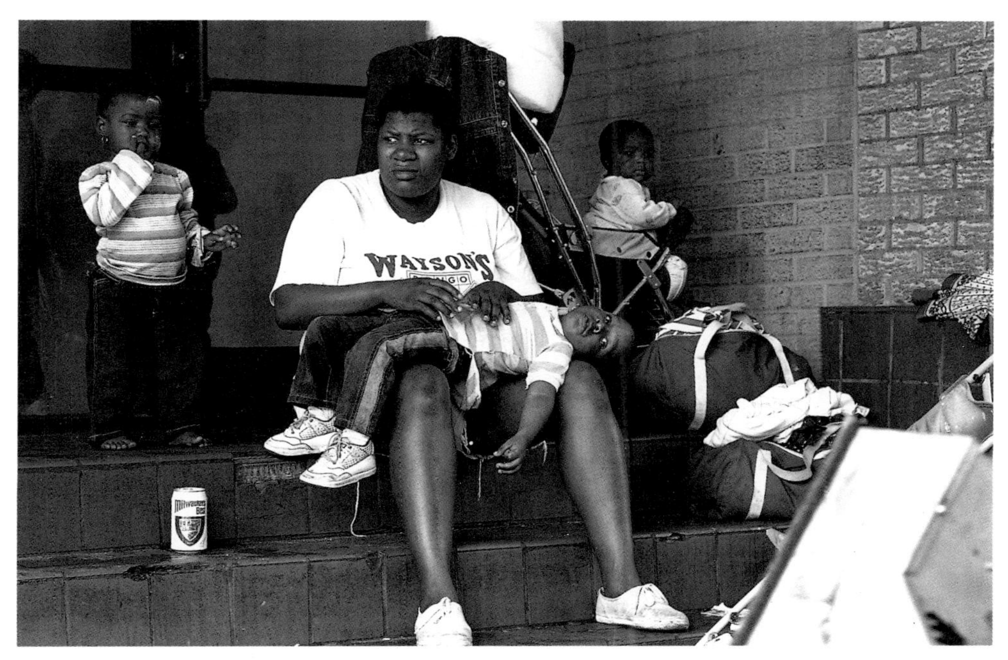
WAYSON'S

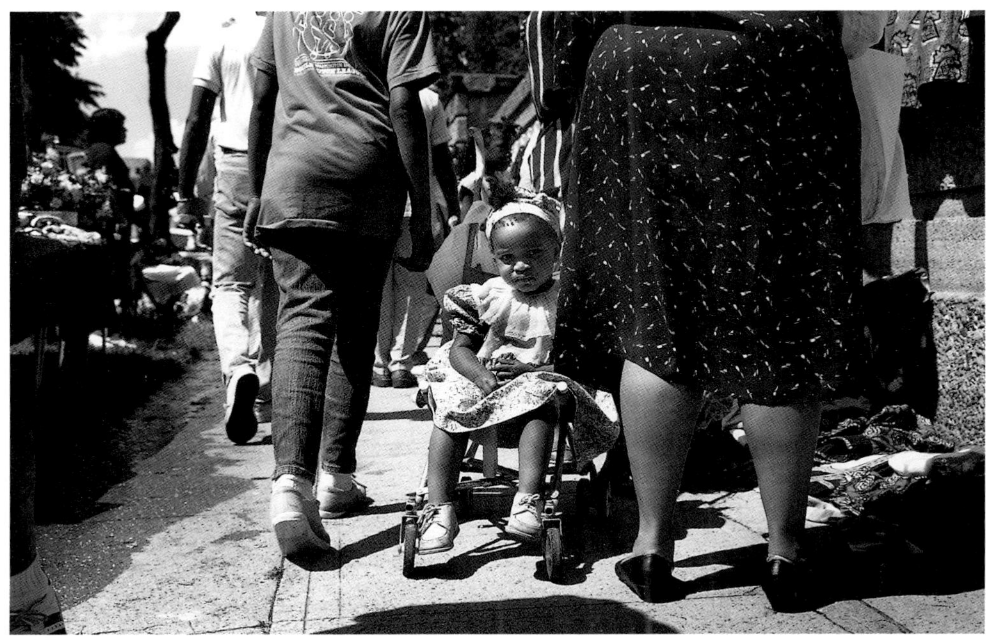

Card game

Albert

Holiday Park Shelter,
Wheaton, Maryland
1989
11" by 14", silver print

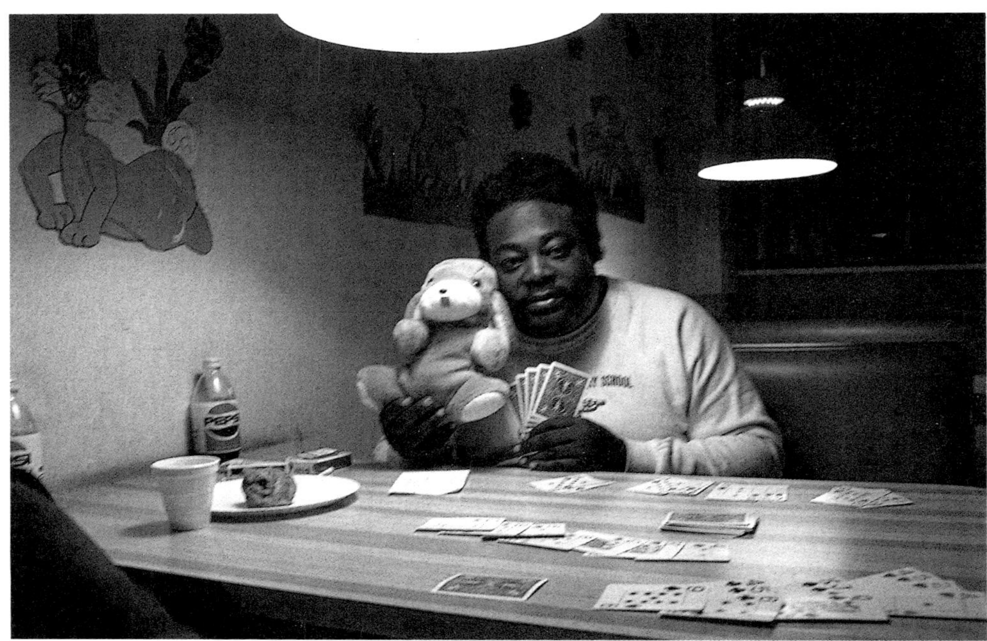

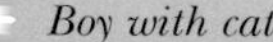

Boy with cat

Columbia Thomas, 11

Pitts Hotel,
Washington, D.C.
1989
16" by 20", silver print

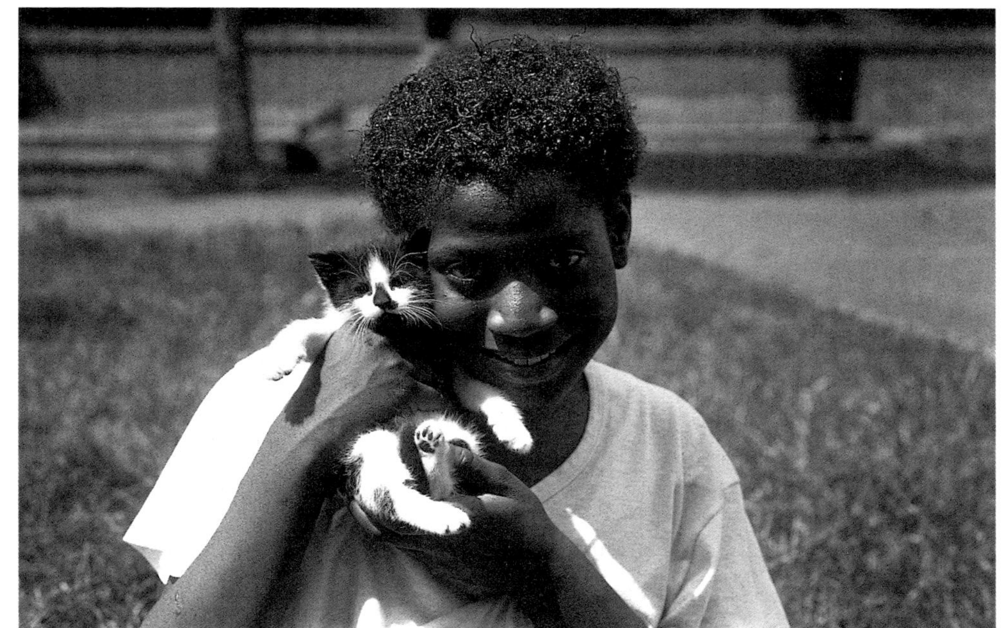

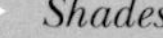

Shades

Dion Johnson, 12

new residence,
Southwest
Washington, D.C.
1990
11" by 14", silver print

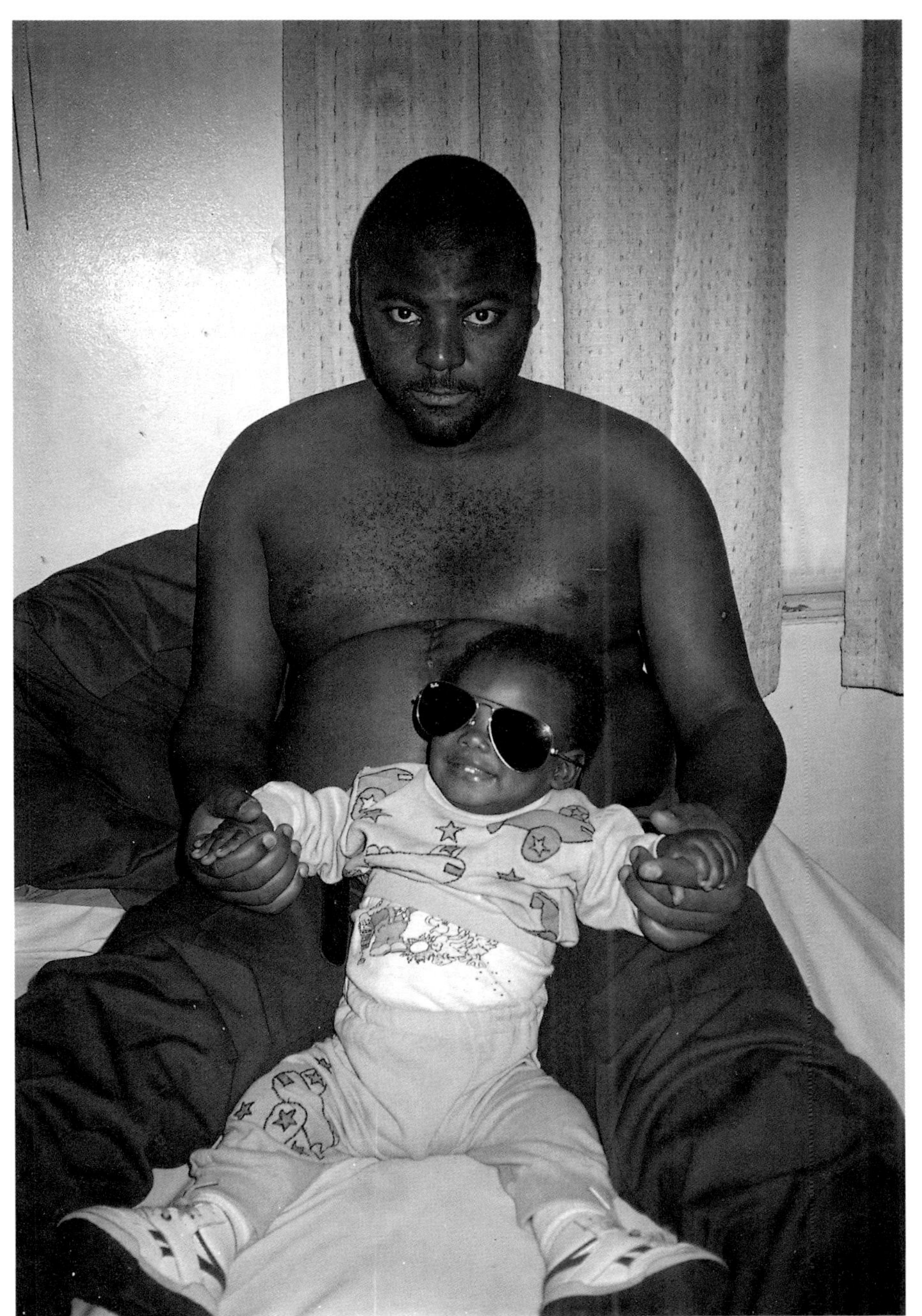

▶ *My baby*

Dion Johnson, 12
new residence,
Southwest
Washington, D.C.
1990
16" by 20", silver print

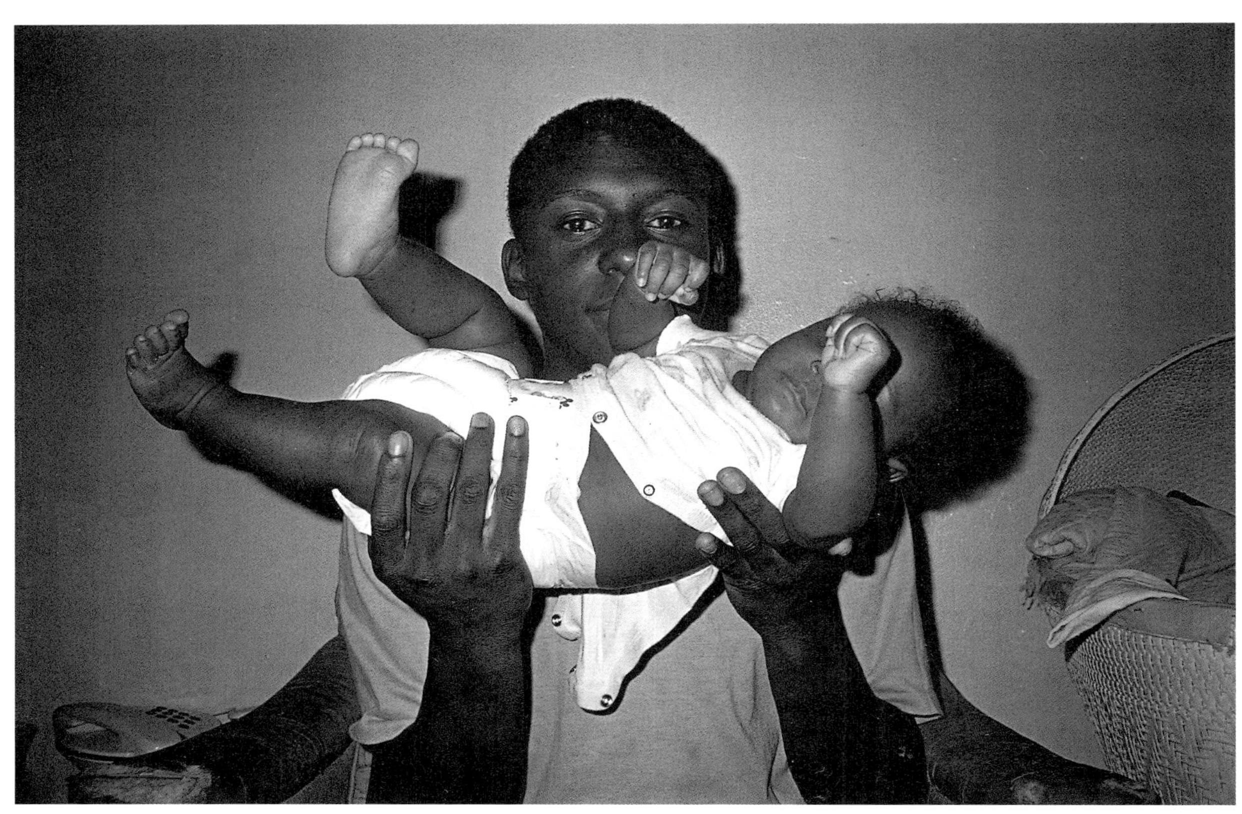

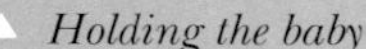 *Holding the baby*

Dion Johnson, 11
new residence,
Southwest
Washington, D.C.
1989
11" by 14", silver print

▶▼ *Laundry room*

Atiba Grey, 16
The Carpenter's
Shelter,
Alexandria, Virginia
1990
16" by 20", silver print

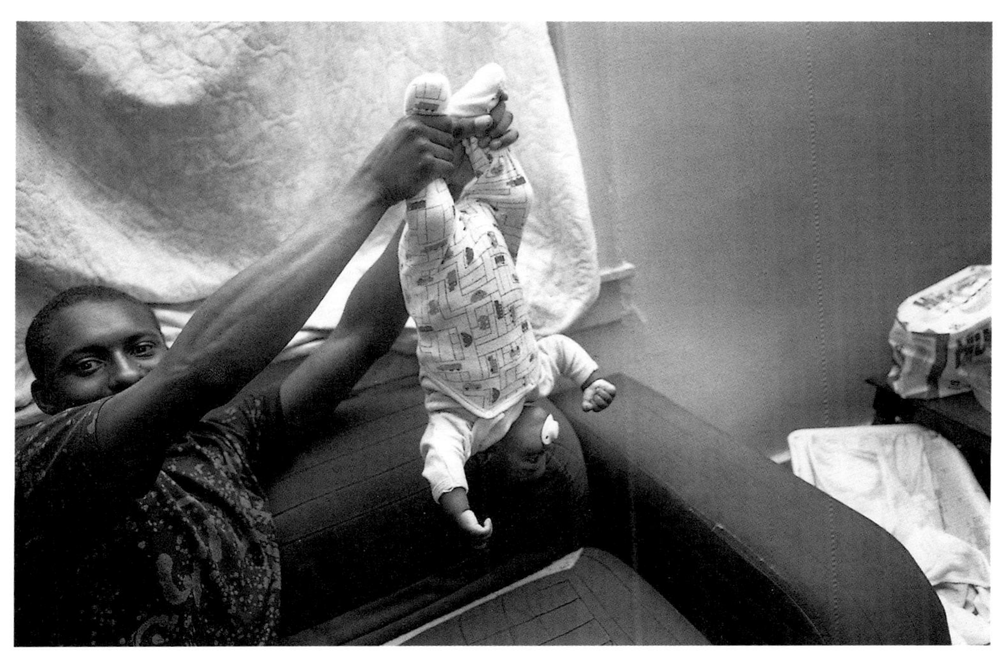

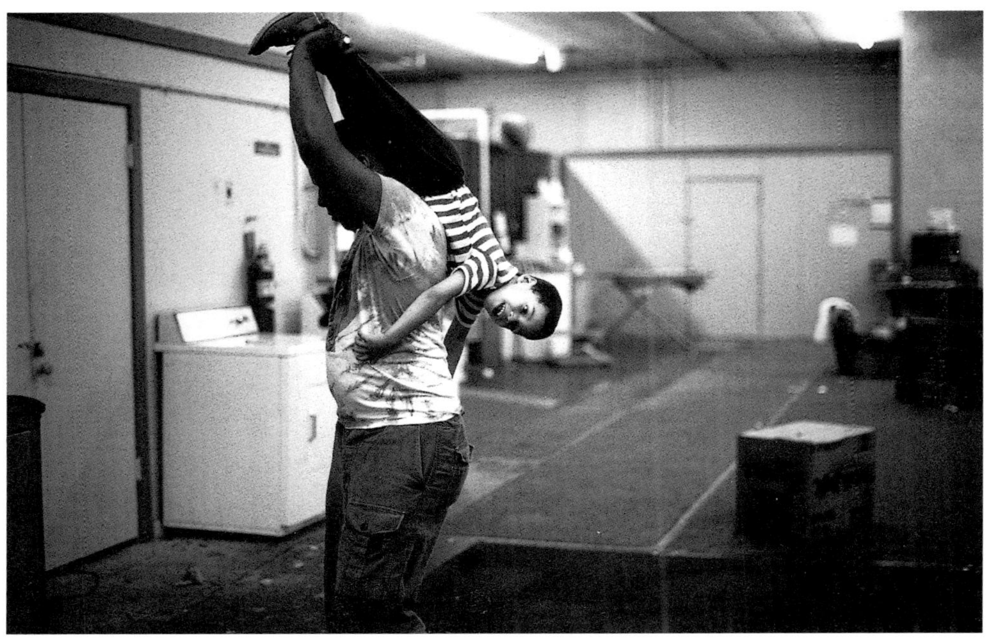

▶ *Kids on car*

Joe Andrews, 15
Capitol City Inn,
Washington, D.C.
1989
16" by 20", silver print

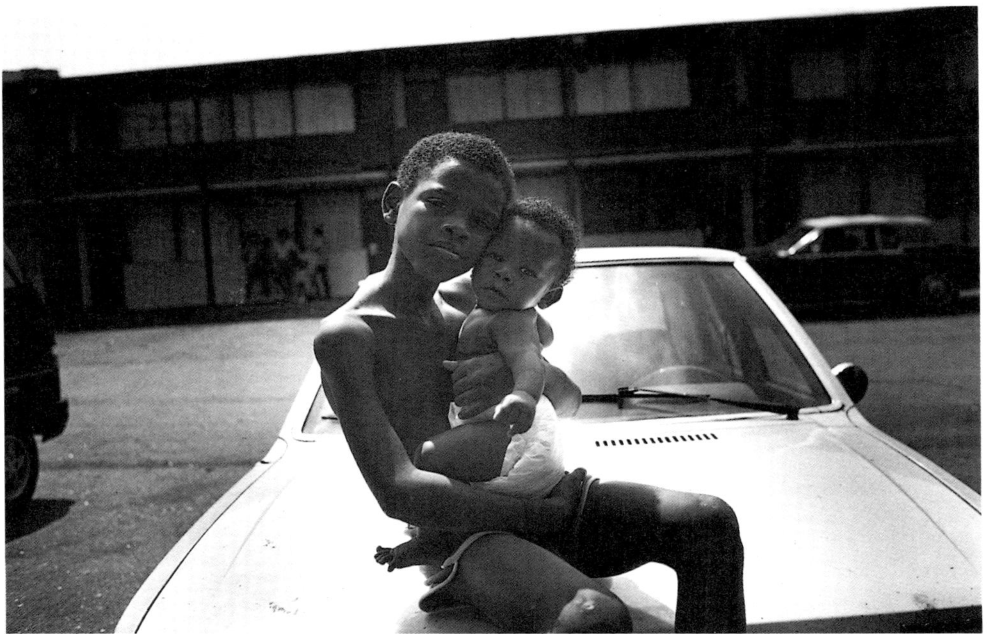

▶ *Family in room*

Calvin Stewart, 17
Reston Shelter,
Reston, Virginia
1989
11" by 14", silver print

▶▲ *Mother and child*

Daniel Hall, 9
Capitol City Inn,
Washington, D.C.
1989
16" by 20", silver print

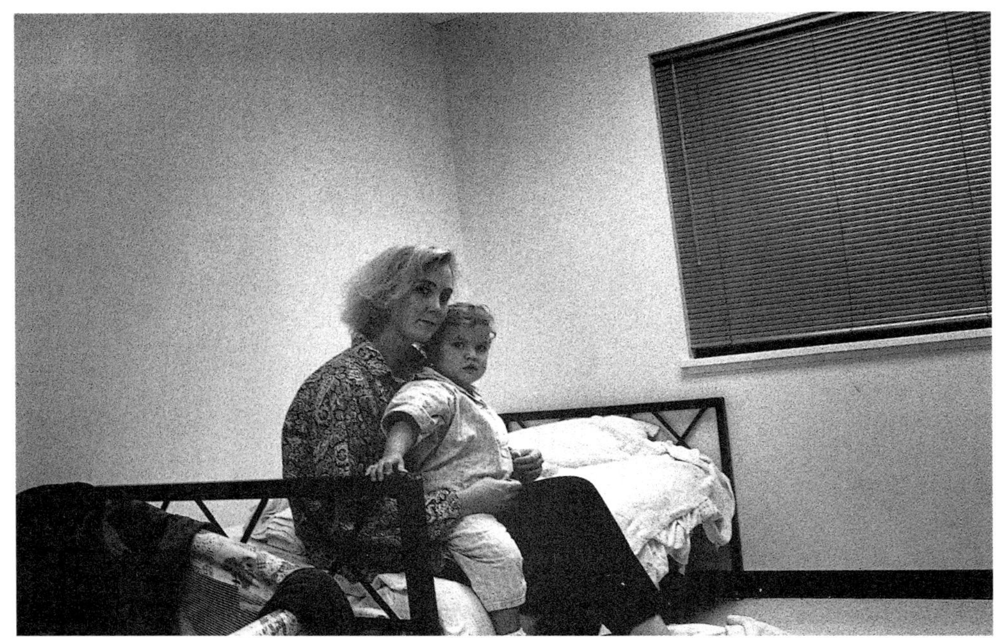

▶▼ *Resting*

Crystal Carlisle
Holiday Park Shelter,
Wheaton, Maryland
1989
16" by 20", silver print

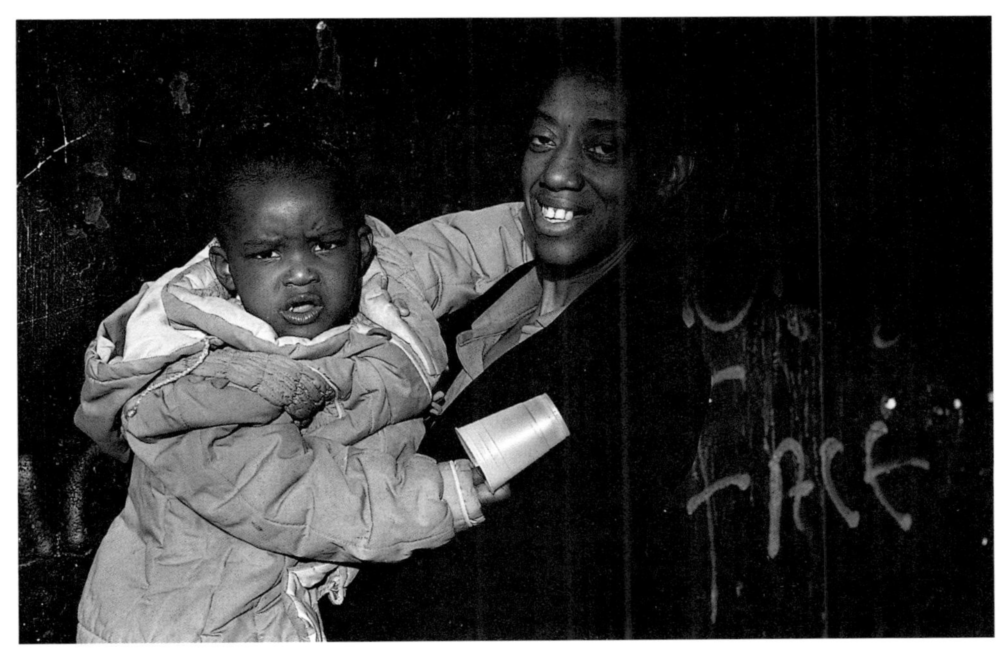

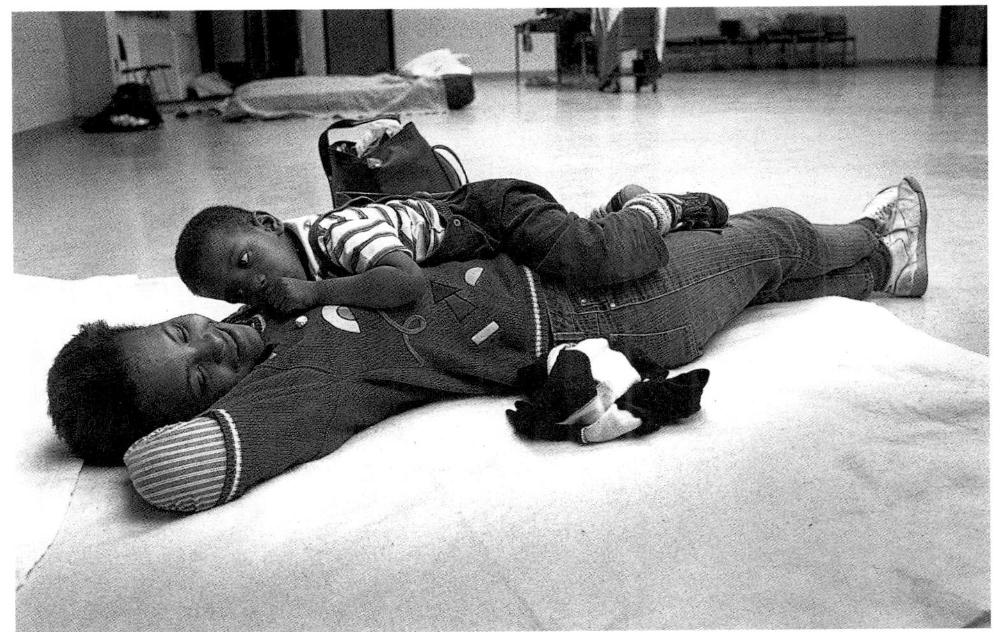

▶ *Twins on bed,*

Daniel Hall, 9

Capitol City Inn,
Washington, D.C.
1989
16" by 20", silver print

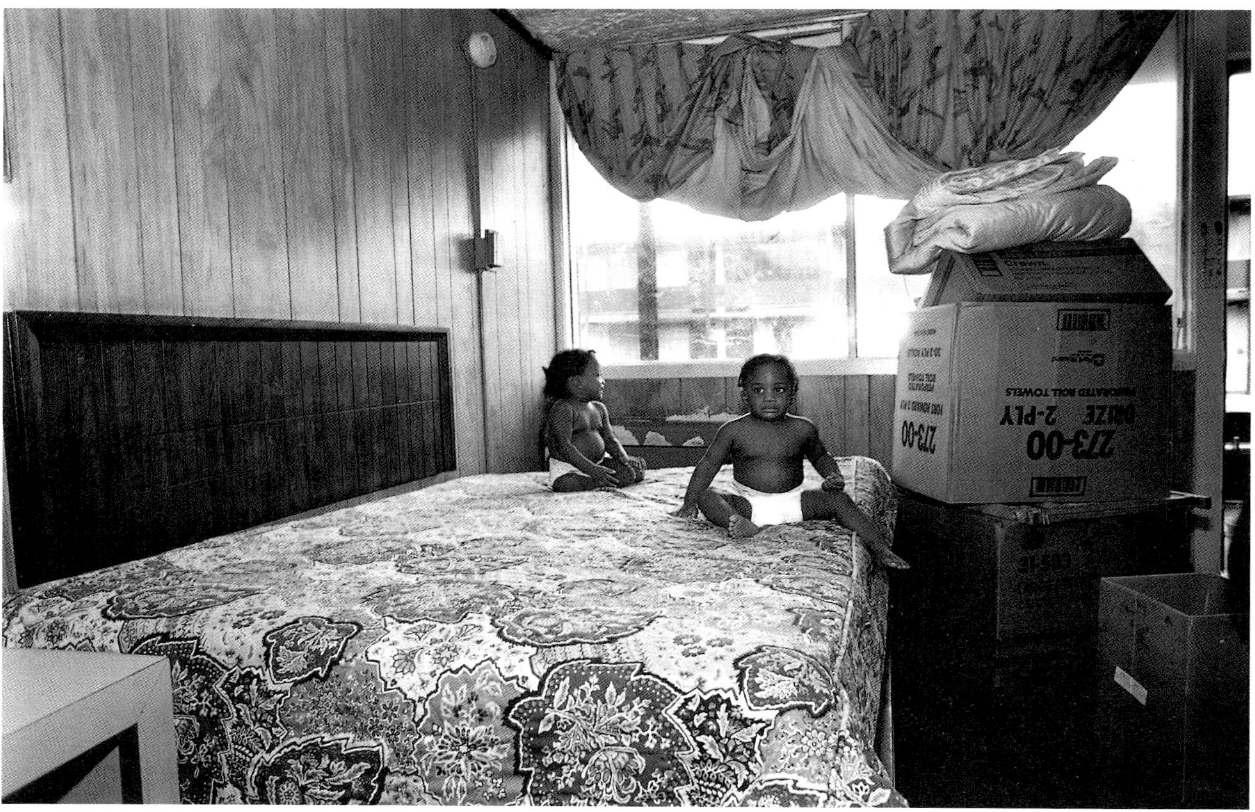

▶▶ *Twins in bath*

Daniel Hall, 9

Capitol City Inn,
Washington, D.C.
1989
11" by 14", silver print

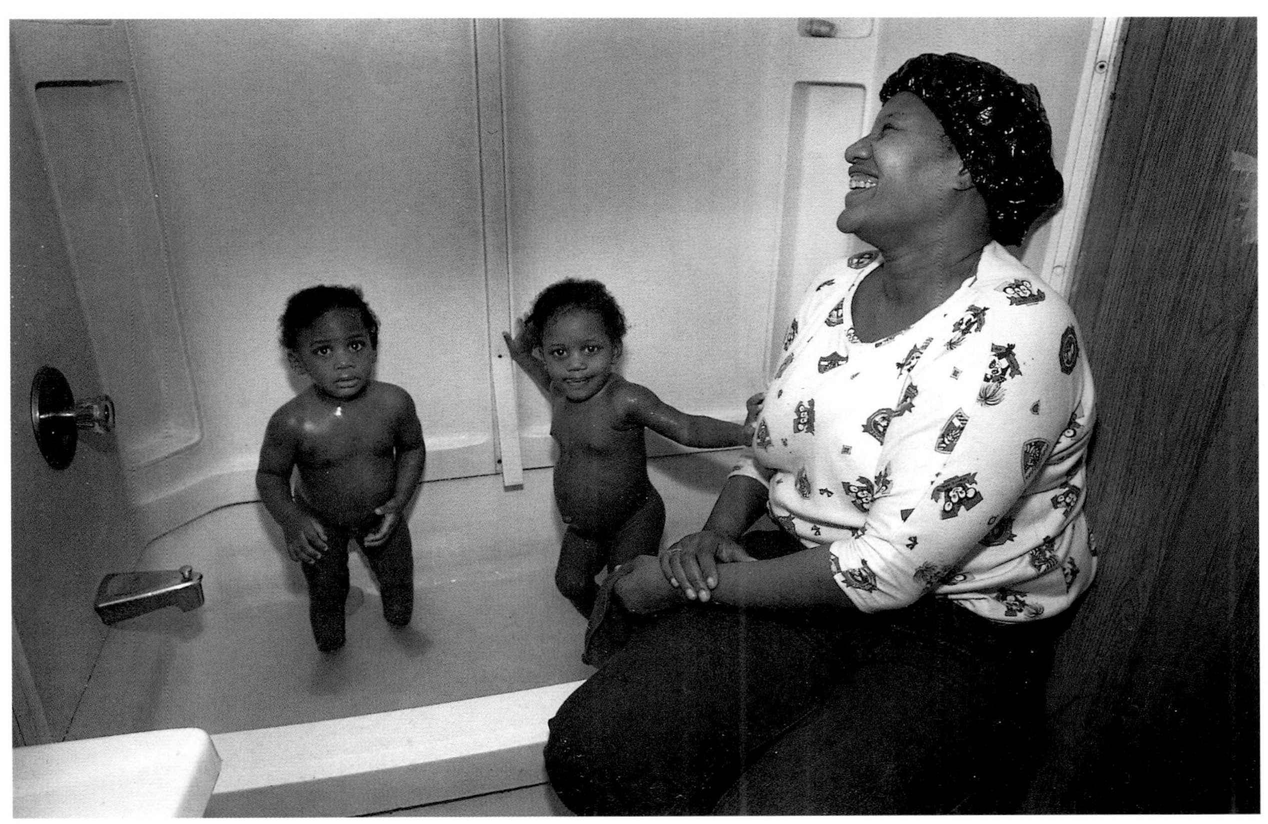

COMMENT FROM SCHOOLCHILD **This exhibit shows the way homeless people want us to see them not the way magazines want us to.**

▶ *Bath in sink*

Shawn Nixon, 18

The Carpenter's Shelter,
Alexandria, Virginia
1990
11" by 14", silver print

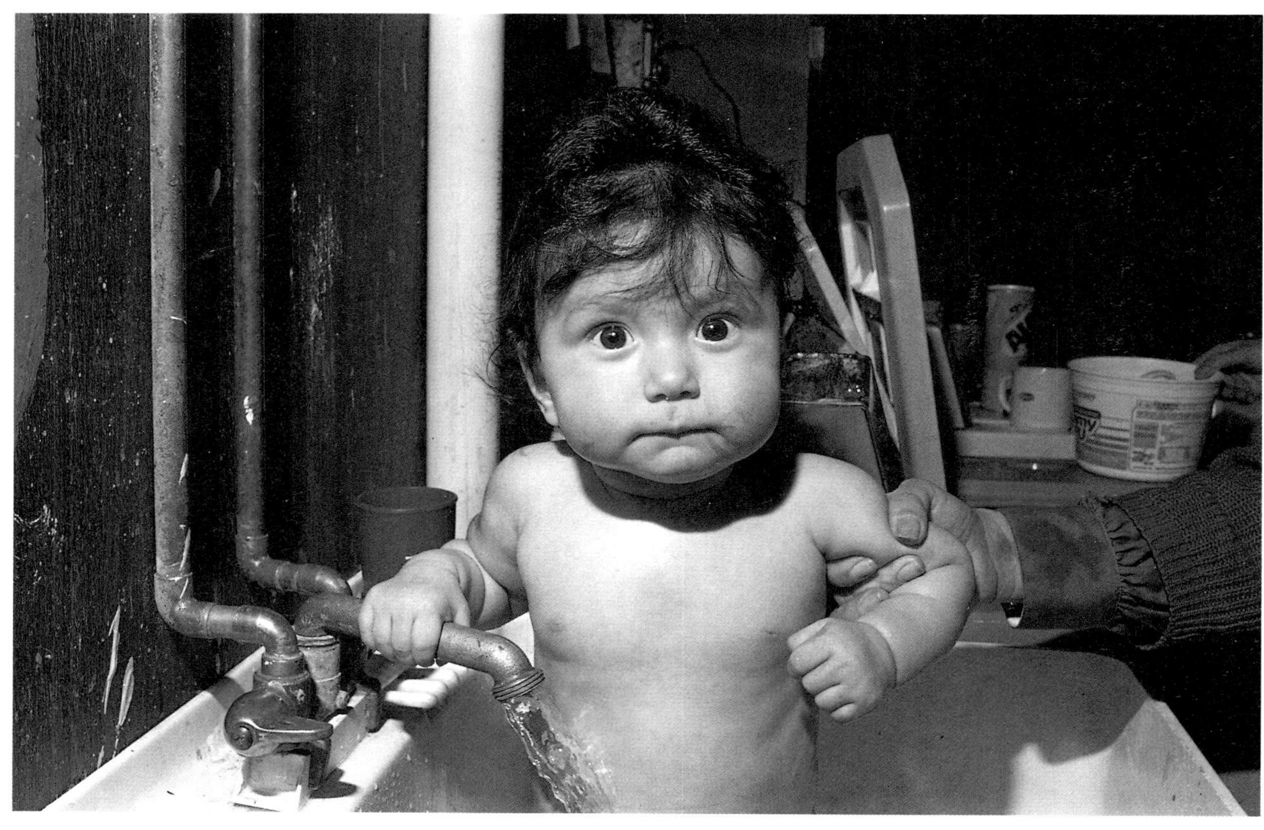

▶▶ *Bath in sink*

Shawn Nixon, 18

The Carpenter's Shelter,
Alexandria, Virginia
1990
16" by 20", silver print

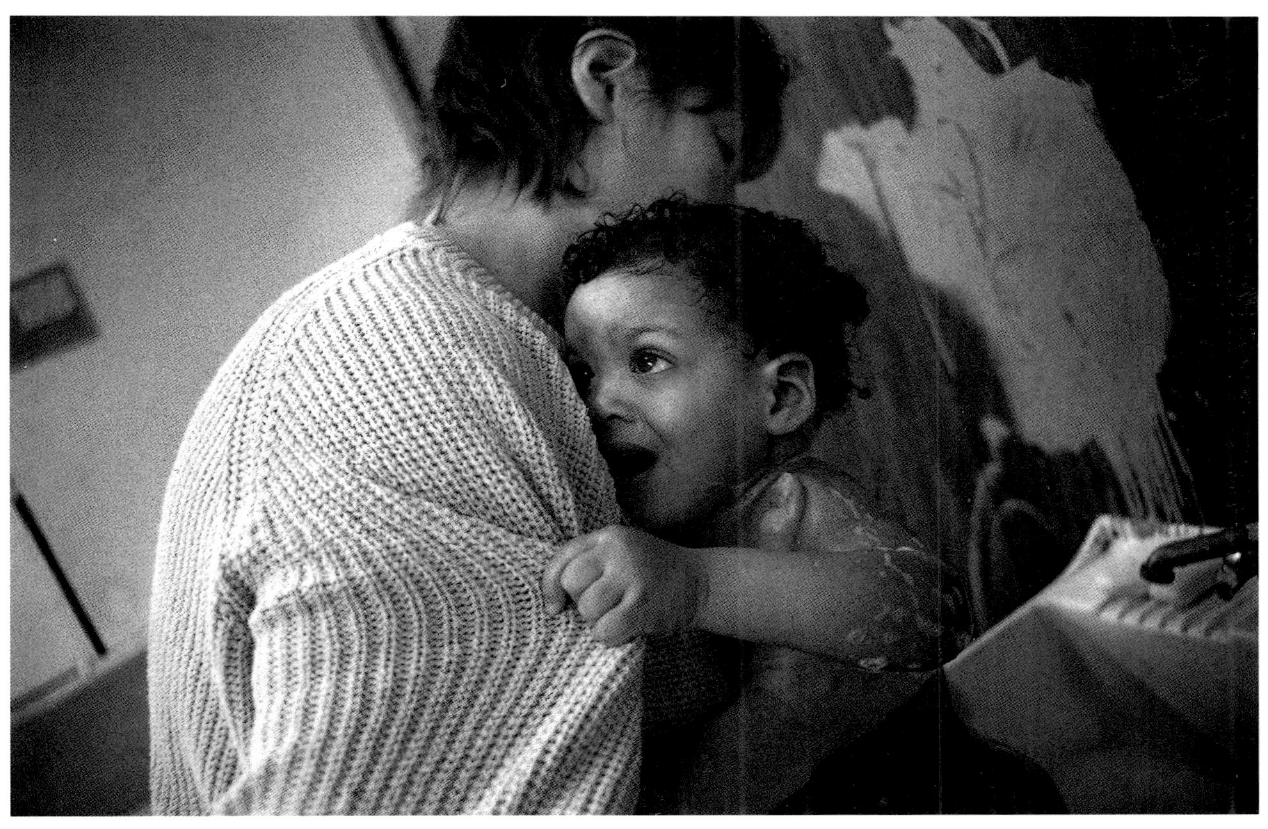

SHAWN TALKING WITH JIM **A lot of the pictures that I had— I had sold them. Those pictures you all had blown up for me last time.** *You sold them?* **Yeah—to the people I took the pictures of.** *The pictures you took of people here you sold to the people?* **Yeah.** *You are becoming a major businessman. I mean, I never heard of such a great thing. You were formerly selling crack. Now you are selling photographs. You may not make quite as much money, you probably won't get shot, you probably won't go to prison for selling photographs, plus it's a creative thing, follow? I'm going to help you on this, if you let me.*

▸ *Used clothes arrive*

Daniel Hall, 9

Capitol City Inn,
Washington, D.C.
1989
11" by 14", silver print

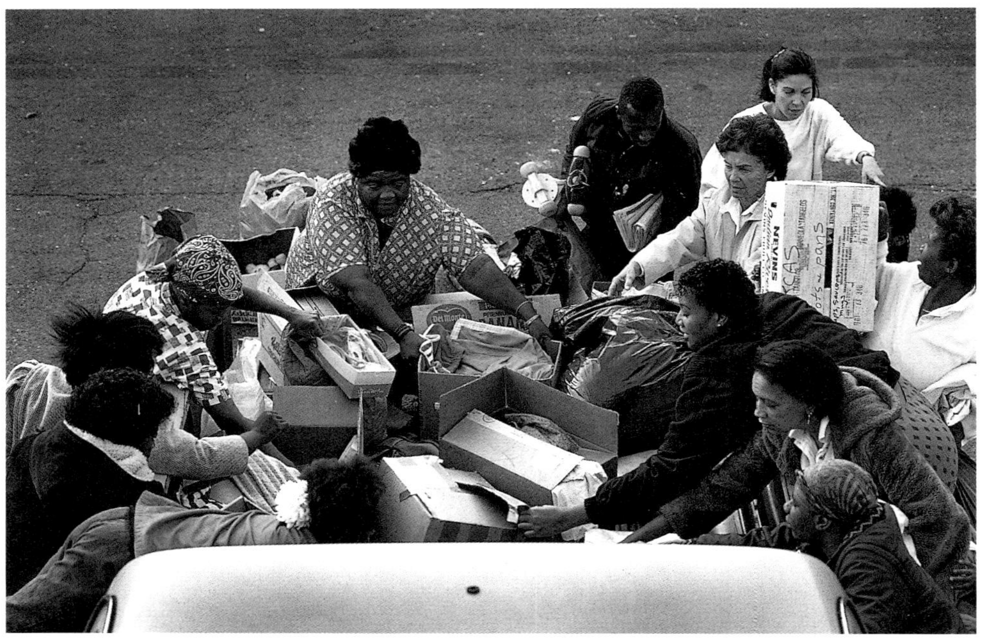

▸ *Christmas gifts*

Dion Johnson, 11

new residence,
Southwest
Washington, D.C.
1990
11" by 14", silver print

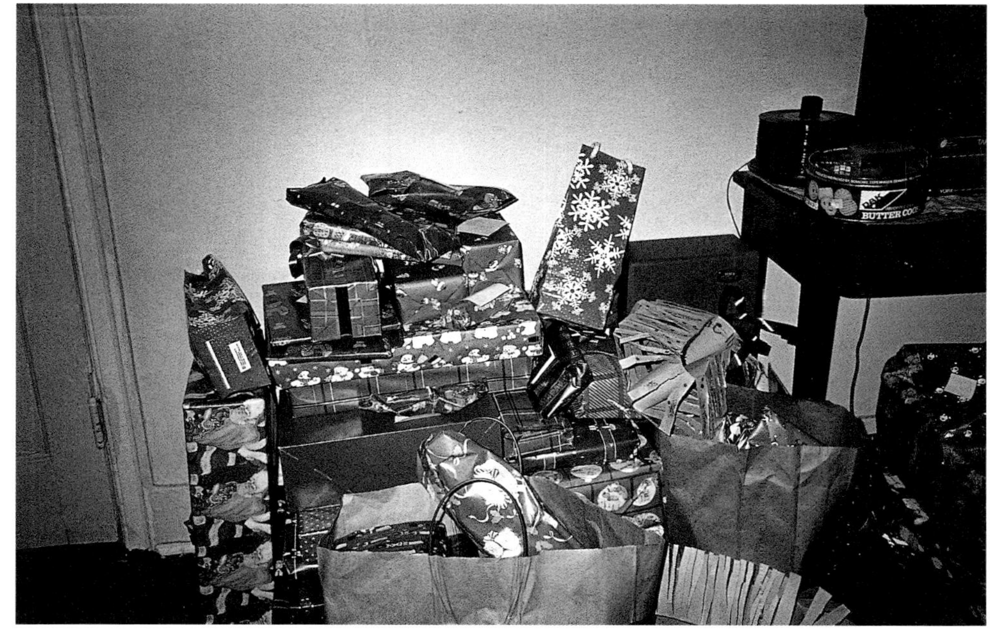

▸▸ *Vanessa Johnson family in their new home after move from CapitolCity Inn*

Dion Johnson, 11

Capitol City Inn,
Southwest
Washington, D.C.
1989
16" by 20", silver print

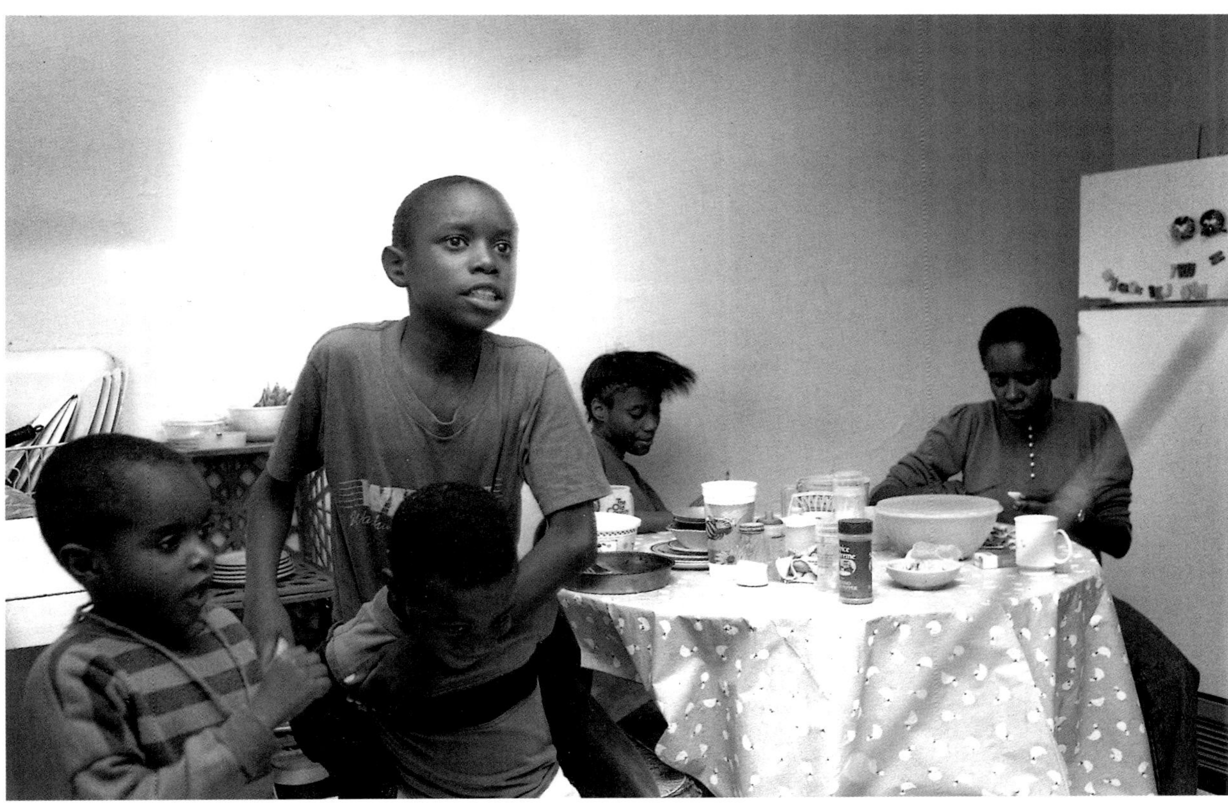

COMMENT FROM VANESSA JOHNSON (DION'S MOTHER) I have been able to be a proud mother because of the achievements the children have made.

This year I put living in the shelter behind me—the physical part—but the mental part and the emotional part of living in the shelter take awhile to get away from. If I forget all the things I went through [in the shelter] then I'm going to forget that there's other people out there that's in the same situation, will be in the same situation, and I want to be able to say, well, look, this happened to me, I've experienced it, I can show you the things that I've been through. It's tough when you first get out there because you're still going through it.

It was bad being in there but good things come out of it, if you use your mind, if you encourage each other. Now we got each other's phone numbers and we've been visiting each other and keeping up with each other, reminding each other of what we did.

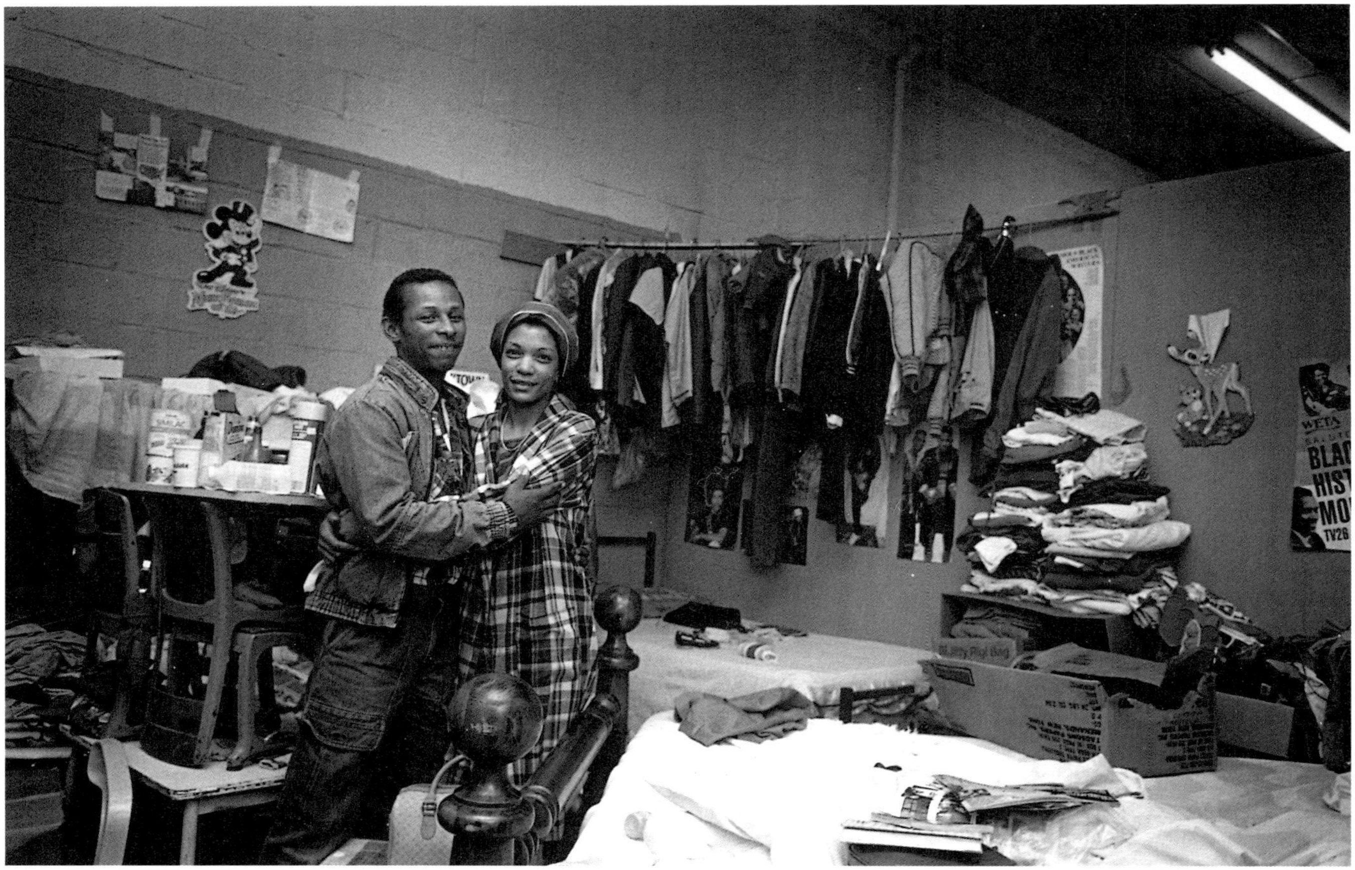

▶ *Man and woman in room*

Marvin Edwards, 11

The Carpenter's Shelter,
Alexandria, Virginia
1990
16" by 20", silver print

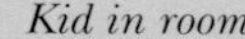

Kid in room

Chris Heflin, 9

The Carpenter's Shelter,
Alexandria, Virginia
1990
11" by 14", silver print

▶▼ *Family*

Rajaee Grey, 11

The Carpenter's Shelter,
Alexandria, Virginia
1990
11" by 14", silver print

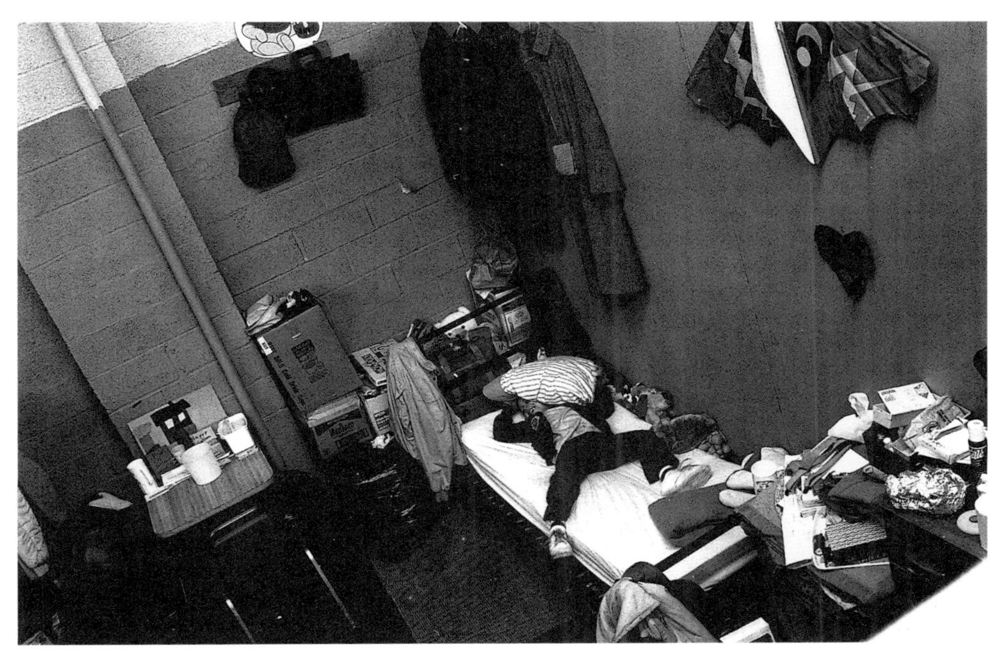

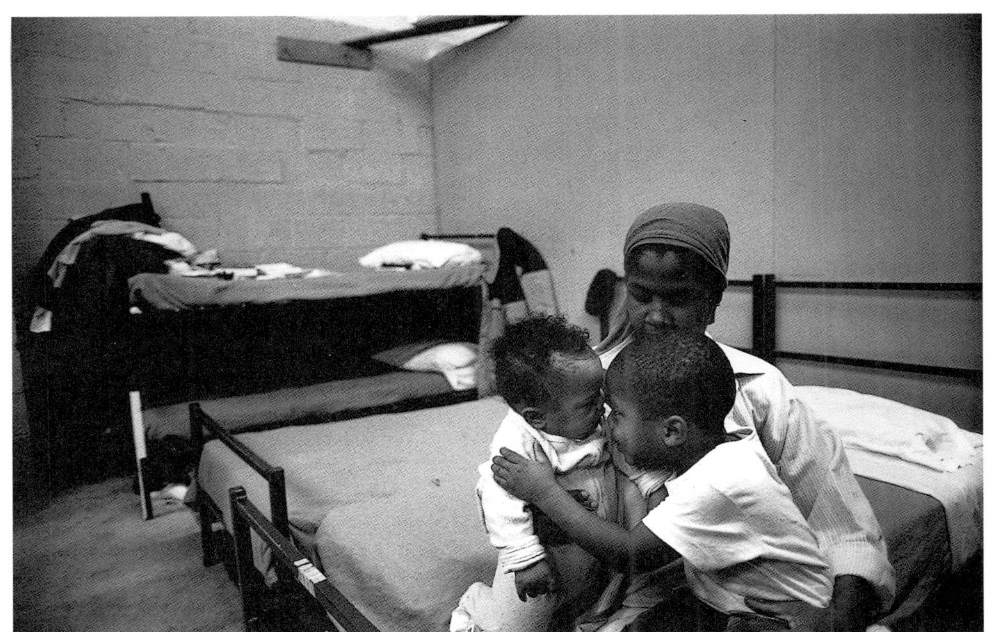

▶ *Man and woman in room*

Granada Brown

Capitol City Inn,
Washington, D.C.
1989
11" by 14", silver print

▶ *Family in shelter*

Chris Heflin, 9

The Carpenter's Shelter,
Alexandria, Virginia
1990
11" by 14", silver print

▶▲ *Magic castle*

Marvin Edwards, 11

The Carpenter's Shelter,
Alexandria, Virginia
1990
16" by 20", silver print

▶▼ *Reading II*

Marvin Edwards, 11

The Carpenter's Shelter,
Alexandria, Virginia
1990
11" by 14", silver print

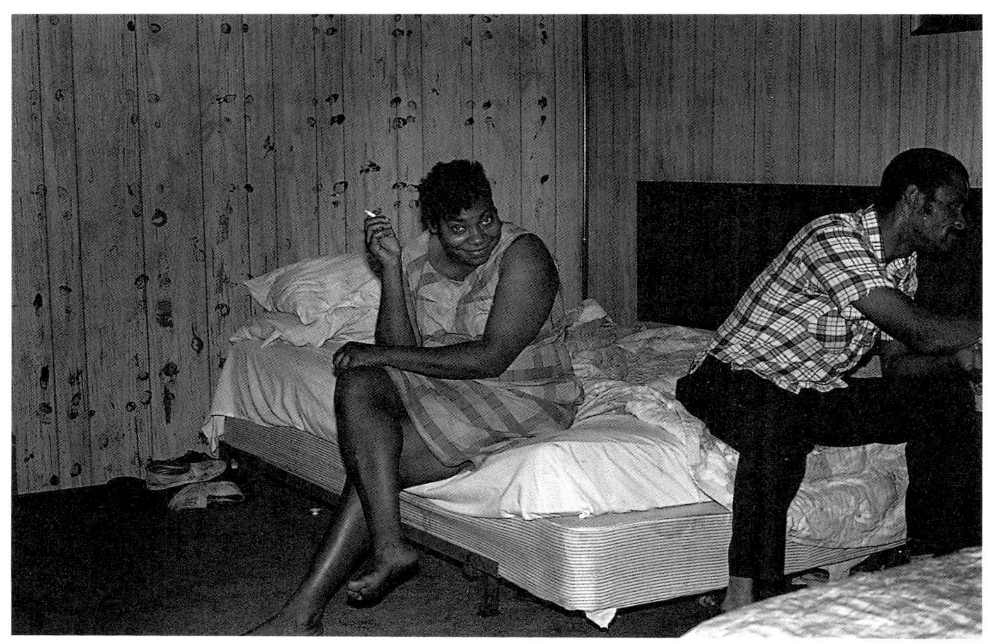

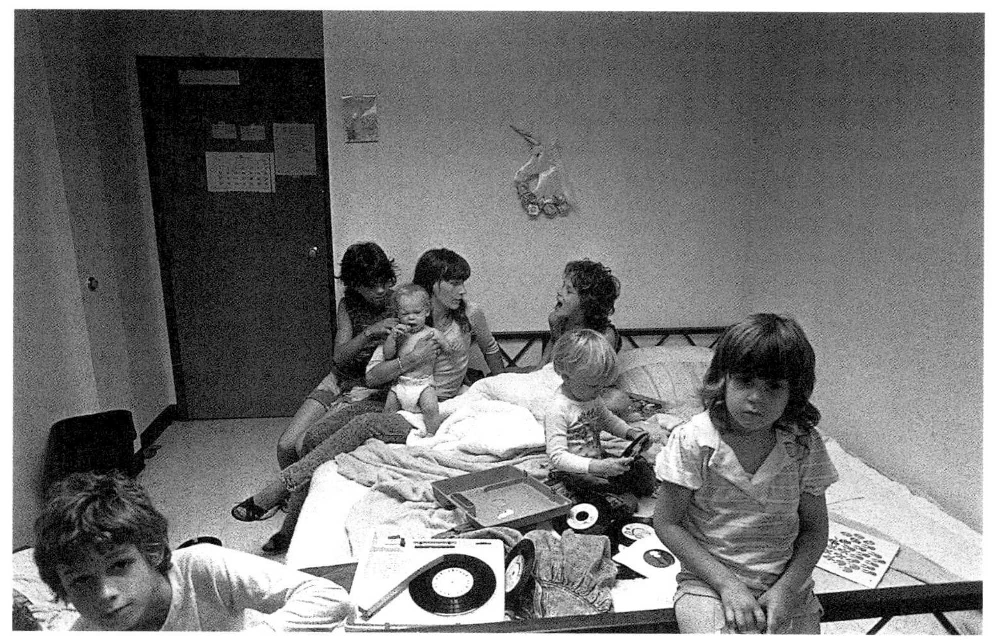

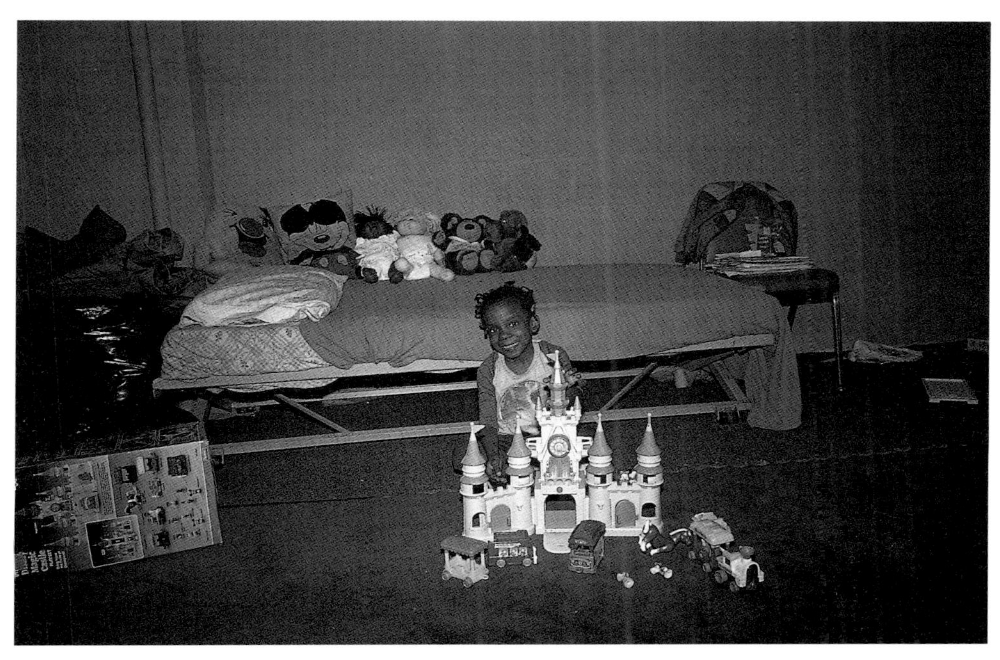

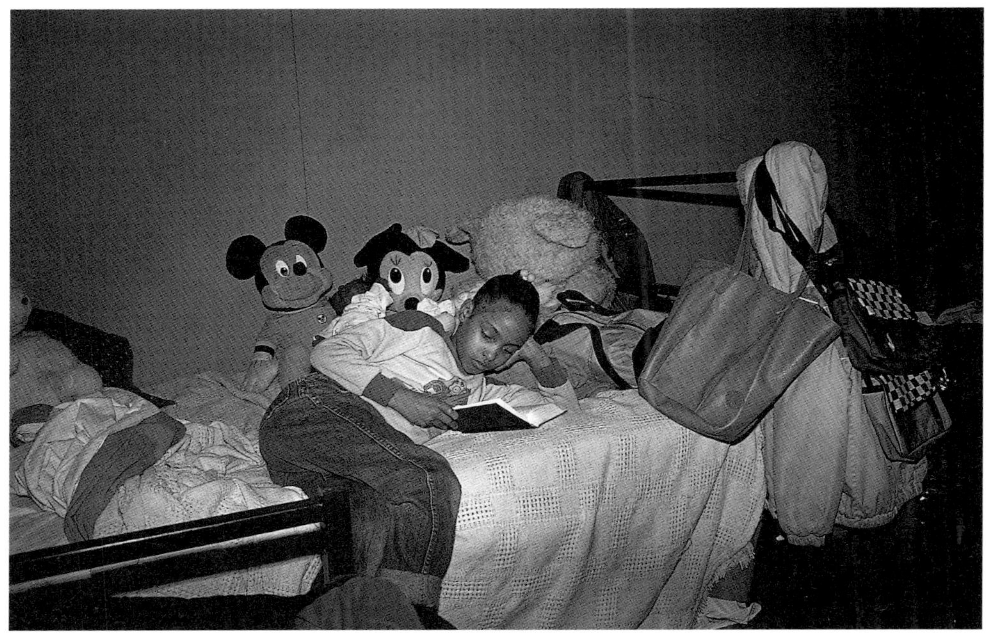

▶ *Mother and child*

Shawn Brooks, 11

The Carpenter's Shelter, Alexandria, Virginia 1990

11" by 14", silver print

▶▶ *Child in shelter*

Chris Heflin, 9

The Carpenter's Shelter, Alexandria, Virginia 1990

11" by 14", silver print

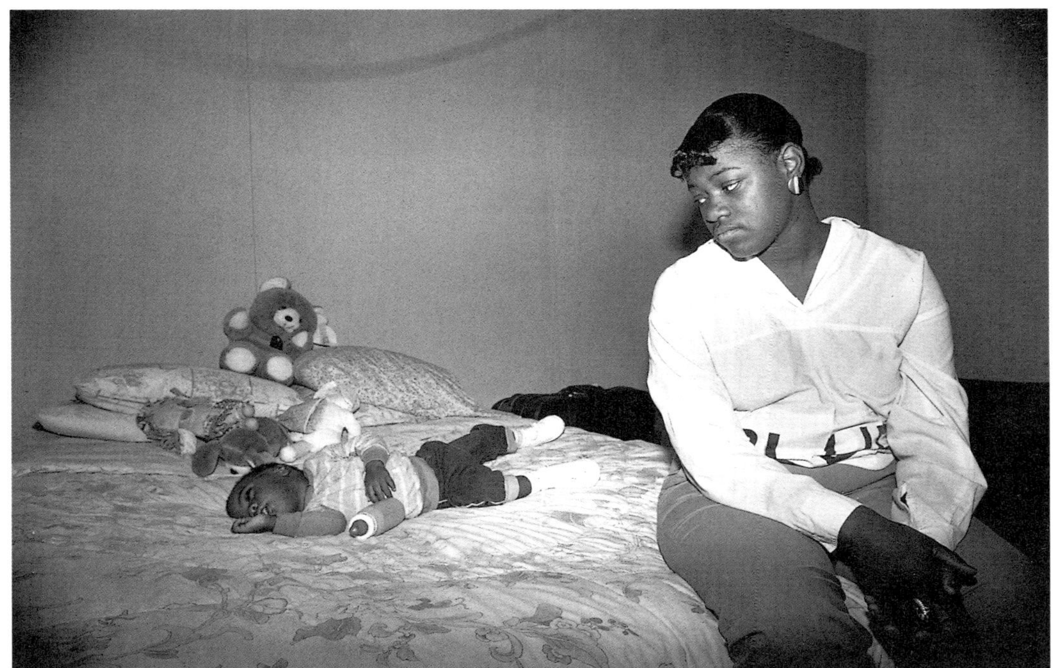

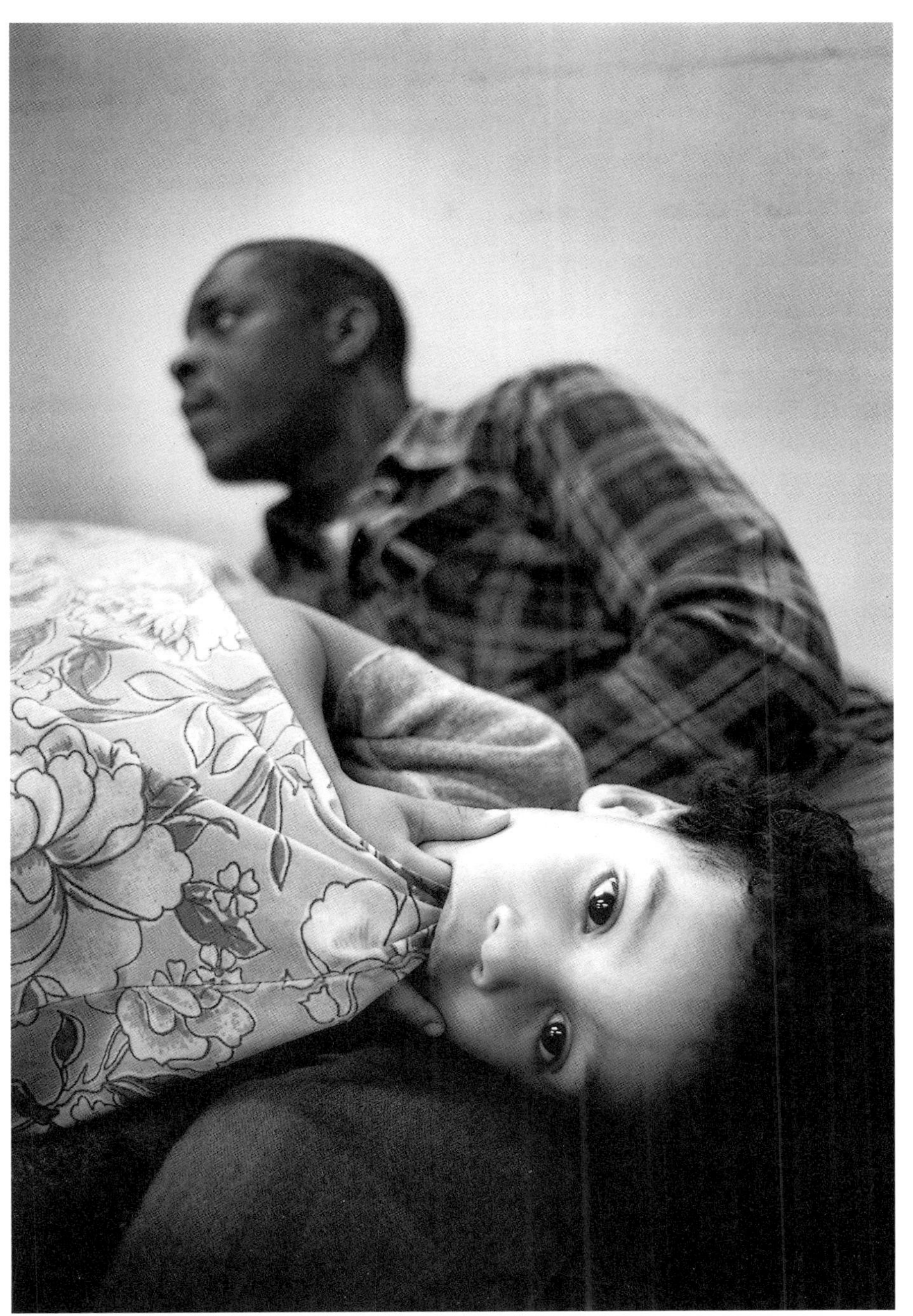

Legs

Morgan Paul, 10
Capitol City Inn,
Washington, D.C.
1989
11" by 14", silver print

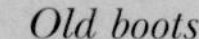

Old boots

David Burch, 12
Capitol City Inn,
Washington, D.C
1989
11" by 14", silver print

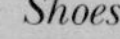

Shoes

Dion Johnson, 11
new residence,
Southwest
Washington, D.C.
1989
11" by 14", silver print

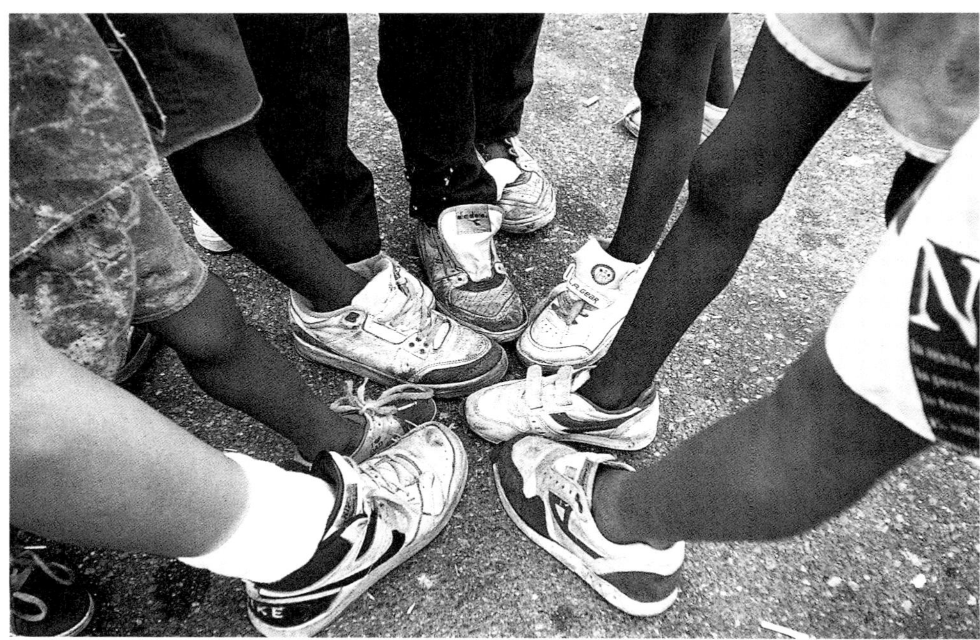

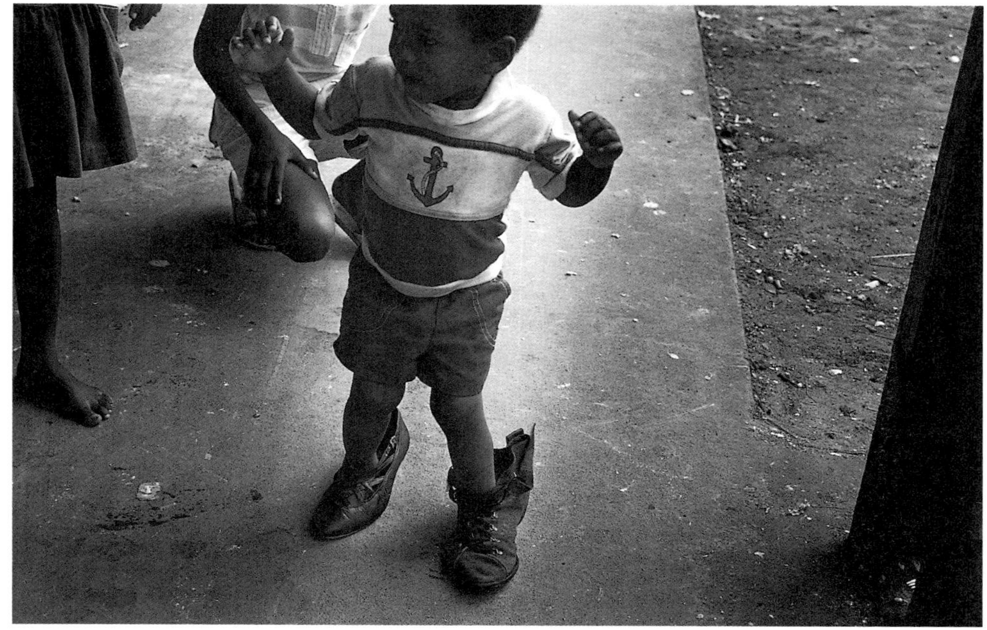

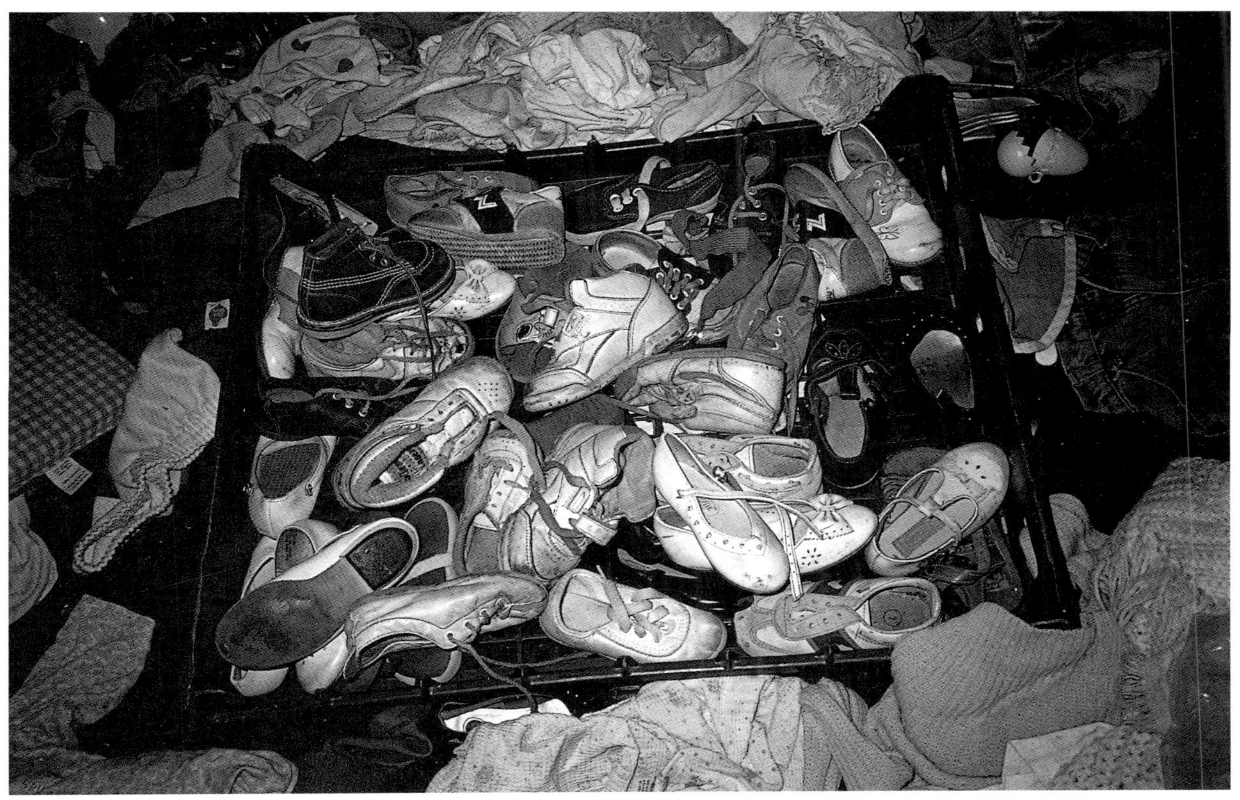

COMMENT FROM DION At my house, there's my Aunt Pat, she's got Robin, Morgan, Barry, and Marquita, that's five. Me, Big David, Little David, Kim, Sonny, Little Vanessa, Frank, Brandon. So how much is that? Fifteen.Me and Barry sleep on the top bunk. Brandon and them sleep on the bottom bunk. Kim, Marquita, and the girls sleep downstairs on the sofa bed. My mother sleeps in her bed with Big David; Little David sleeps anywhere he wants, sometimes with me.

▶ *Corridor*

Calvin Stewart, 17
Reston Shelter,
Reston, Virginia
1989
11" by 14", silver print

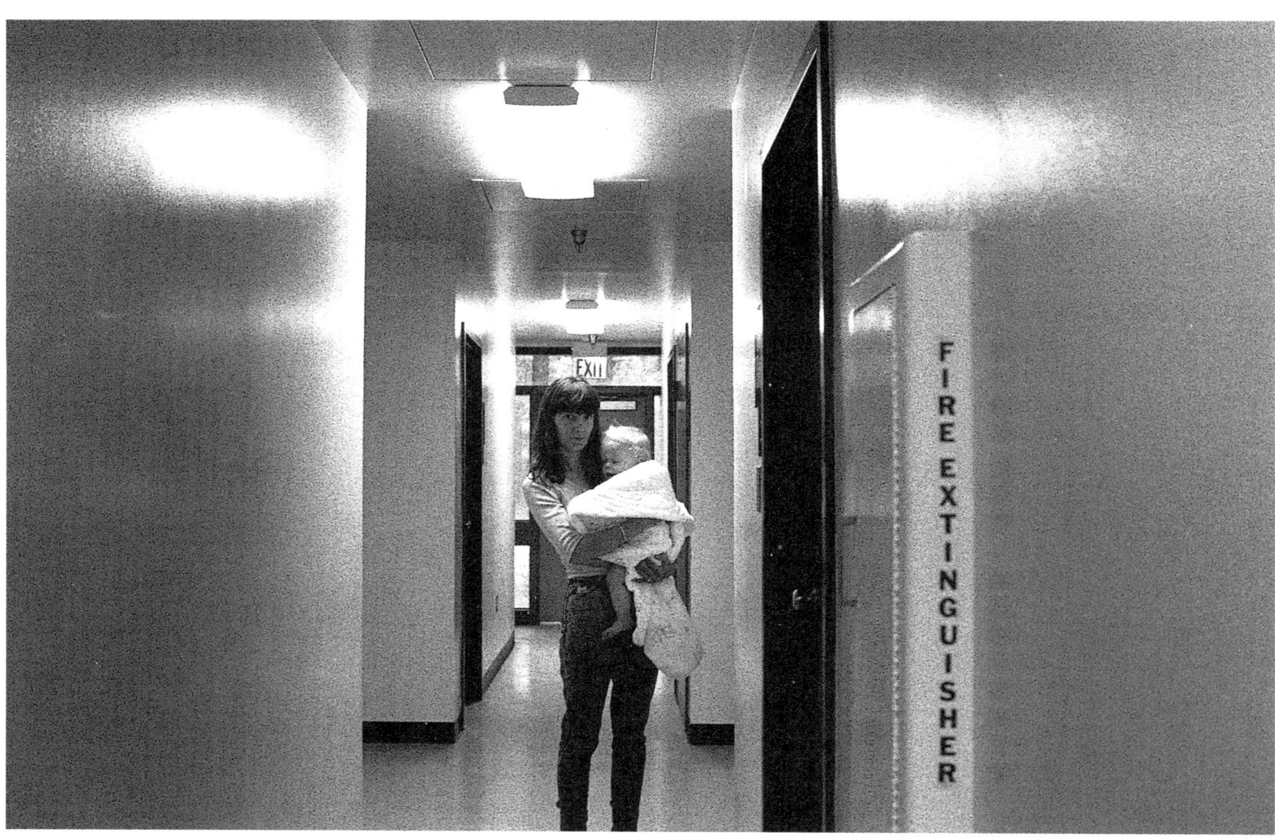

▶▲ *Baby in common living area*

Calvin Stewart, 17
Reston Shelter
Reston, Virginia
1989
11" by 14", silver print

▶▼ *Television*

Calvin Stewart, 17
Reston Shelter,
Reston, Virginia
1989
11" by 14", silver print

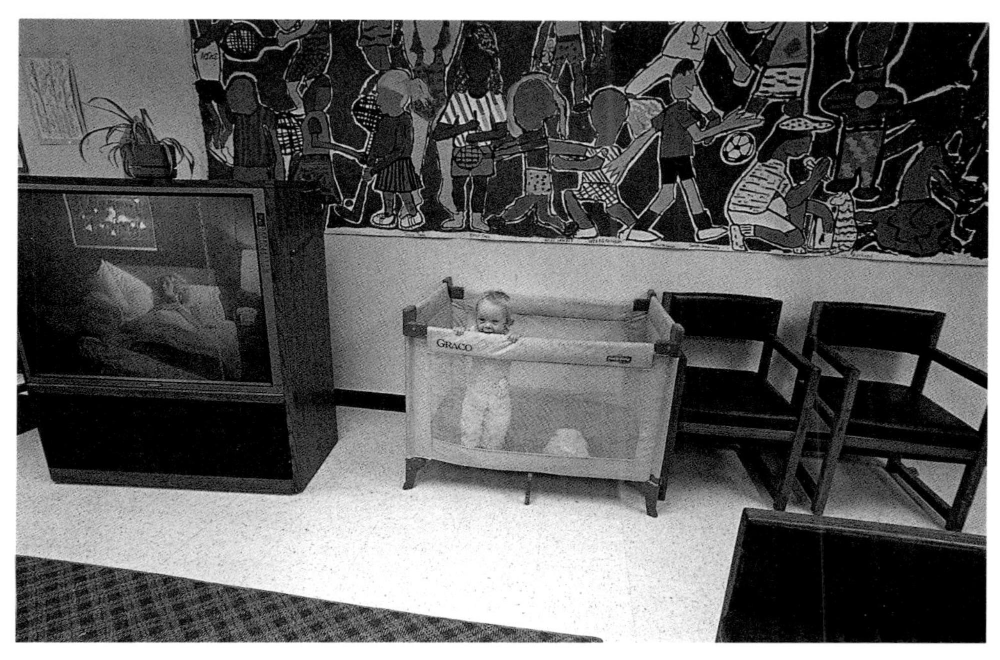
GRACO

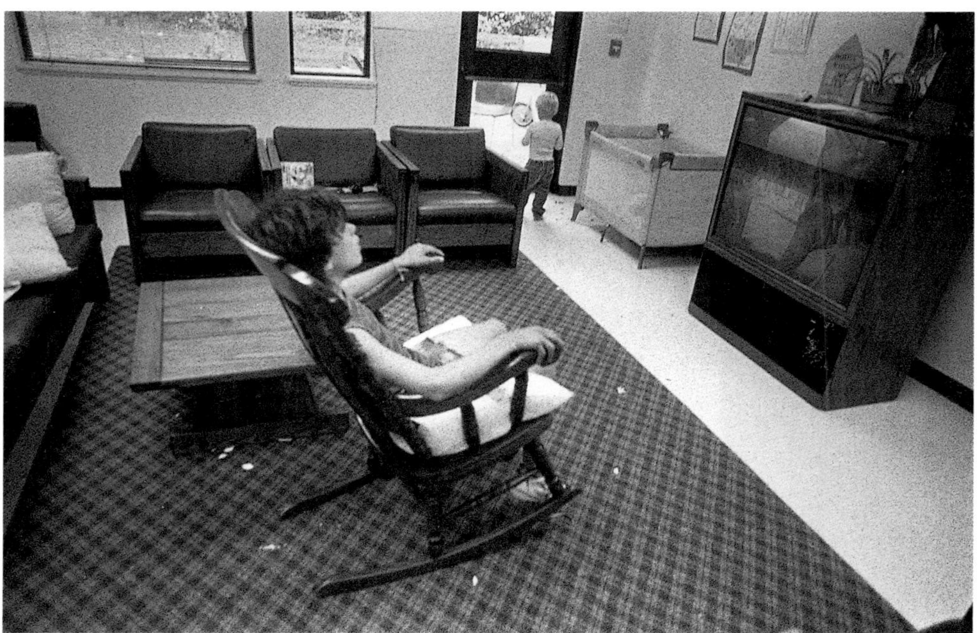

▶ *Family in shelter*

Chris Heflin, 9

The Carpenter's Shelter,
Alexandria, Virginia
1990
11" by 14", silver print

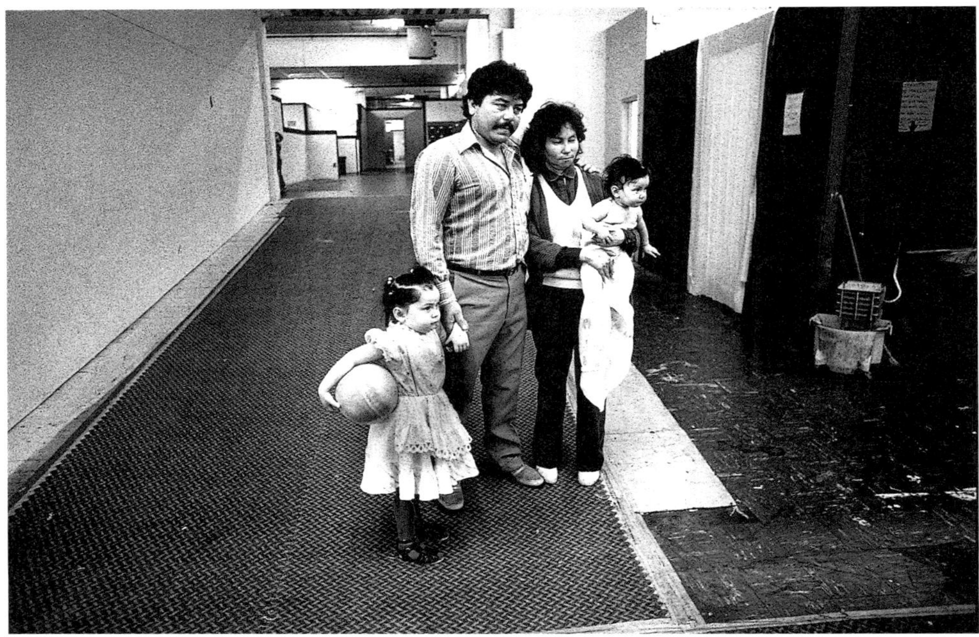

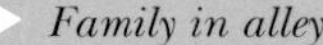 *Family in alley*

Yolanda Mitchell

Community of Hope,
Washington, D.C.
1989
16" by 20", silver print

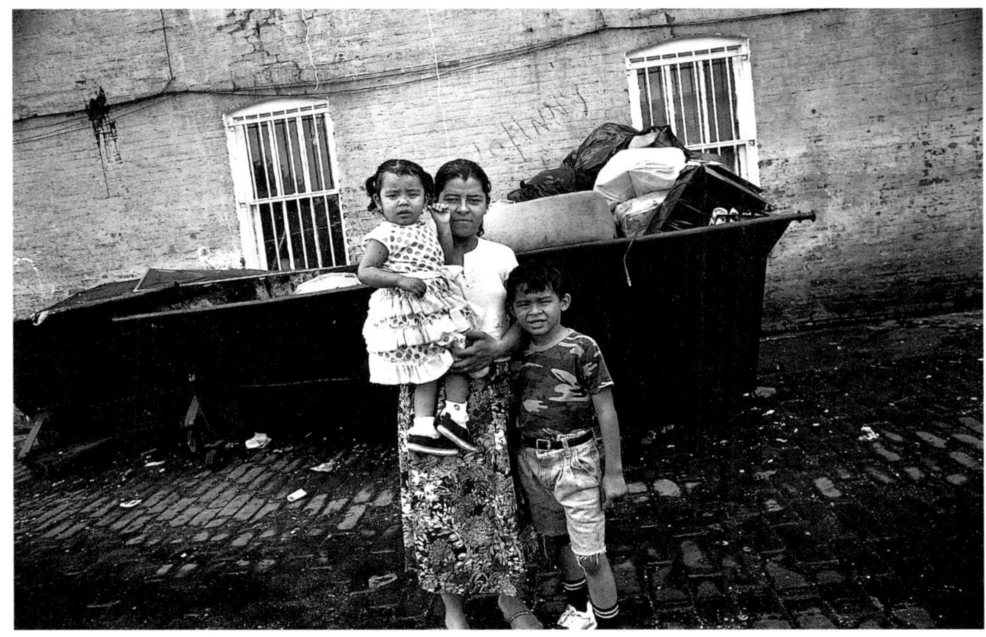

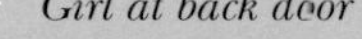 *Girl at back door*

Norman Heflin, 8

The Carpenter's Shelter,
Alexandria, Virginia
1990
11" by 14", silver print

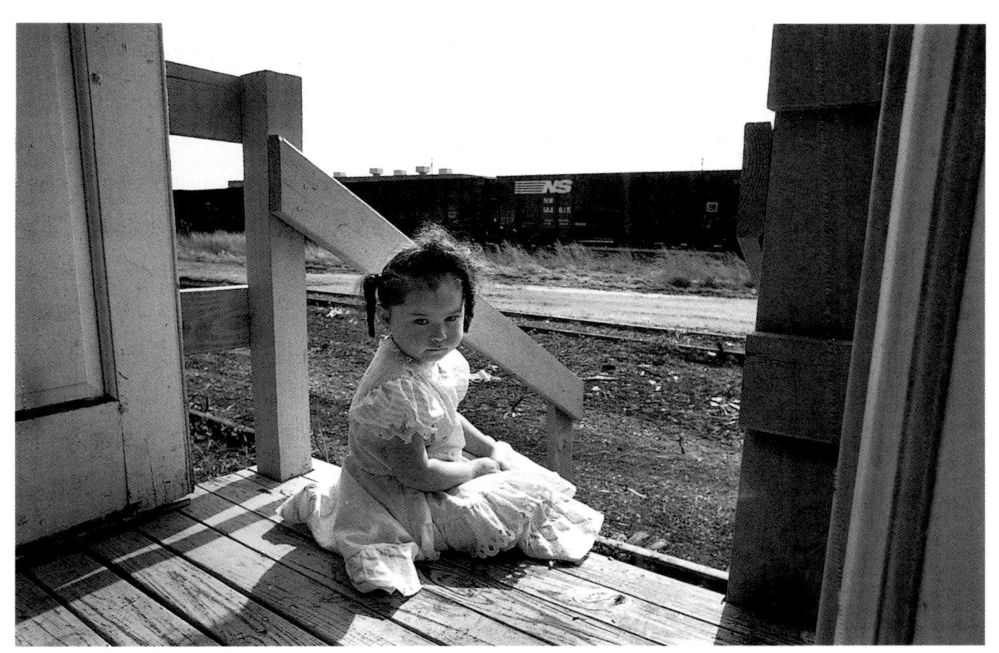
NS

▶ *Mother and son*

Calvin Stewart, 17
Reston Shelter,
Reston, Virginia
1989
11" by 14", silver print

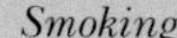 *Smoking*

Calvin Stewart, 17
Reston Shelter,
Reston, Virginia
1989
11" by 14", silver print

▶▼ *Television*

Norman Heflin, 8
The Carpenter's
Shelter,
Alexandria, Virginia
1990
11" by 14", silver print

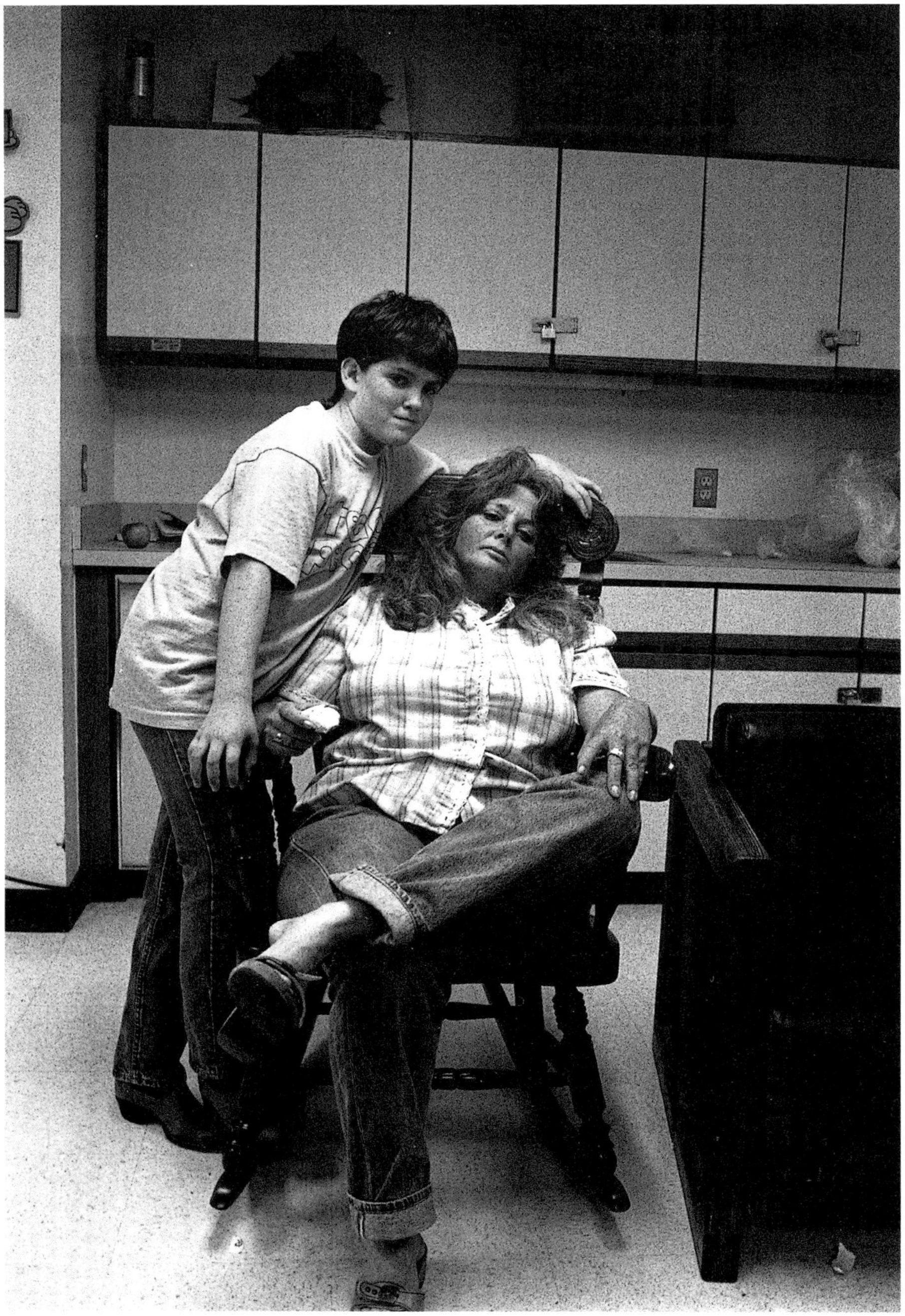

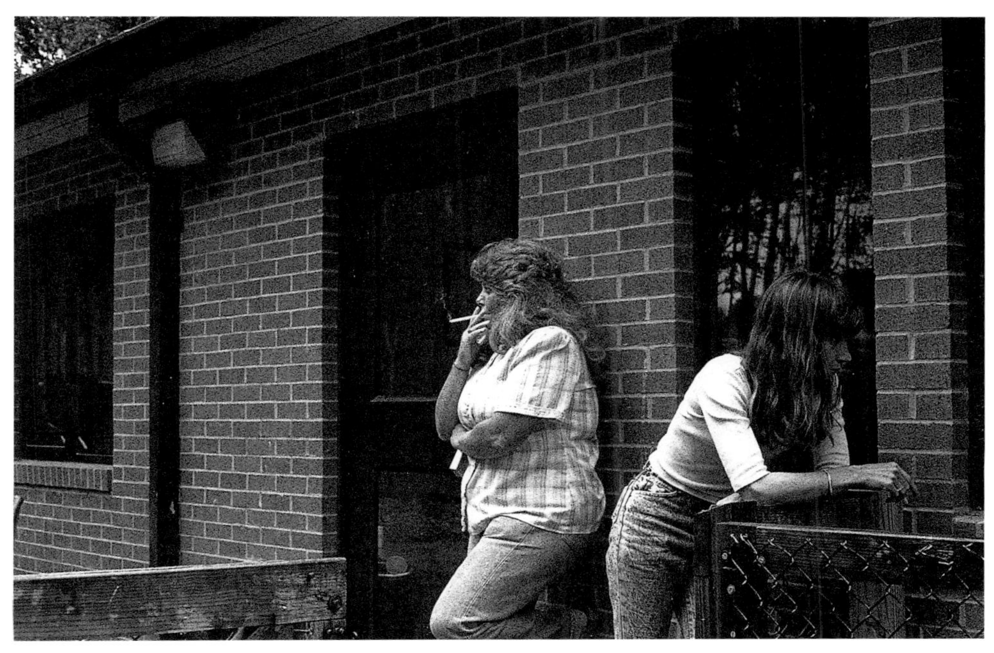

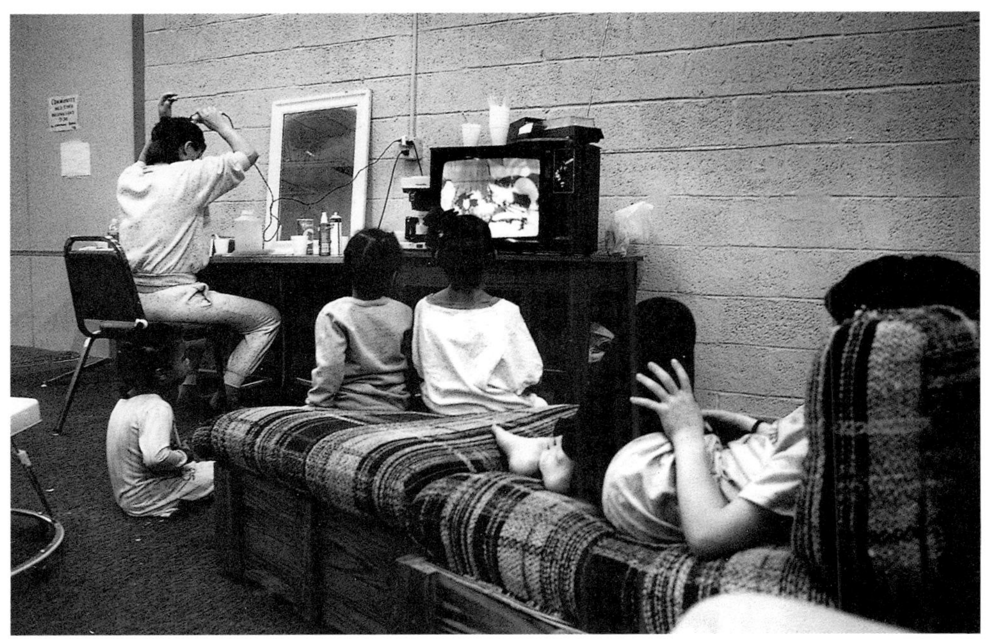

Kitchen

Calvin Stewart, 17
Reston Shelter,
Reston, Virginia
1989
11" by 14", silver print

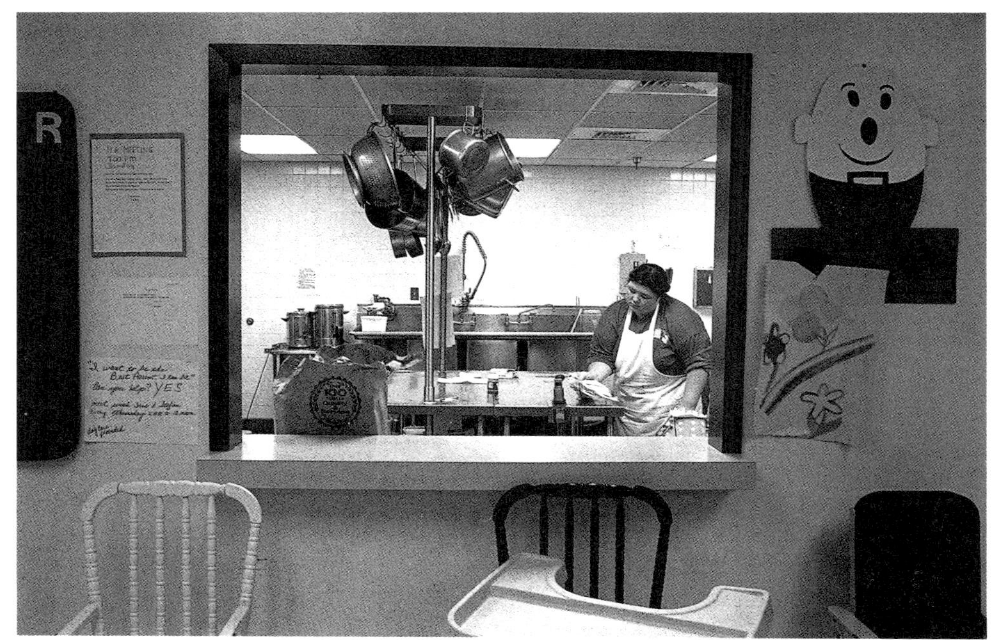

Cook

Robyn Turner, 7
Reston Shelter,
Reston, Virginia
1989
11" by 14", silver print

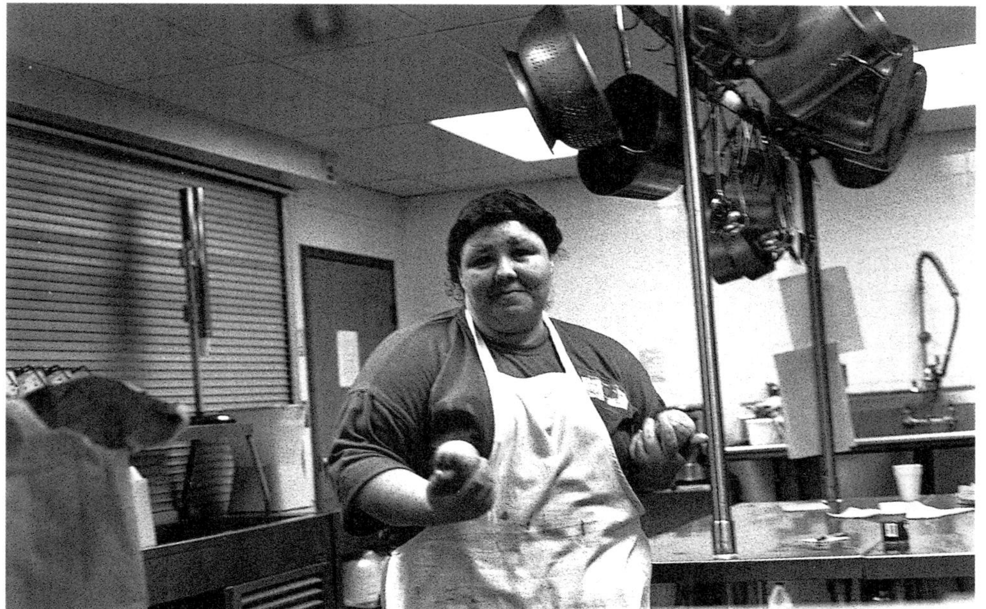

Baby with apple

Calvin Stewart, 17
Reston Shelter,
Reston, Virginia
1989
11" by 14", silver print

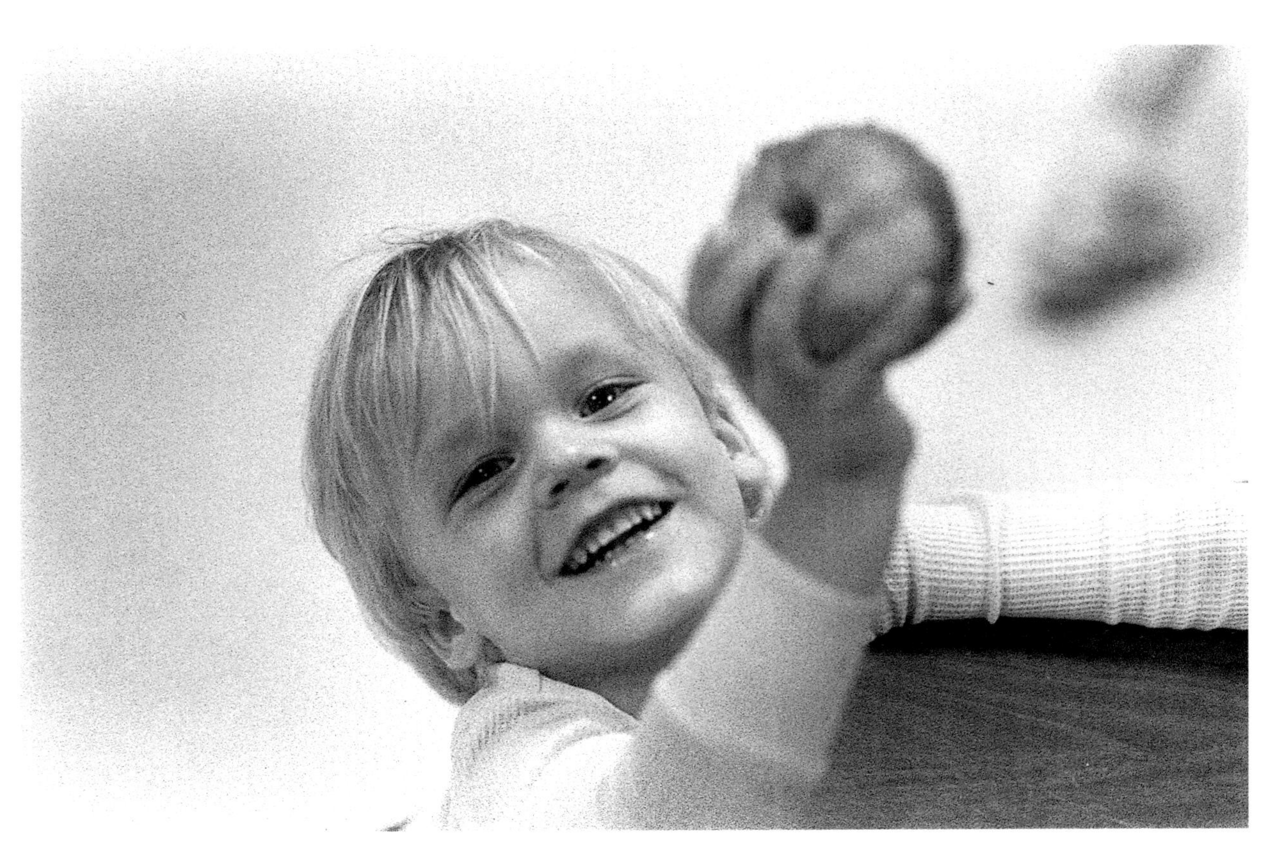

▶ *Malcolm X Park*

Calvin Stewart, 17
Pitts Hotel,
Washington, D.C.
1989
16" by 20", silver print

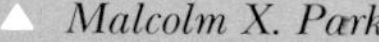
Malcolm X. Park

Daniel Hall, 9
Pitts Hotel,
Washington, D.C.
1989
11" by 14", silver print

▶▼ *Family in park*

Daniel Hall, 9
Pitts Hotel,
Washington, D.C.
1989
11" by 14", silver print

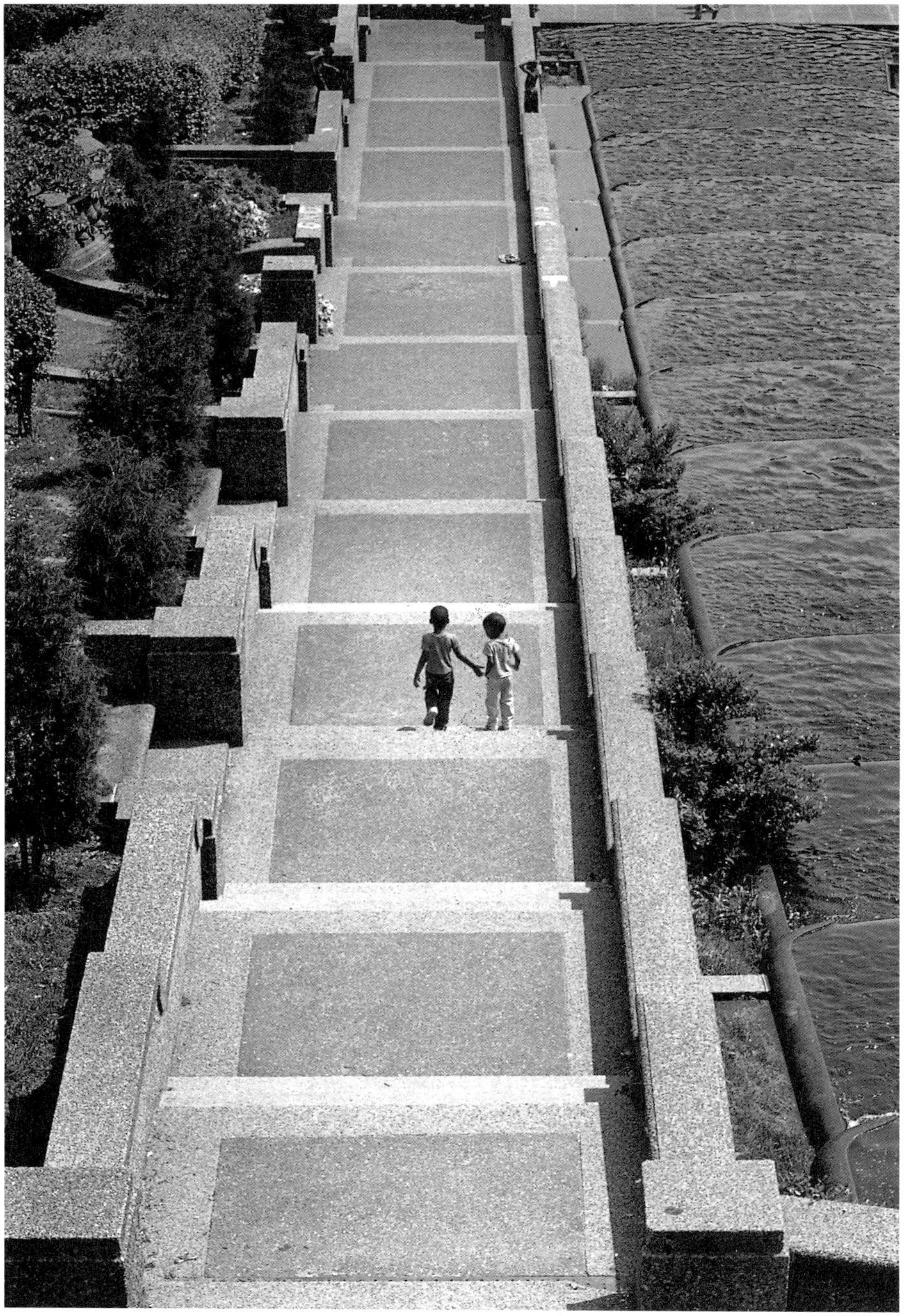

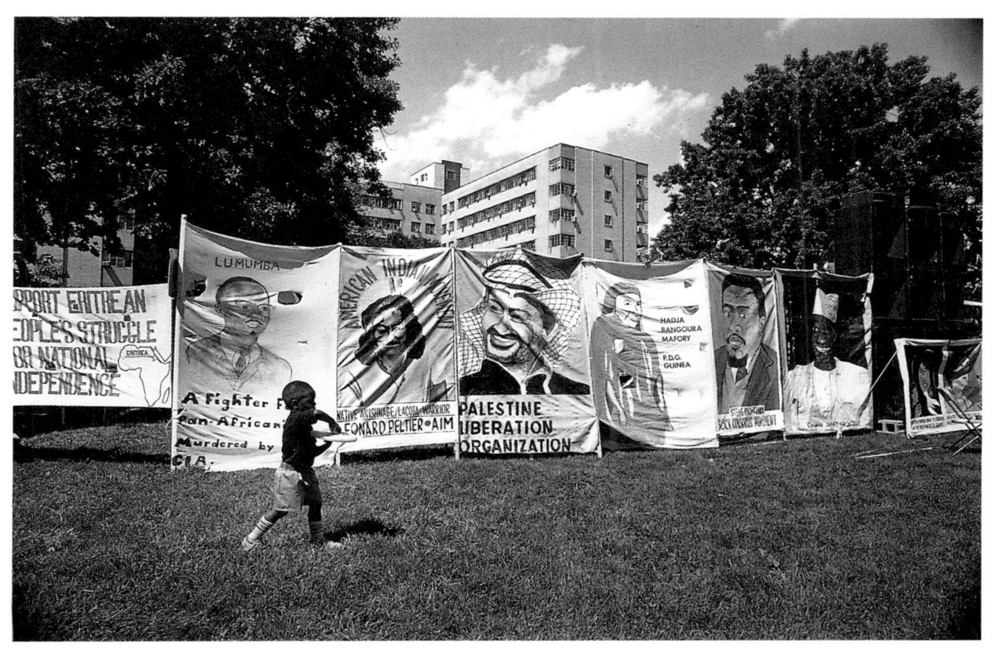
PPORT ERITREAN
EOPLE'S STRUGGLE
OR NATIONAL
NDEPENDENCE
ERITREA
LUMUMBA
A Fighter F
Pan-African
Murdered by
CIA.
AMERICAN INDIAN
NATIVE ANISHNABE/LACOTA WARRIOR
EONARD PELTIER • AIM
PALESTINE
LIBERATION
ORGANIZATION
HADJA
BANGOURA
MAFORY
P.D.G.
GUINEA

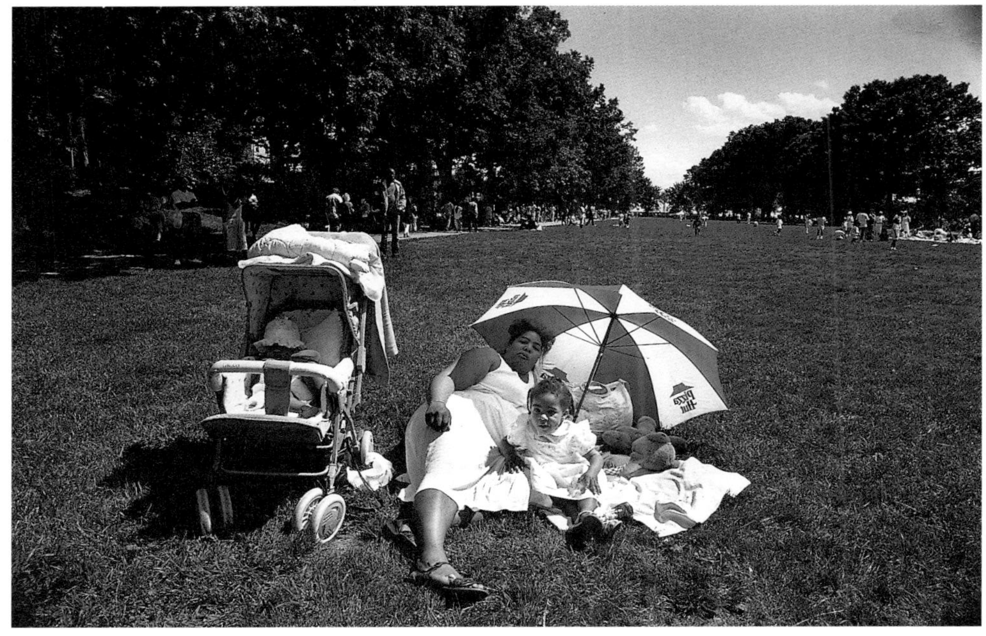

Washington Homes Limited

Calvin Stewart, 17

General Scott Hotel, Washington, D.C.
1989
11" by 14", silver print

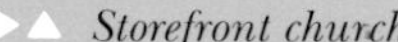 *Storefront church*

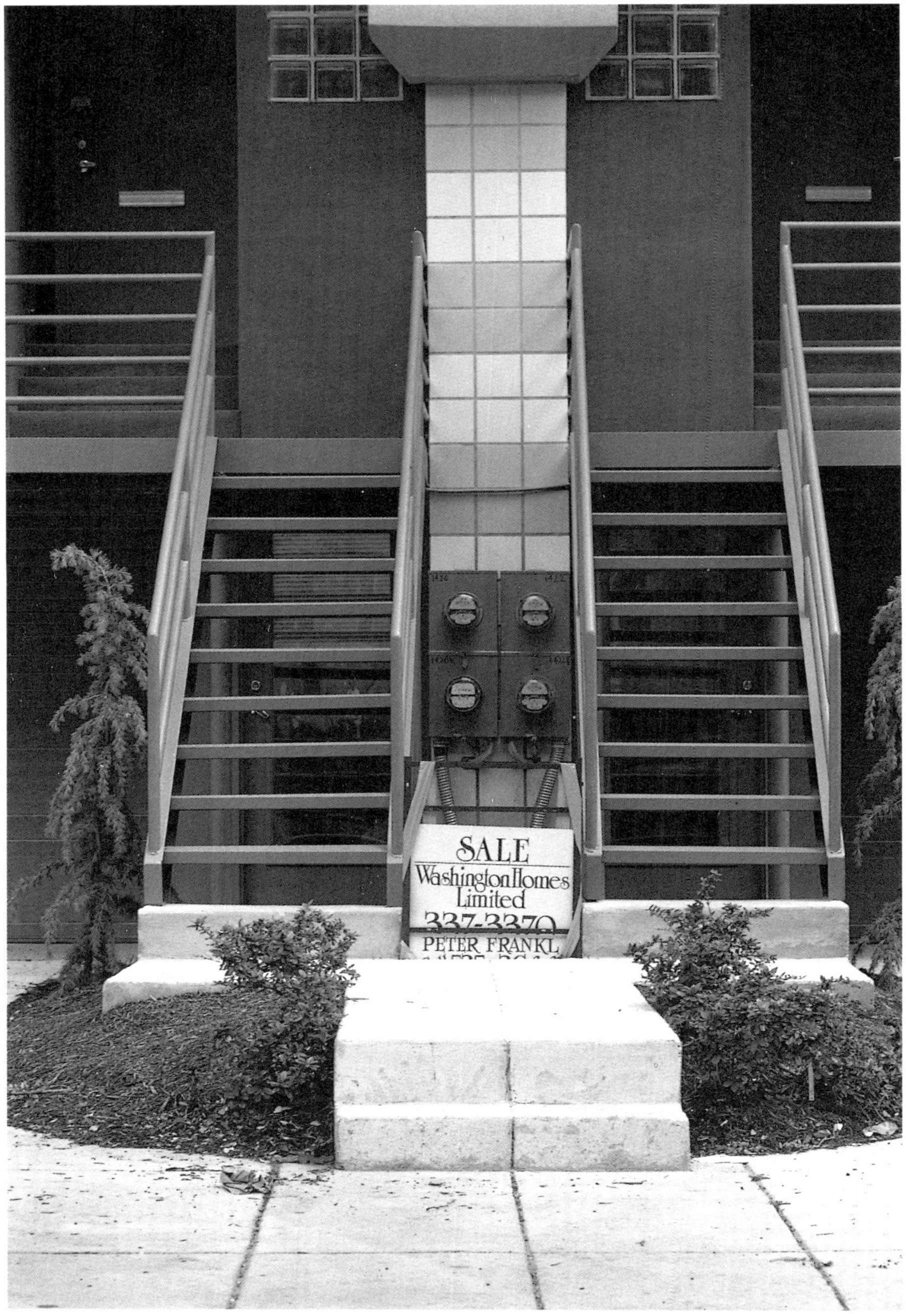

Arthur Taylor, 10

Community of Hope, Washington, D.C.
1989
11" by 14", silver print

Watchtower

Tamicka Hodge, 12

General Scott Hotel, Washington, D.C.
1989
11" by 14", silver print

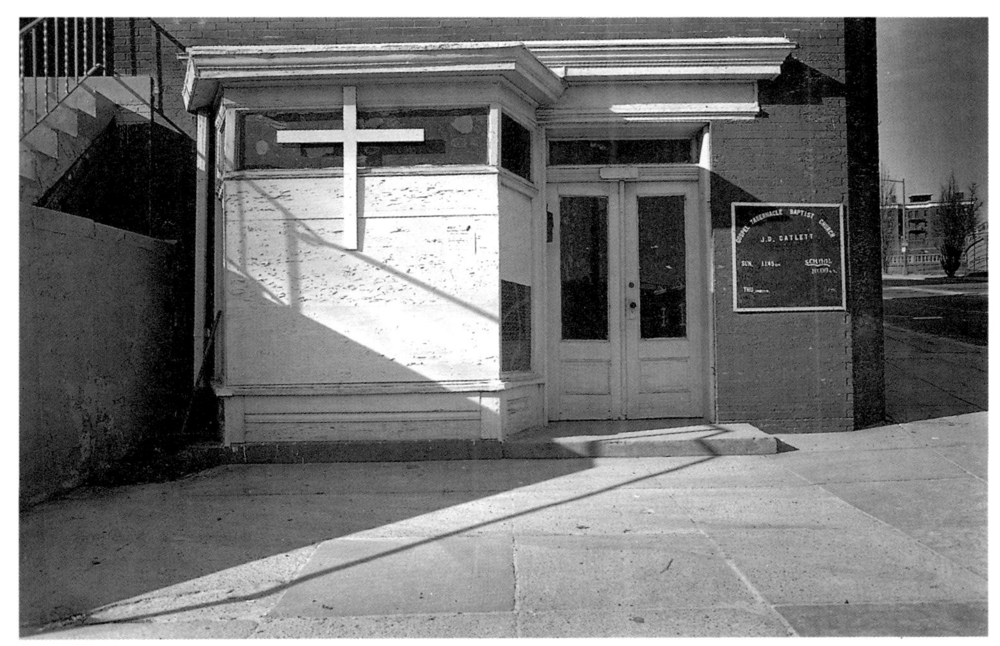
GOSPEL TABERNACLE BAPTIST CHURCH
J.D. CATLETT
SUN.
SCHOOL
THU

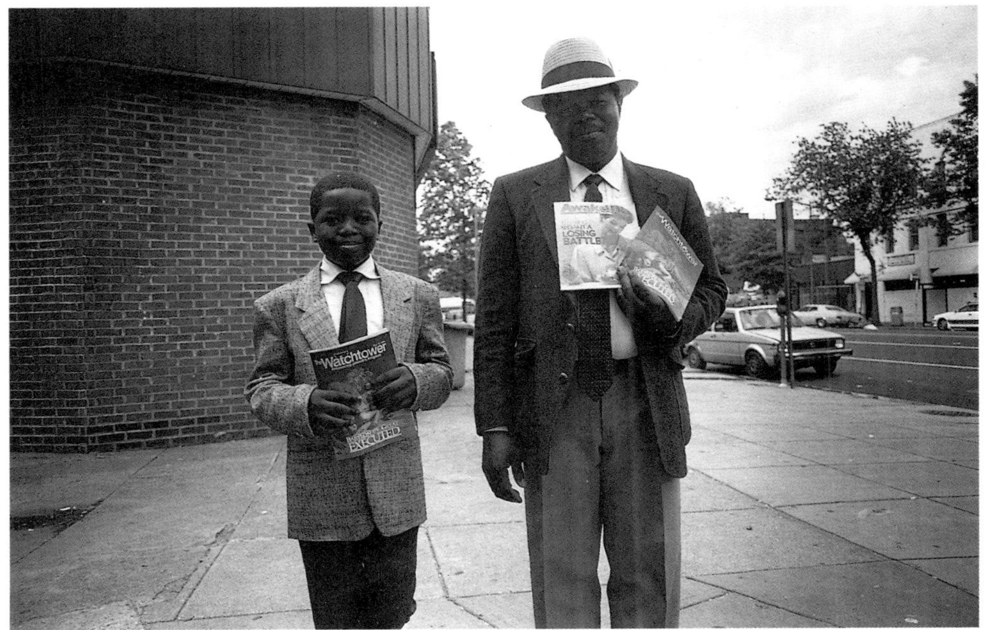
The Watchtower
EXECUTED
LOSING
BATTLE
Watchtower

▶ *Fire escape*

Calvin Stewart, 17

Community of Hope,
Washington, D.C.
1989
11" by 14", silver print

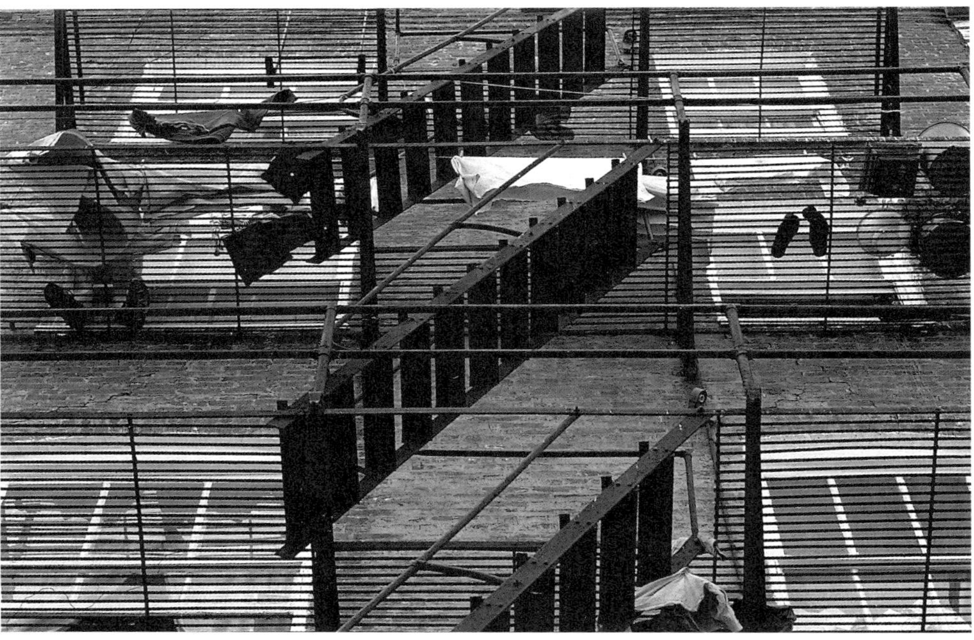

▶ *Cleaning*

Chris Heflin, 9

The Carpenter's
Shelter,
Alexandria, Virginia
1990
11" by 14", silver print

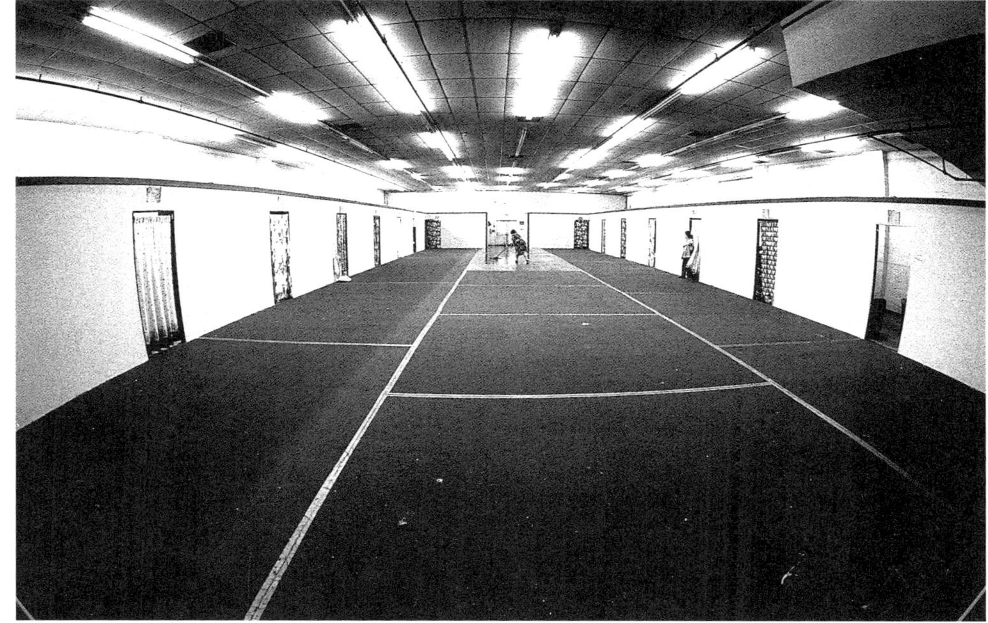

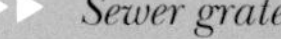

Sewer grate

Mario Lamont, 12

Pitts Hotel,
Washington, D.C.
1989
16" by 20", silver print

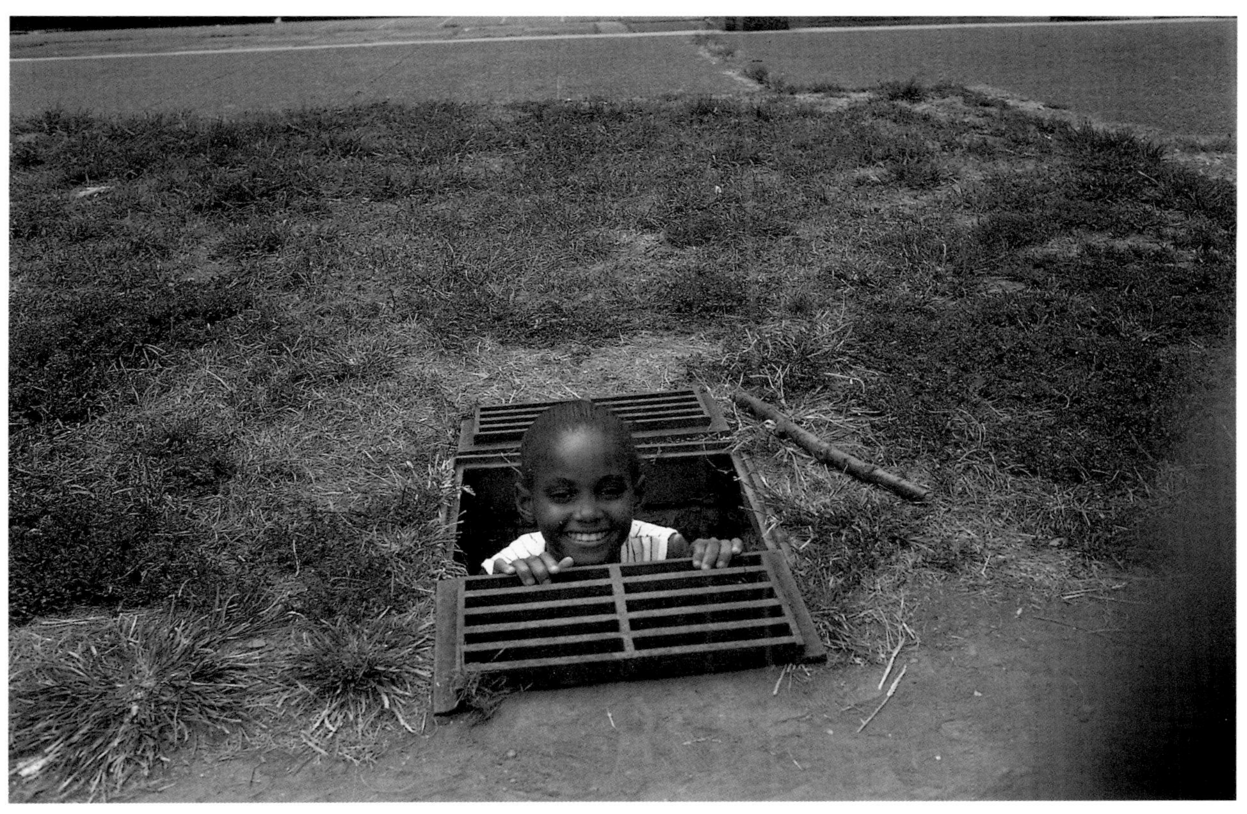

COMMENT FROM SCHOOLCHILD I really admire how they still have fun even though they don't have much.

Police line, aftermath of fire that claimed a child's life

Dion Johnson, 11
Capitol City Inn,
Washington, D.C.
1989
11" by 14", silver print

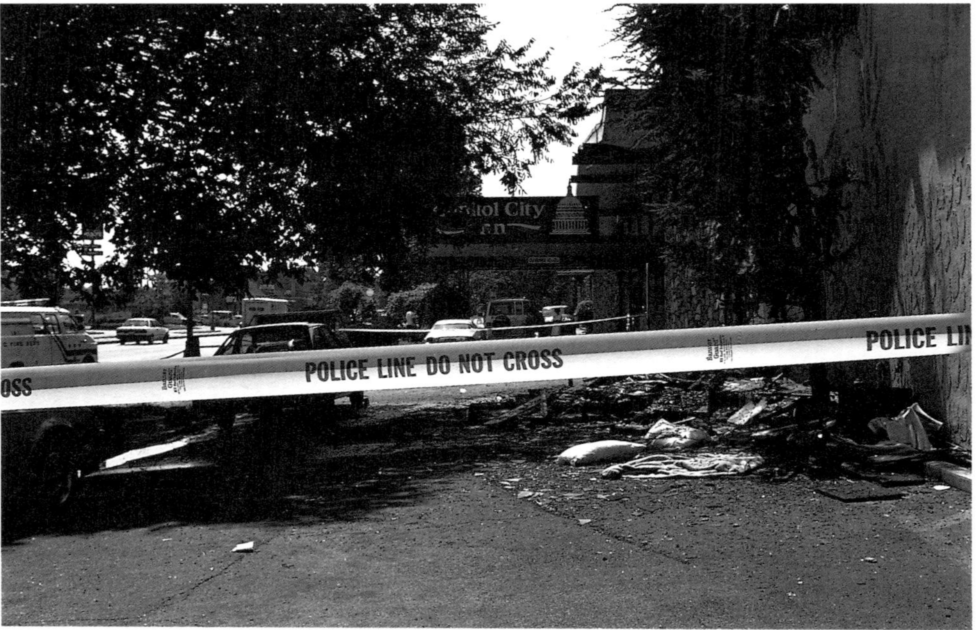

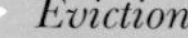
Eviction

Calvin Stewart, 17
Community of Hope,
Washington, D.C.
1989
11" by 14", silver print

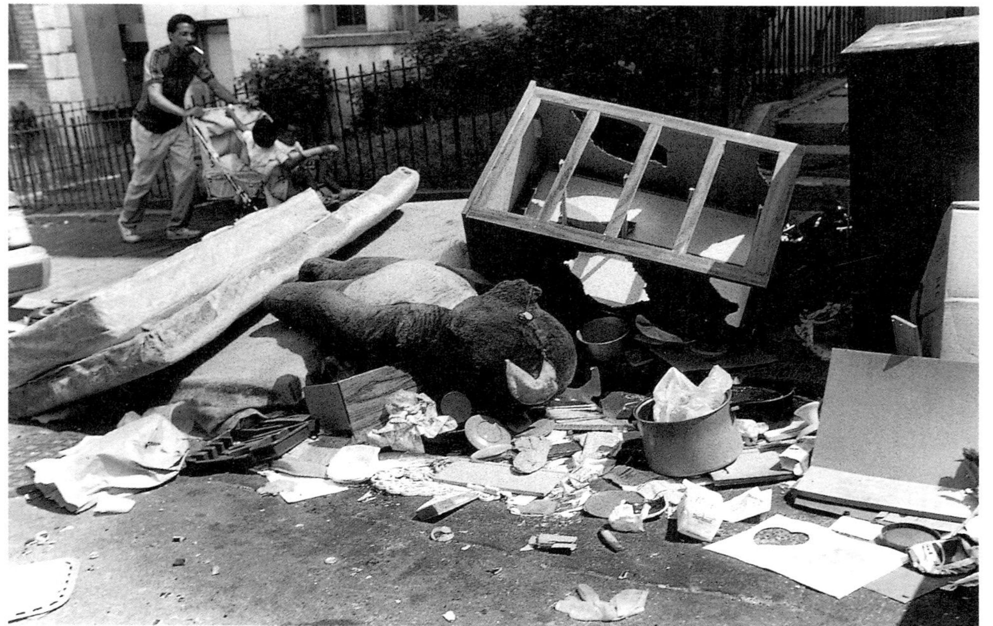

Aftermath of fire that claimed a child's life

Dion Johnson, 11
Capitol City Inn,
Washington, D.C.
1989
11" by 14", silver print

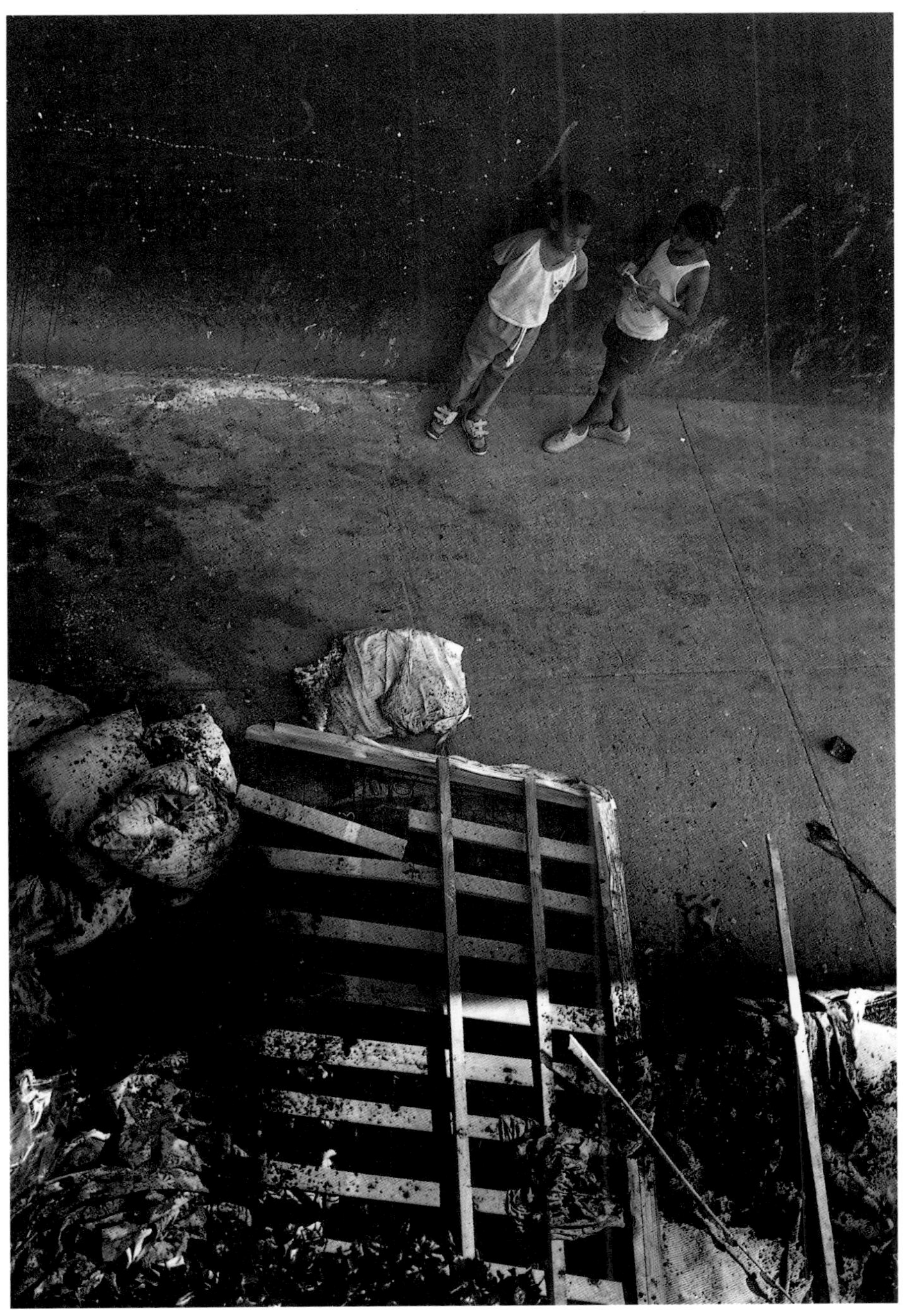

DION'S COMMENT It was sad. At first, I didn't want to take pictures of where it had burned. But then I did. Sometimes it's like a news story. Your pictures tell people what it was like. That's important.

▶ *Girl on street*

Carissa Etheridge, 15
Community of Hope,
Washington, D.C.
1989
11" by 14", silver print

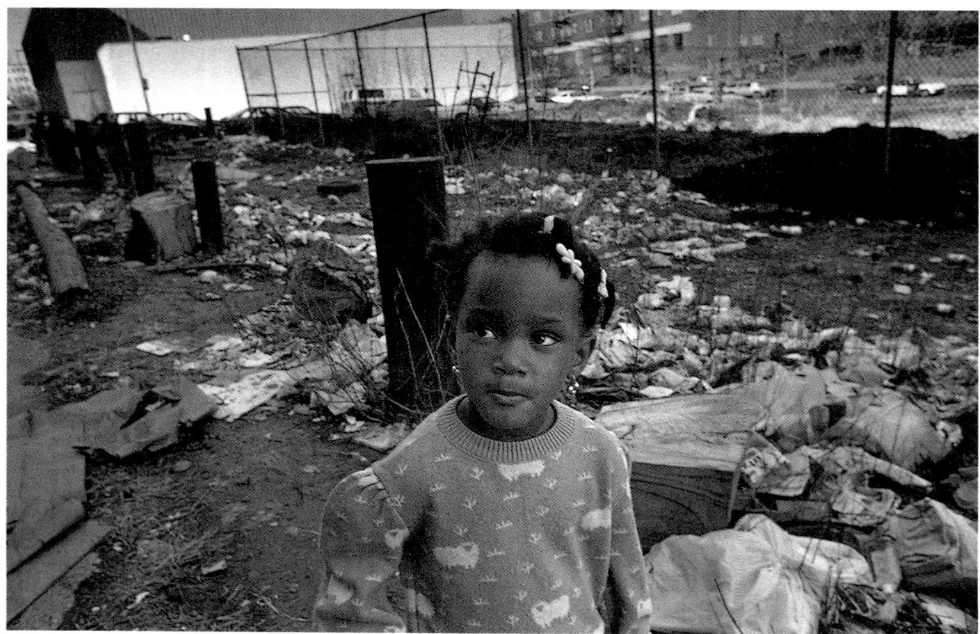

▶ *Boy in street*

Arthur Taylor, 10
Community of Hope,
Washington, D.C.
1989
16" by 20", silver print

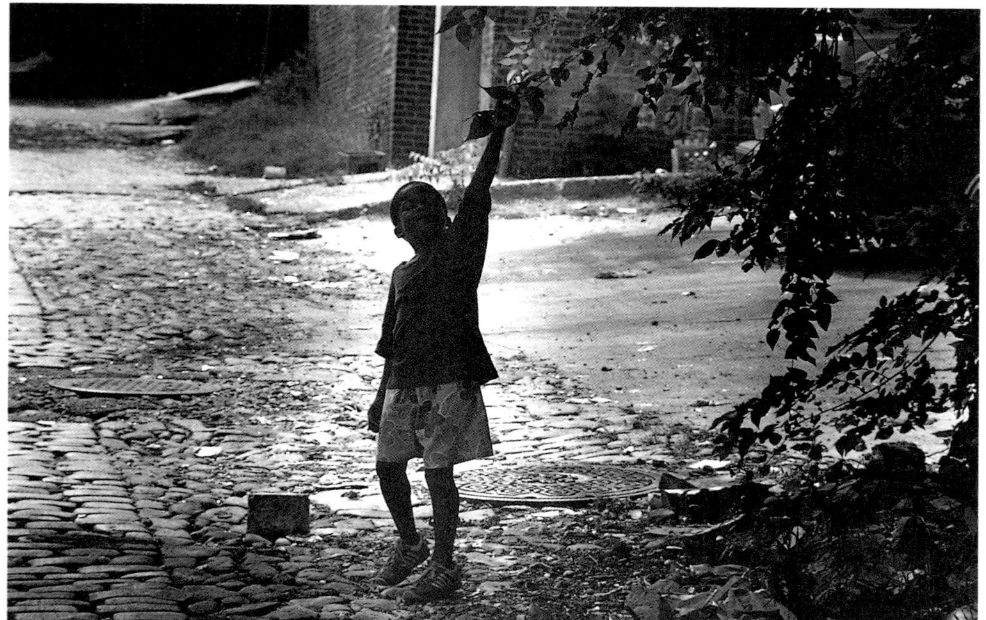

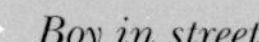

Washington monument

Arthur Taylor, 10
Community of Hope,
Washington, D.C.
1989
16" by 20", silver print

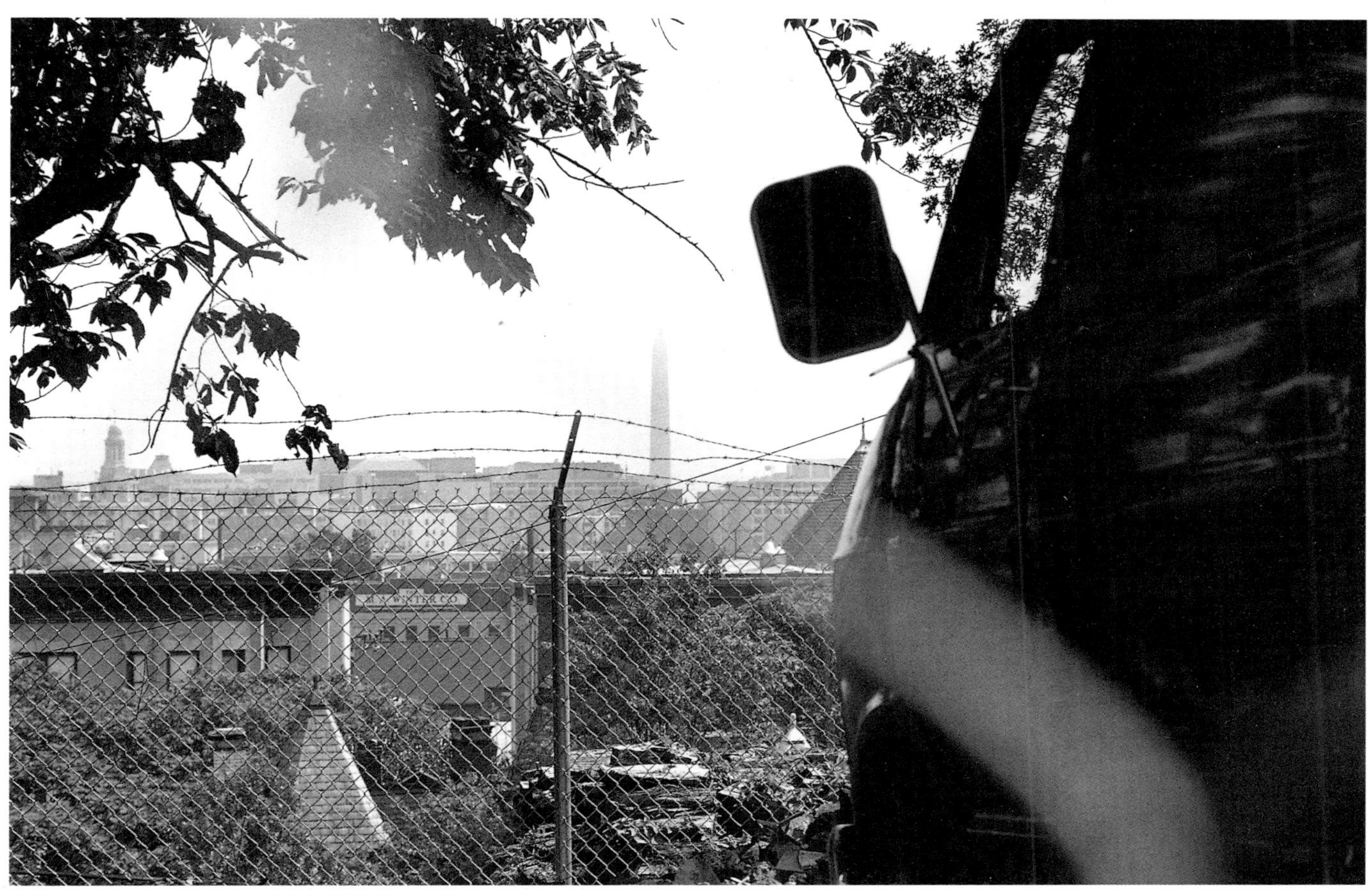

COMMENT TO ARTHUR FROM SCHOOLCHILD The monument is so far away yet and most likely you won't reach what it symbolizes. I live in NYC and I understand the meaning.

Dog

Dion Johnson, 12
new residence,
Southwest
Washington, D.C.
1990
11" by 14", silver print

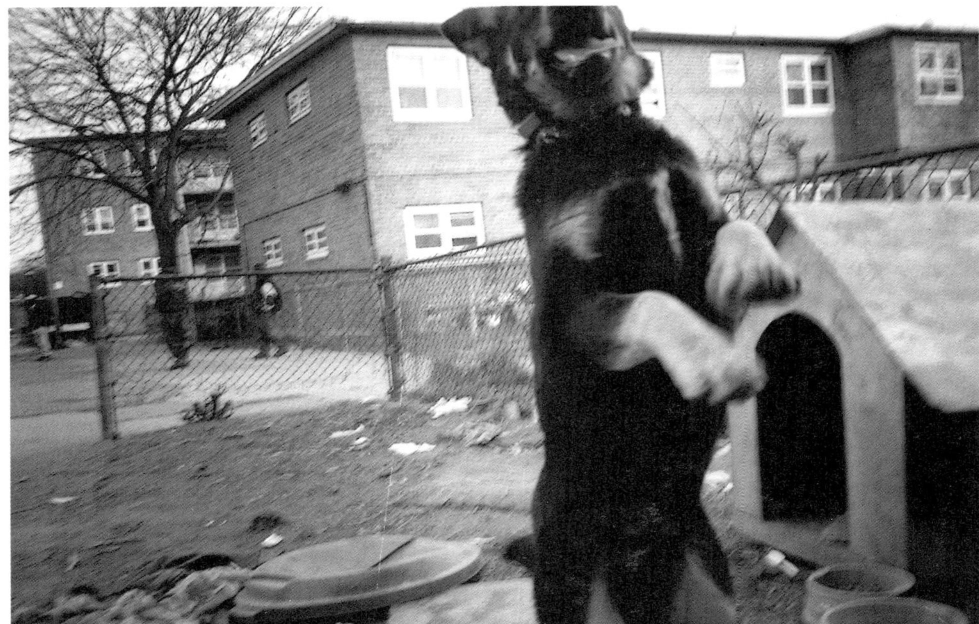

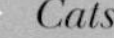 *Cats*

Carissa Etheridge, 15
Community of Hope,
Washington, D.C.
1989
11" by 14", silver print

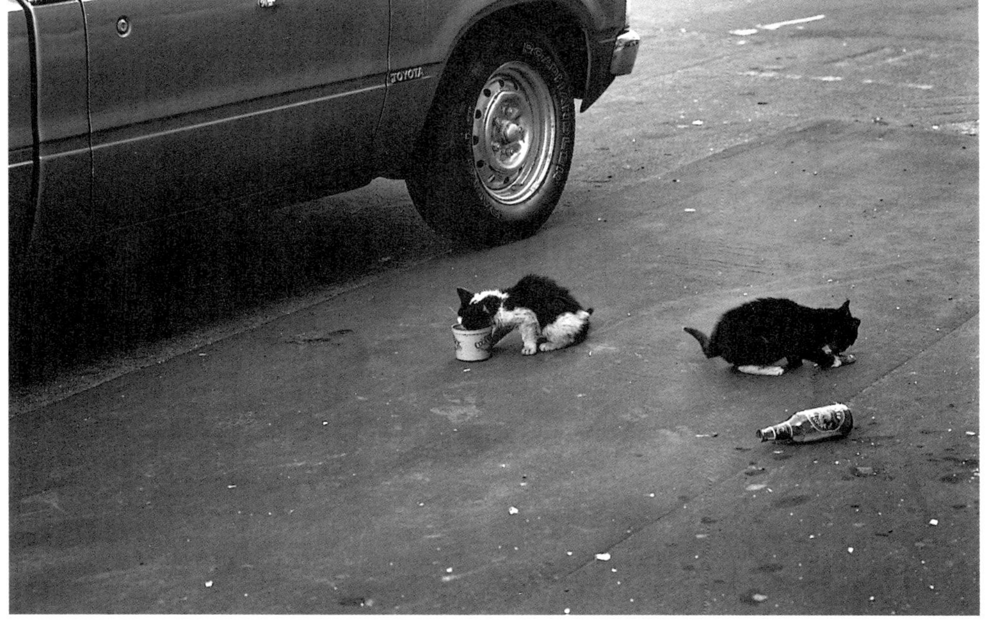

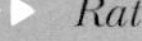 *Rat*

Carissa Etheridge, 15
Community of Hope,
Washington, D.C.
1989
11" by 14", silver print

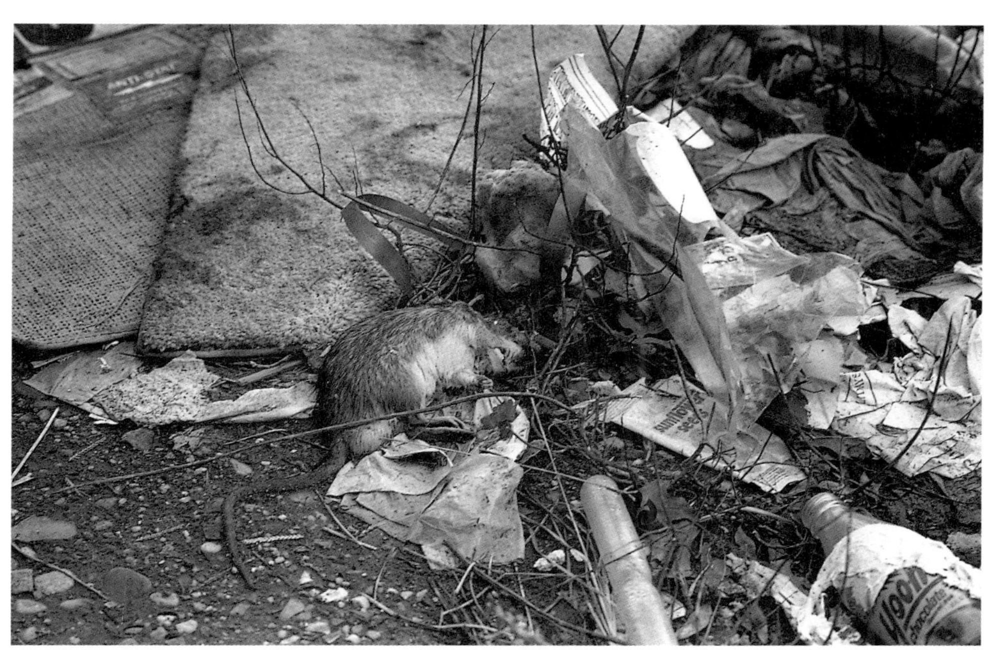

Man in shelter

Tikela Findley, 12
The Carpenter's Shelter,
Alexandria, Virginia
1990
11" by 14", silver print

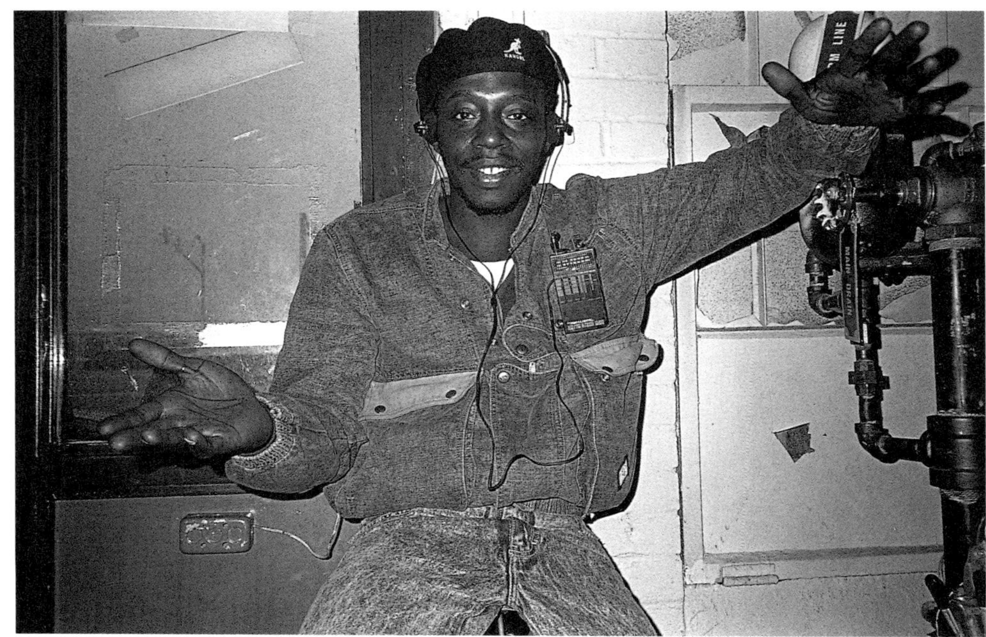

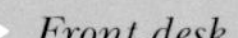

Front desk

Daniel Hall, 9
Capitol City Inn,
Washington, D.C.
1989
11" by 14", silver print

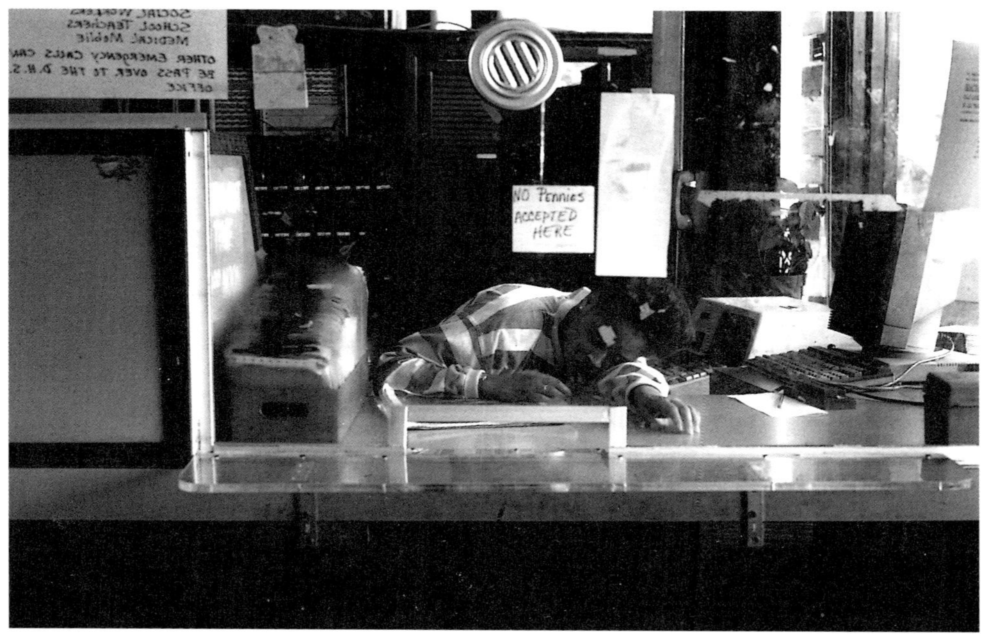

Man out window

Shawn Nixon, 18
The Carpenter's Shelter,
Alexandria, Virginia
1990
16" by 20", silver print

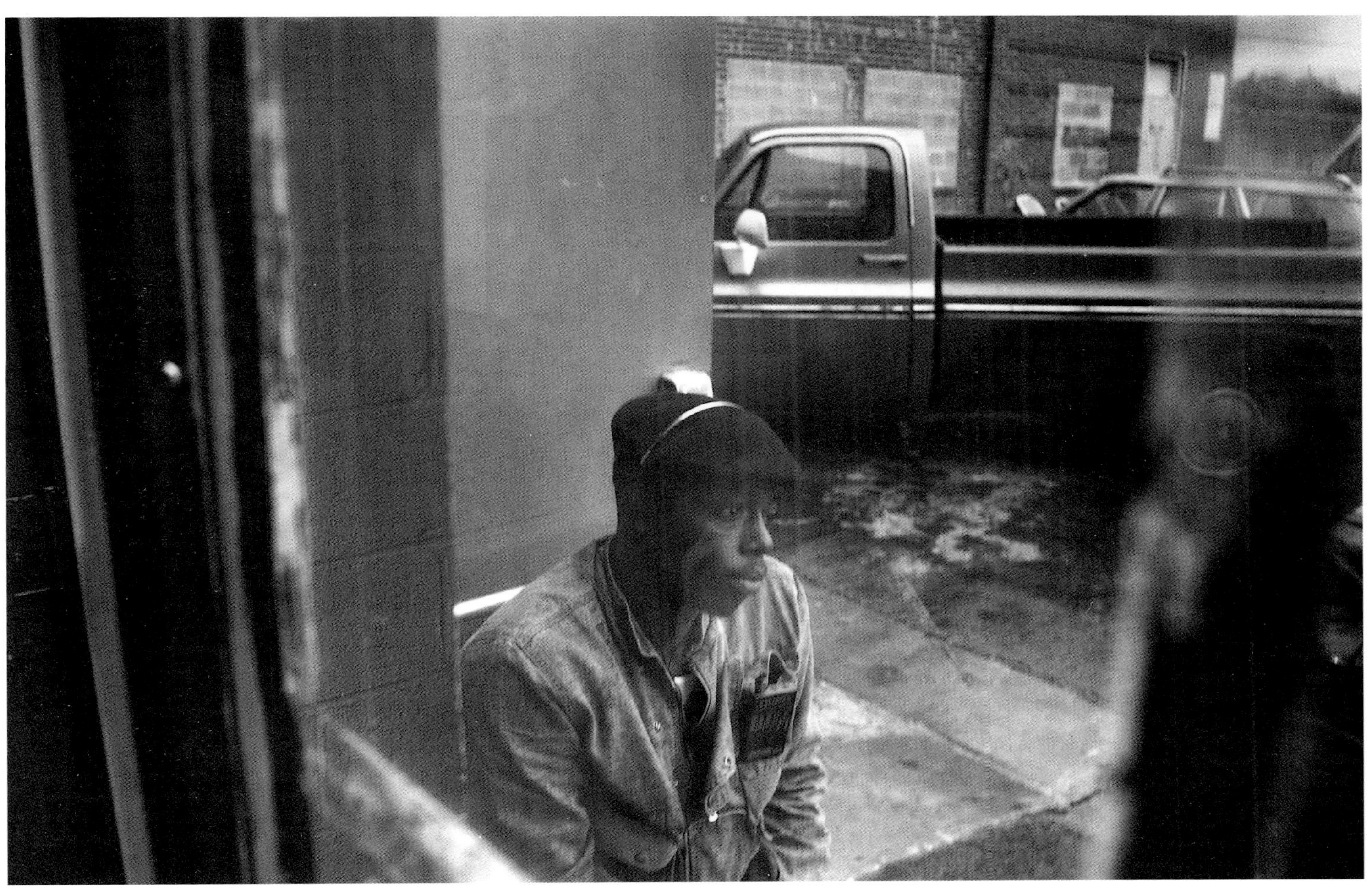

COMMENT FROM TONY, ANOTHER CHILD PHOTOGRAPHER On one Saturday, a homeless man was lost from life. He was asleep on a side of a wall and he was homeless. I felt so sorry to see someone with less than what I have.

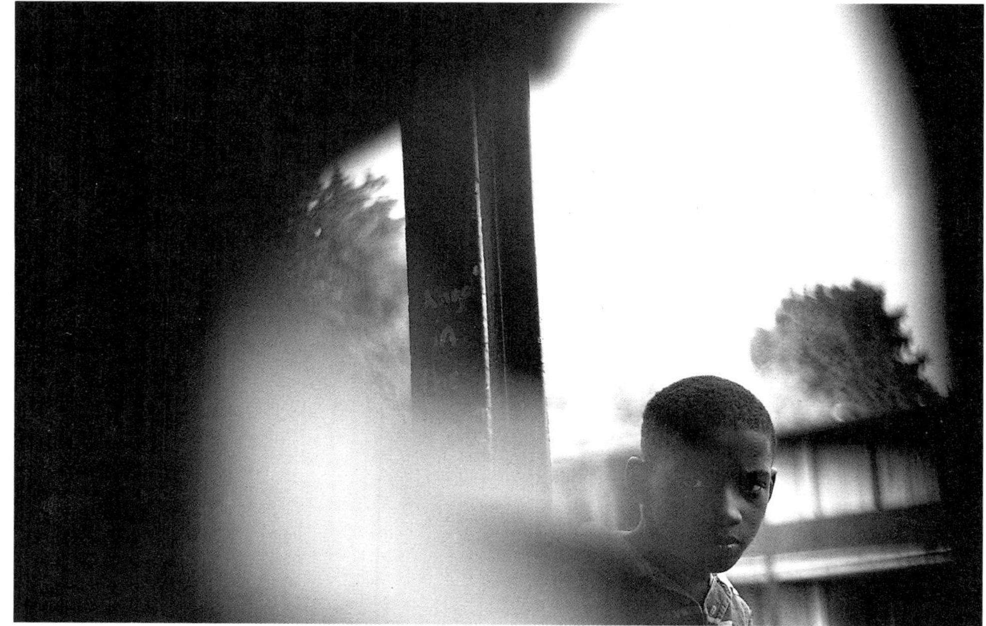

▶ *Angel*

Kevin

Capitol City Inn,
Washington, D.C.
1989
11" by 14", silver print

▶▶ *Boy with gun*

Kevin

Capitol City Inn,
Washington, D.C.
1989
11" by 14", silver print

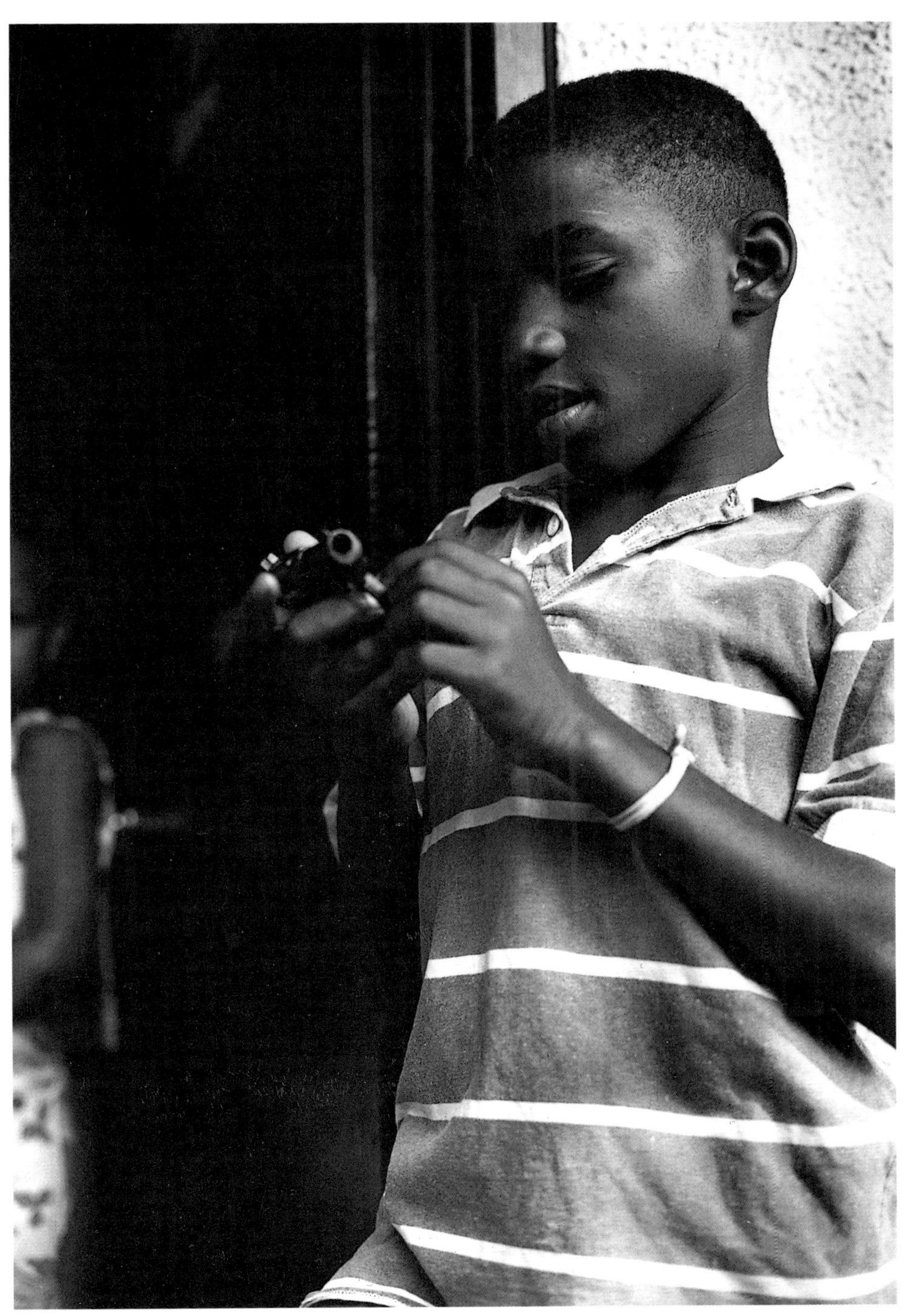

COMMENT TO KEVIN FROM SCHOOLCHILD I live in New York and have seen kids with guns, but never like this, never so calm, and happy. . . . All my teachers say that this picture has a hidden meaning. I don't. You saw a kid with a gun, and you took his picture. It isn't like you were trying to show hardship, and loss of maturity, but the plain truth. Life is scary, and you can die.

Argument

Antwon

Capitol City Inn,
Washington, D.C.
1989
11" by 14", silver print

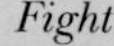

Fight

Daniel Hall, 9

Capitol City Inn,
Washington, D.C.
1989
11" by 14", silver print

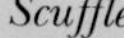

Scuffle

Chris Heflin, 9

The Carpenter's Shelter,
Alexandria, Virginia
1990
11" by 14", silver print

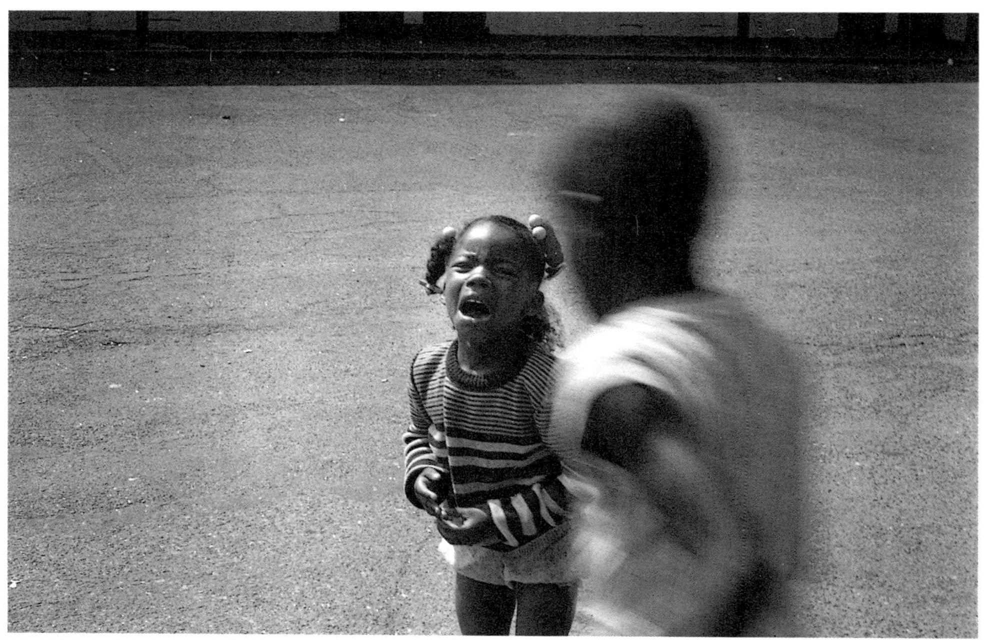

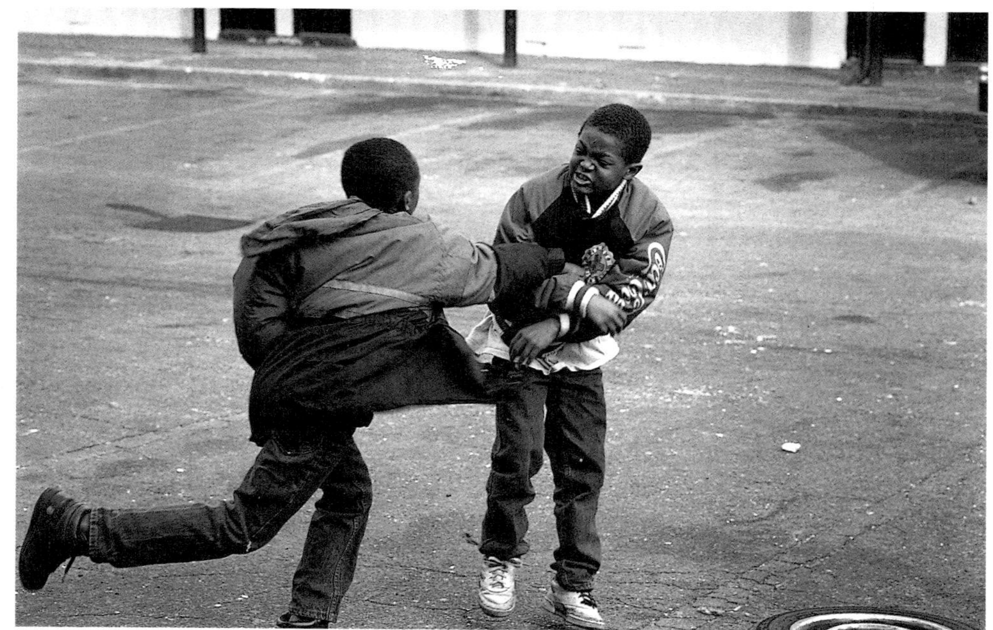

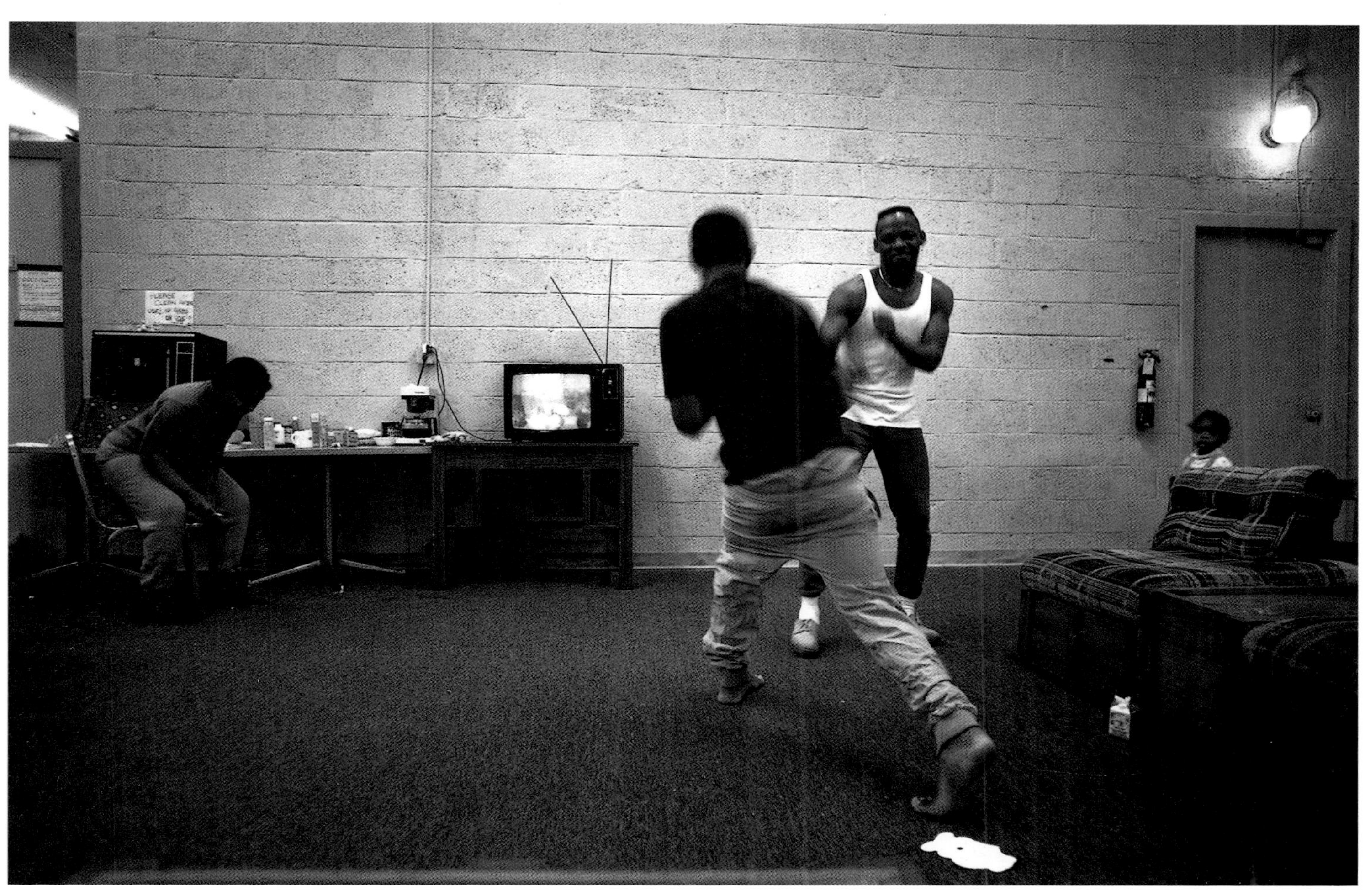

Police

Jermaine

Capitol City Inn,
Washington, D.C.
1989
16" by 20", silver print

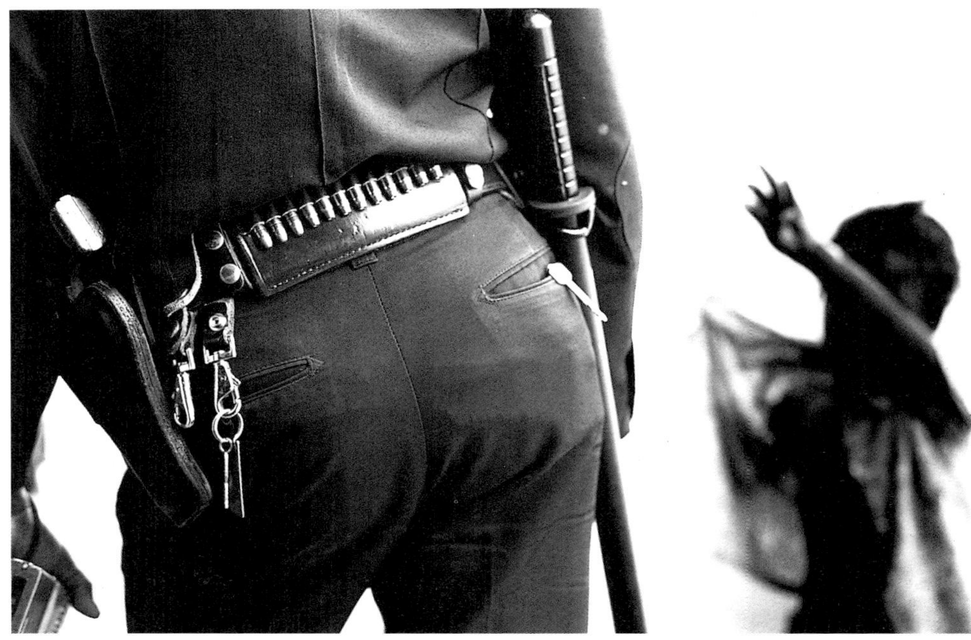

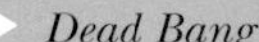

Dead Bang

George Maxie, 10

Community of Hope,
Washington, D.C.
1989
11" by 14", silver print

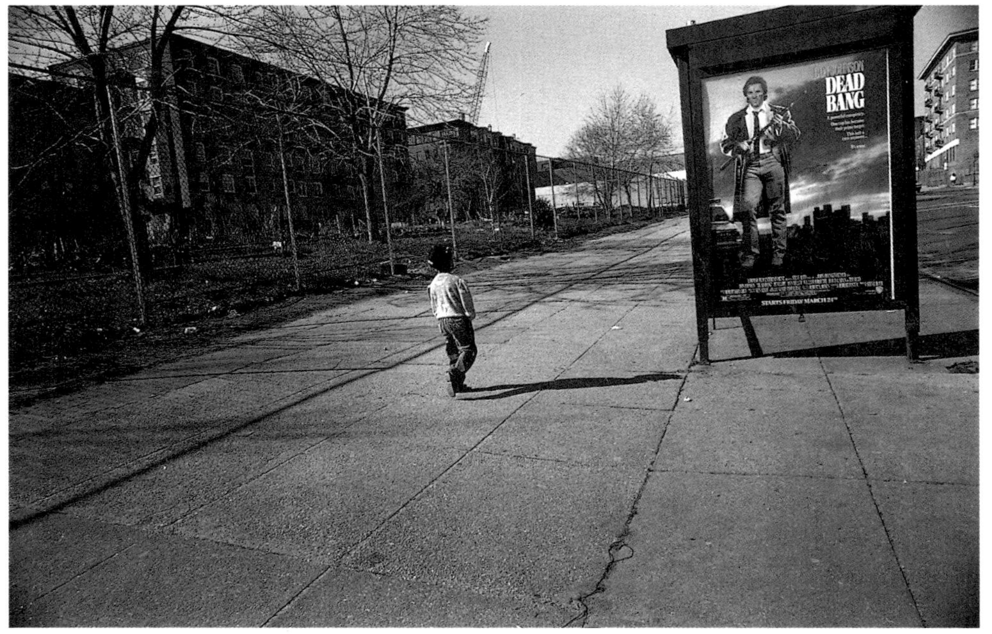

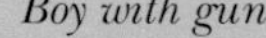

Boy with gun

Daniel Hall, 10

Capitol City Inn,
Washington, D.C.
1990
20" by 24", silver print

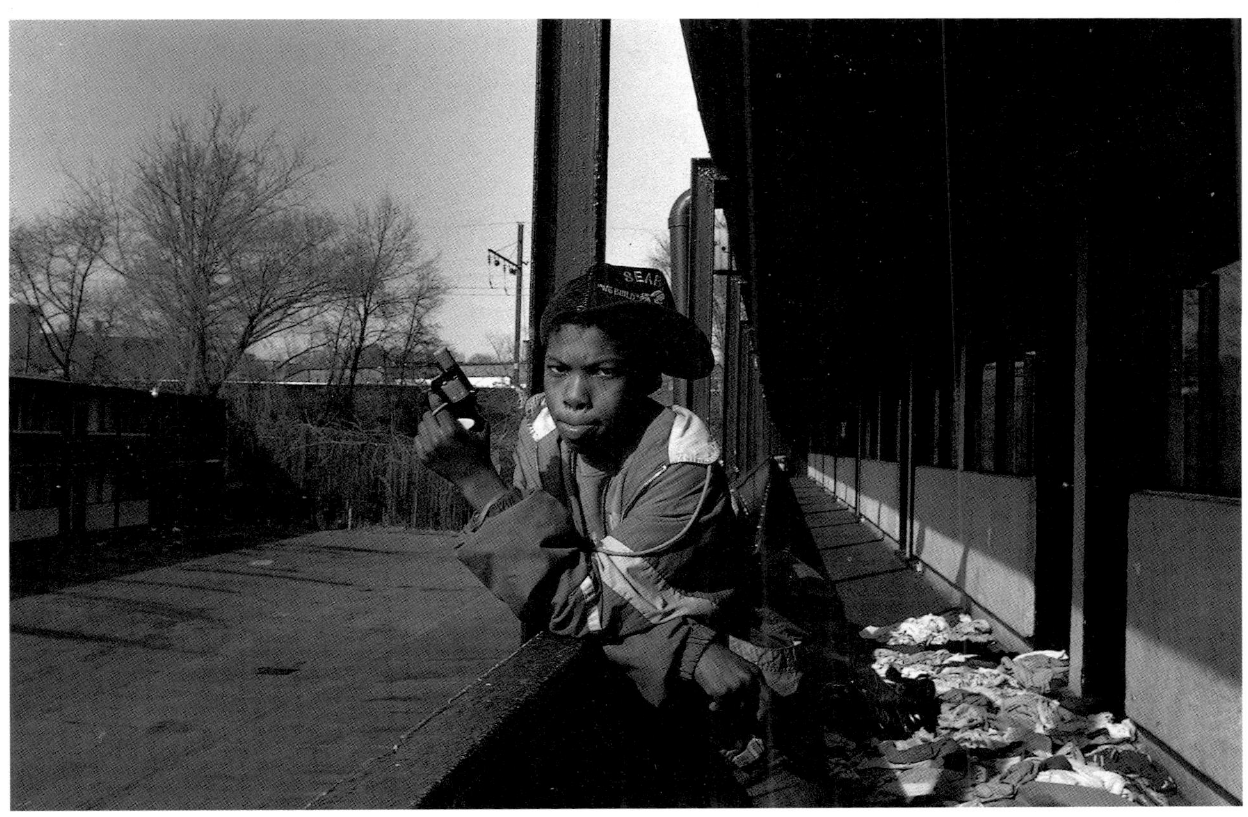

JIM HUBBARD WITH DANIEL *What's up there?* **Bullet holes.** *Do you hear people shooting guns at night in your neighborhood now?* **Yeah. I heard people doing that here, too. People were just running around, doing everything. Sometimes I got scared of people shooting.**

No trespassing

Chris Heflin, 9

The Carpenter's Shelter, Alexandria, Virginia

1990

11" by 14", silver print

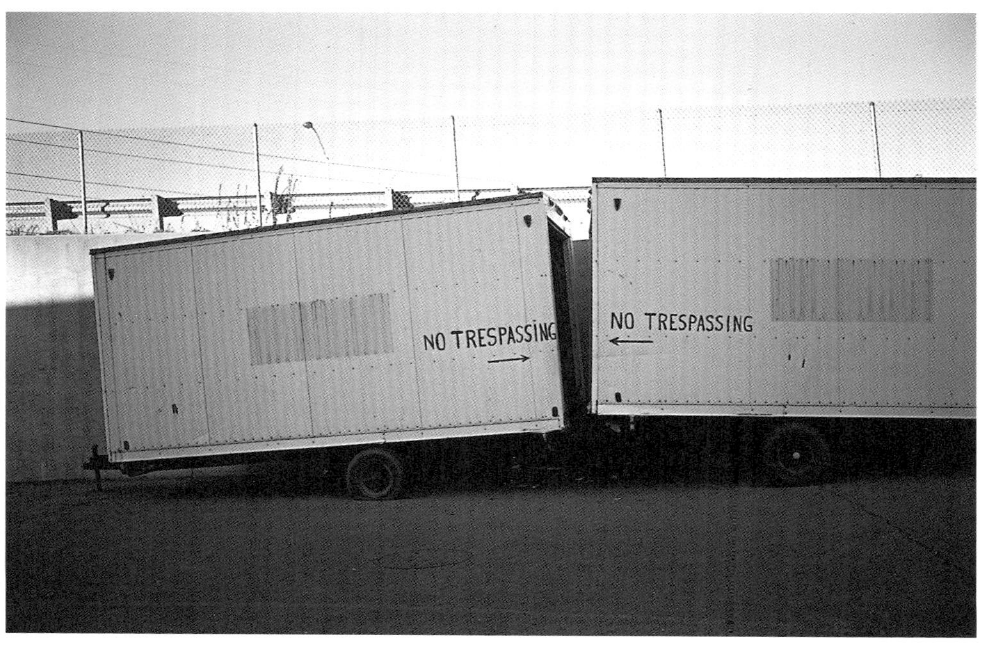

Eviction notice

Yolanda Mitchell

Pitts Hotel, Washington, D.C.

1989

11" by 14", silver print

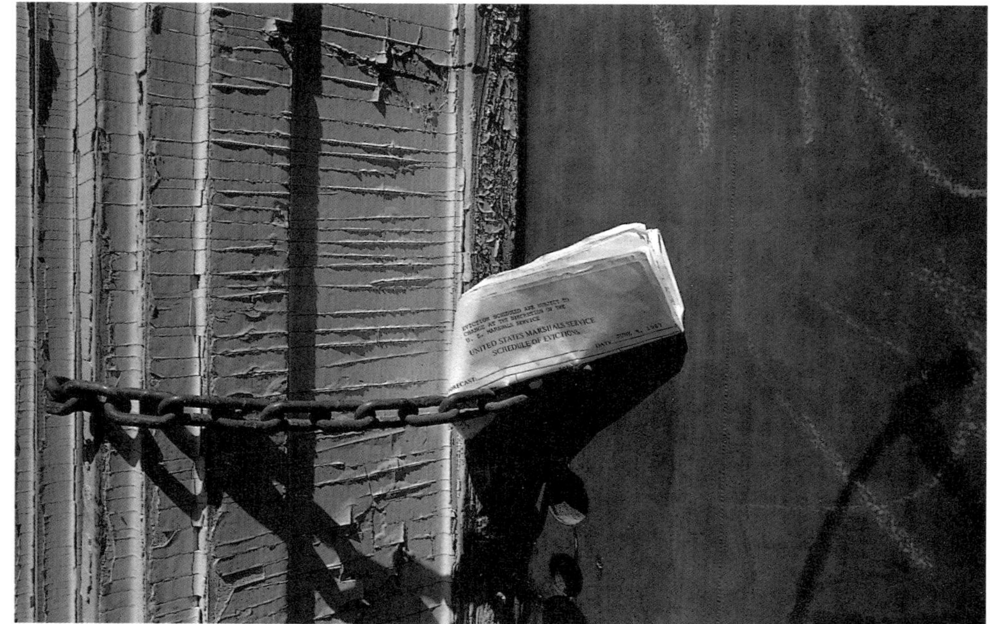

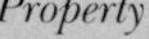 *Property*

Calvin Stewart, 17

Community of Hope, Washington, D.C.

1989

20" by 24", silver print

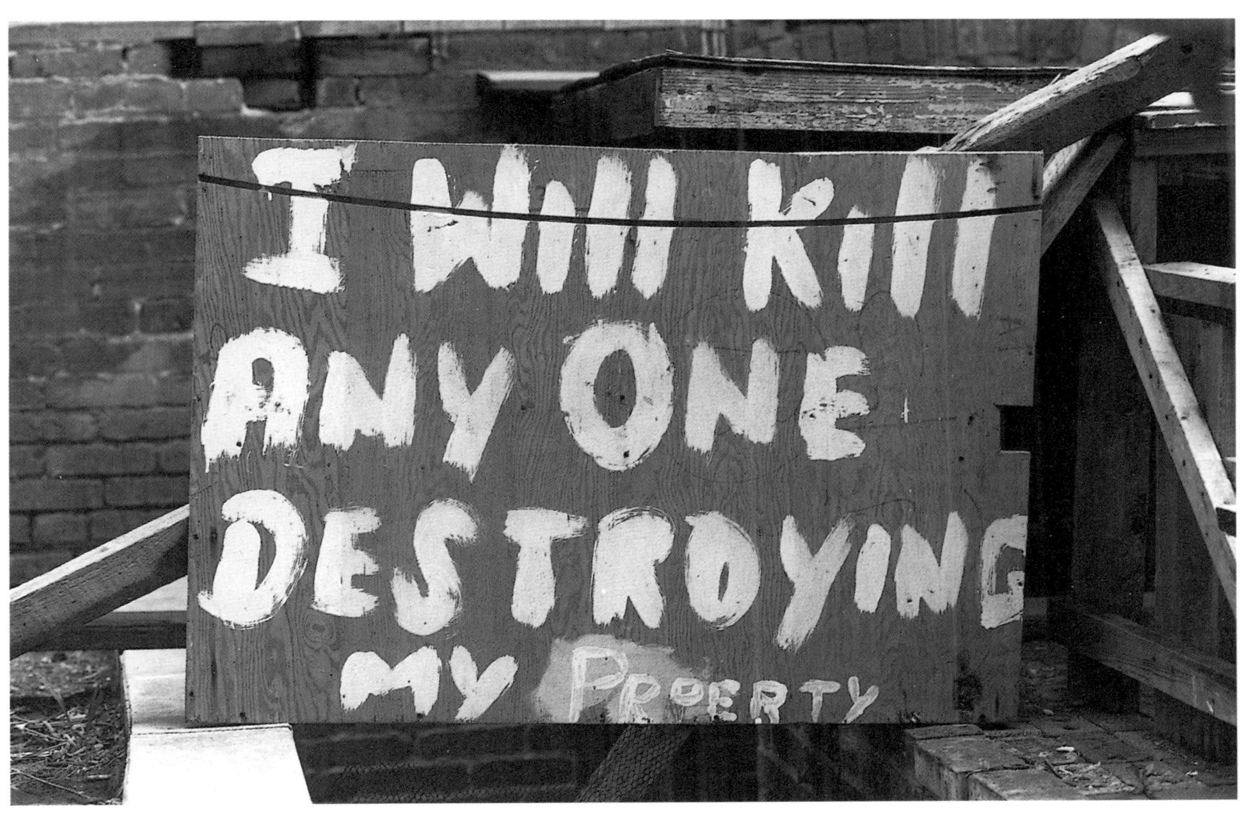

COMMENT FROM CALVIN **When I first met Jim, I was just watching him, and he seemed like he was really into what he was doing. I was trying to learn everything he was trying to teach the kids, so I kept going back every Saturday just to shoot a lot of things around the neighborhood.**

▶ *Common living area*

Jeffrey Turner, 9

Reston Shelter,
Reston, Virginia
1989
11" by 14", silver print

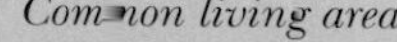

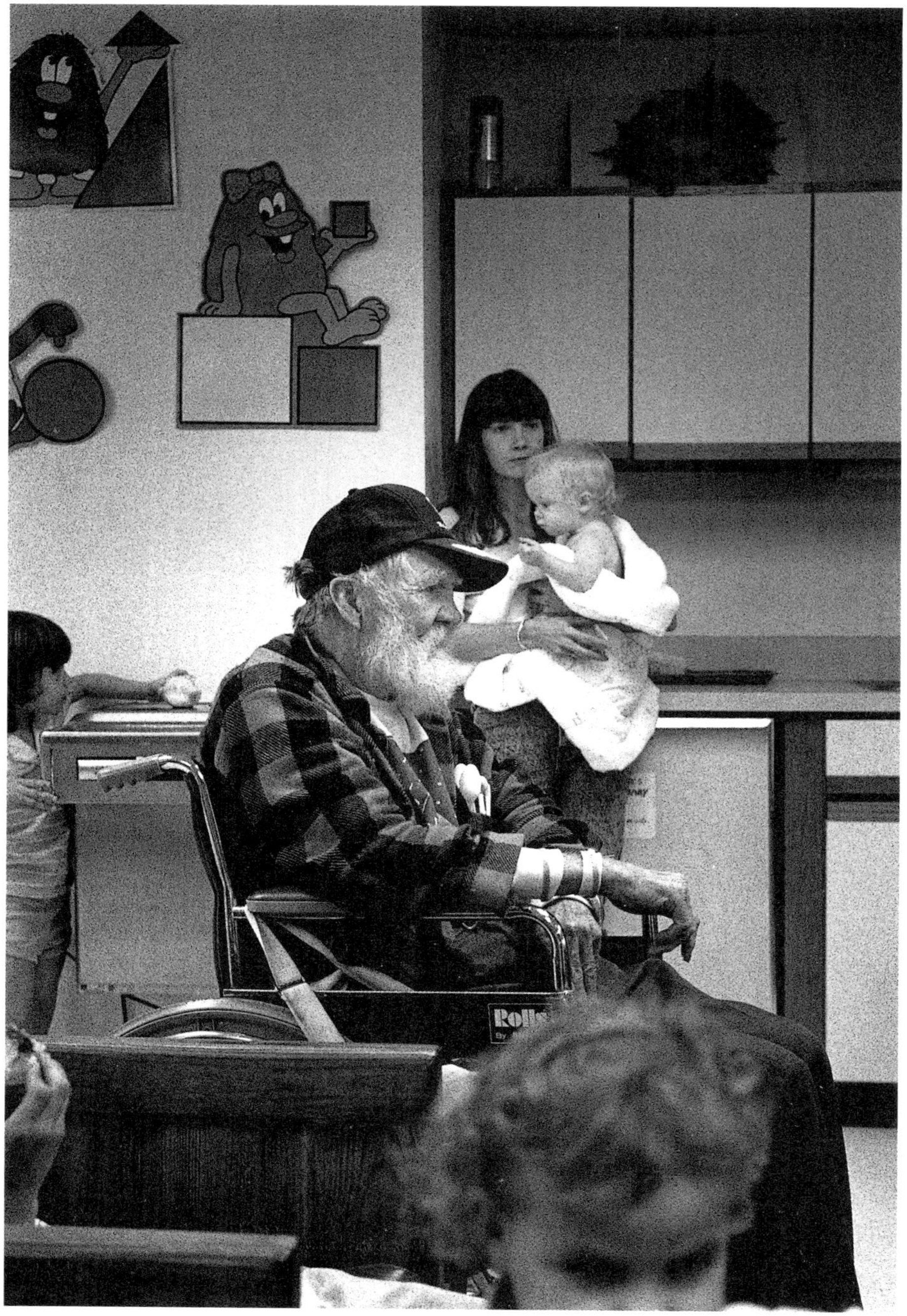

Common living area

Chris Heflin, 9

The Carpenter's
Shelter,
Alexandria, Virginia
1990
11" by 14", silver print

COMMENT FROM CHRIS Now we have our own house, you have your own room and your privacy, that way when you want to play in your own room, or go down to the basement, you have separate places.

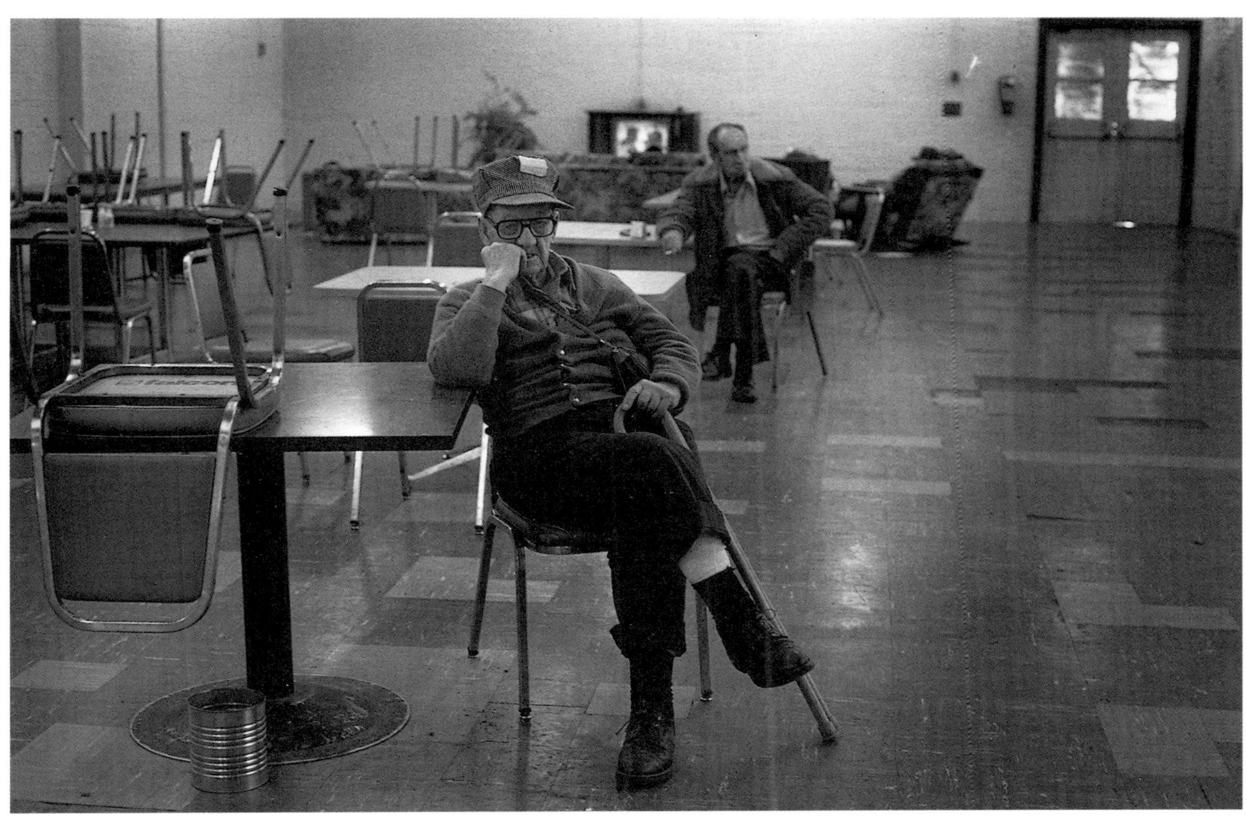

▶ *Woman on phone*

Tikela Findley, 12

The Carpenter's Shelter,
Alexandria, Virginia
1990
11" by 14", silver print

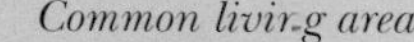

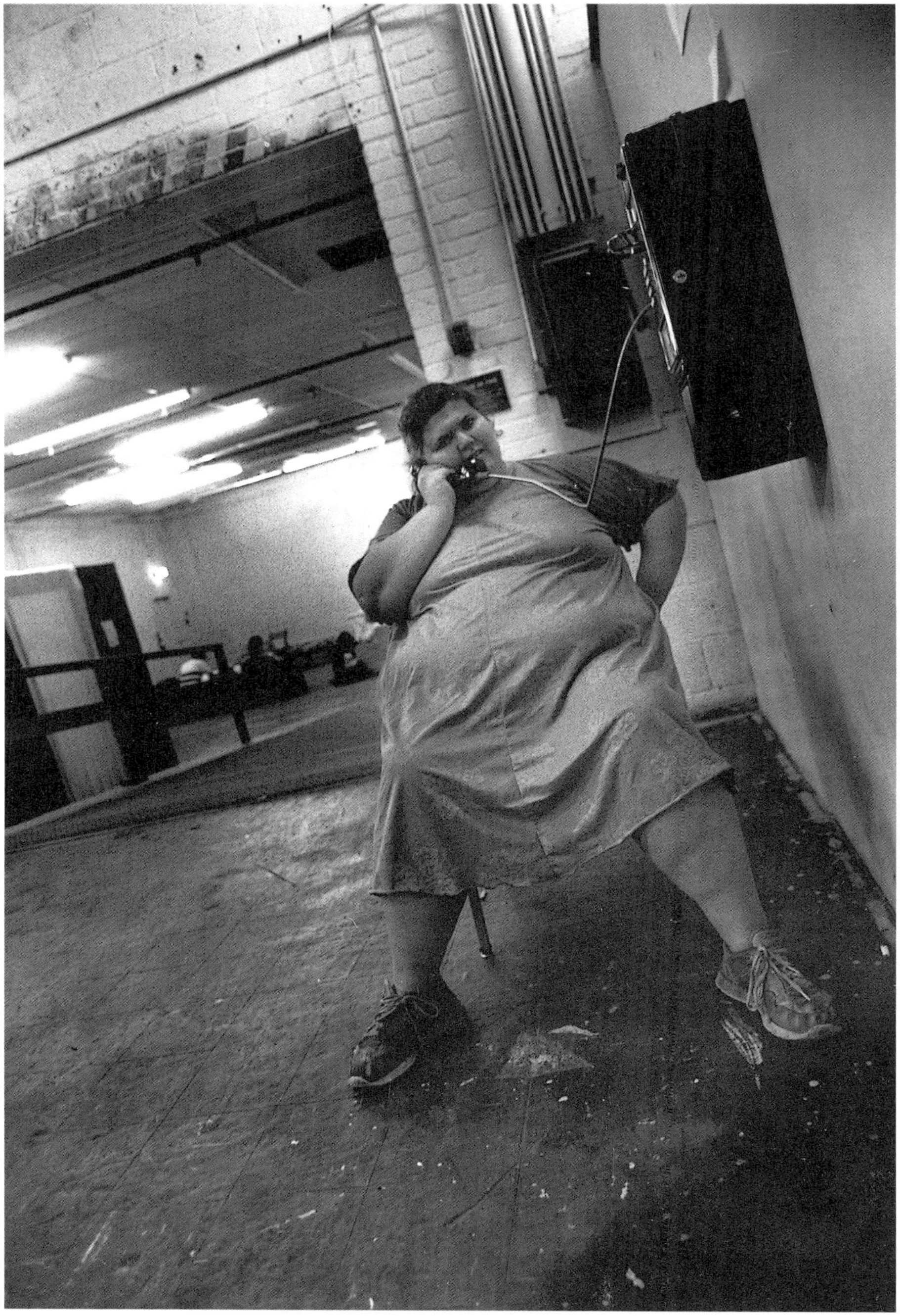

Common living area

Norman Heflin, 8

The Carpenter's Shelter,
Alexandria, Virginia
1990
11" by 14", silver print

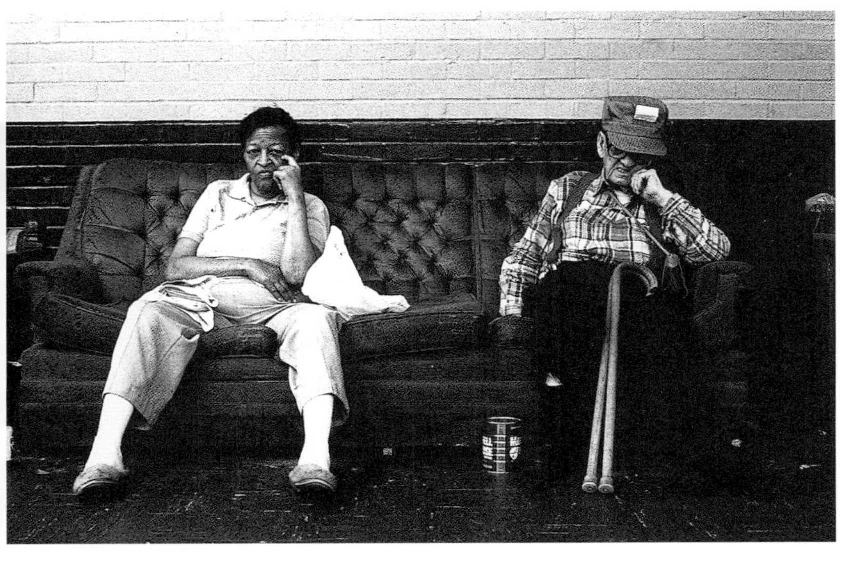
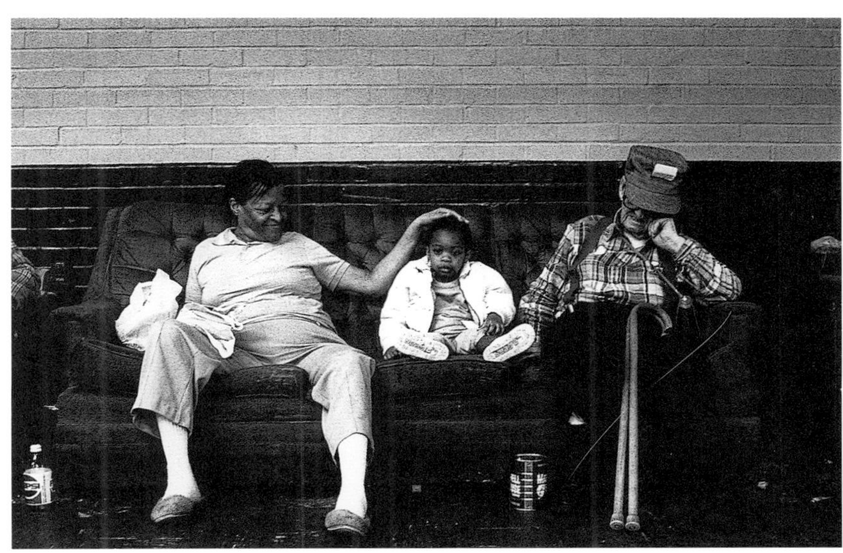
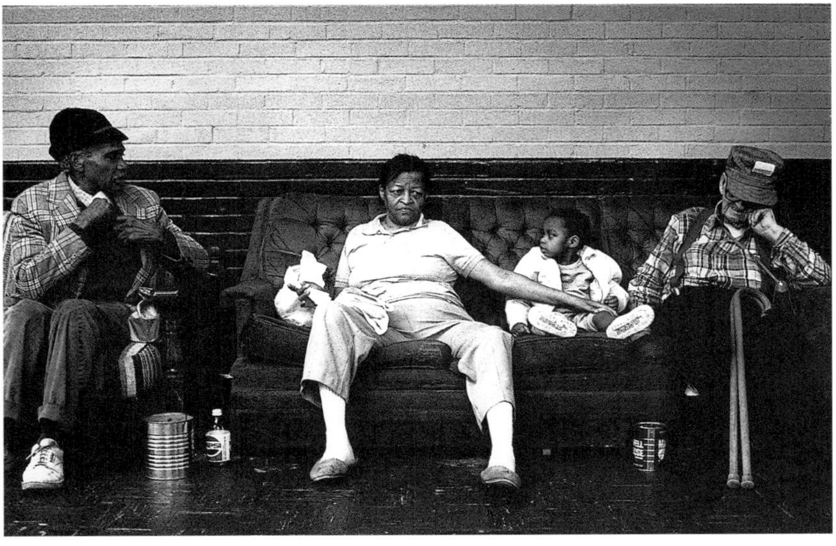
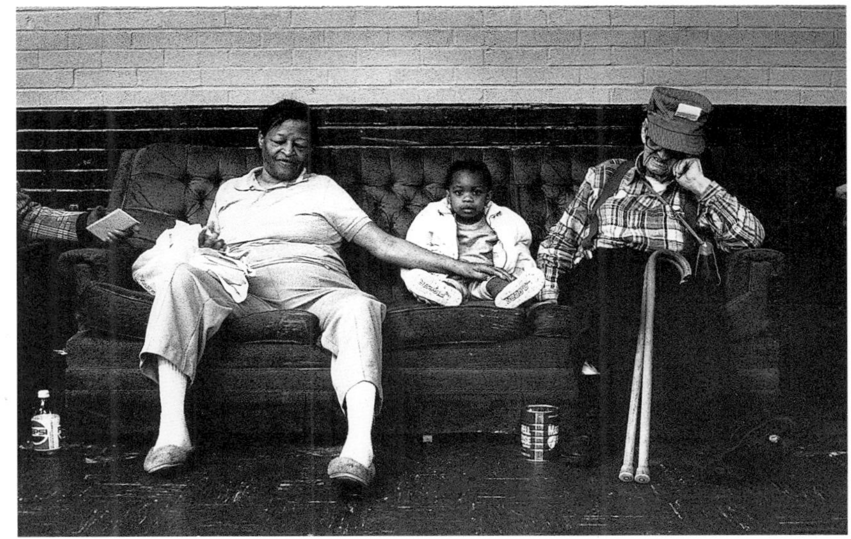

▶ *Girl Sleeping*

Keesha Carroll, 12

Capitol City Inn,
Washington, D.C.
1989
11" by 14", silver print

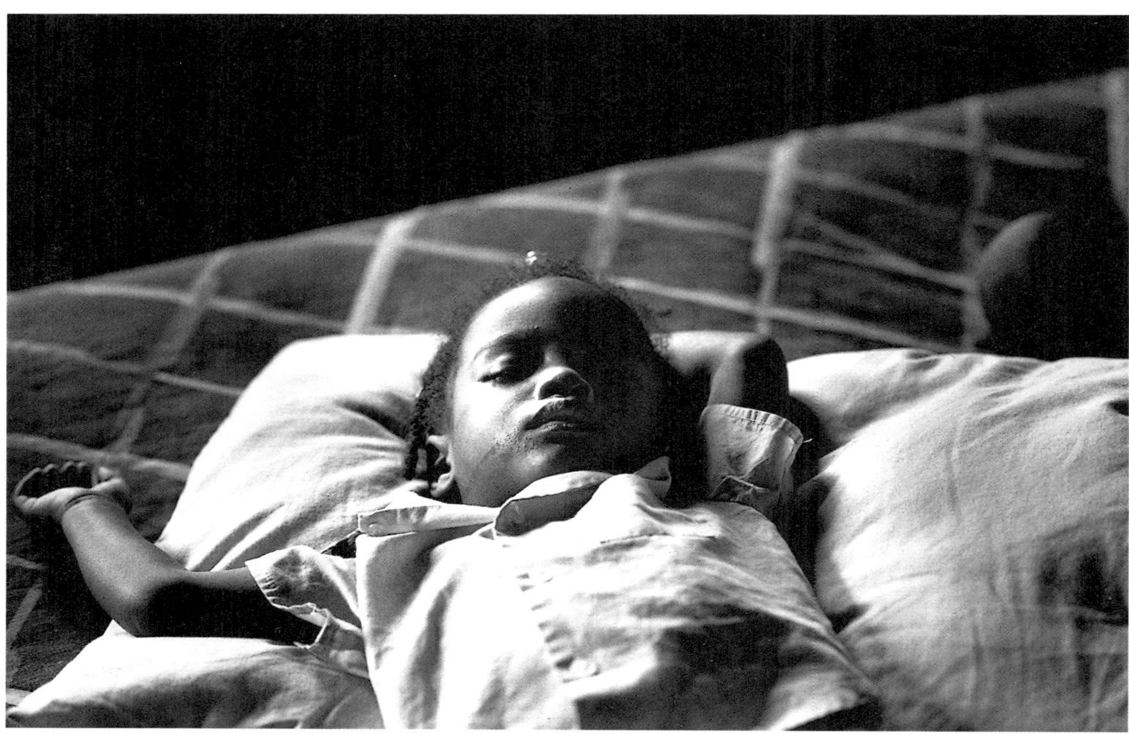

▶▶ *Home on wheels*

Chris Heflin, 9

The Carpenter's
Shelter,
Alexandria, Virginia
1990
11" by 14", silver print

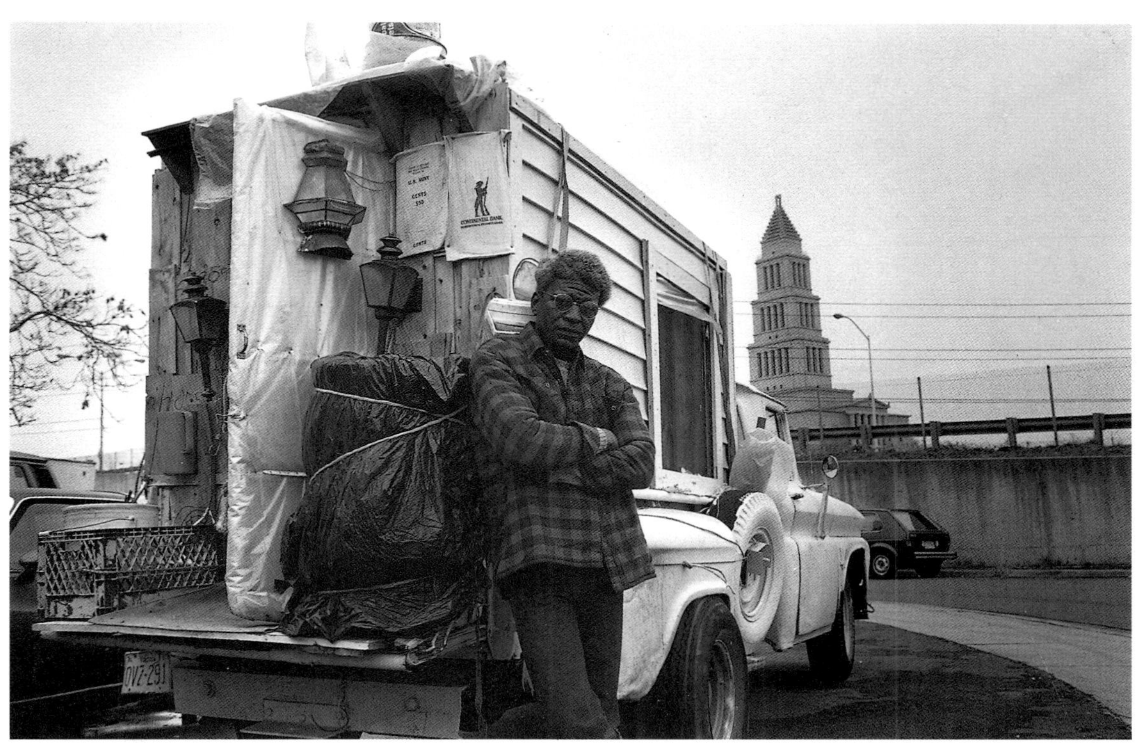

COMMENT FROM CHRIS The reason that people don't have that many homes and they're on the street is because they're knocking the shelters down and building up things for the money. If the President wants to really help, why can't he just give the poor people some money so they can build some houses and then we'd hardly have people on the streets.

▶ *Shadow*

Norman Heflin, 8
The Carpenter's Shelter,
Alexandria, Virginia
1990
11" by 14", silver print

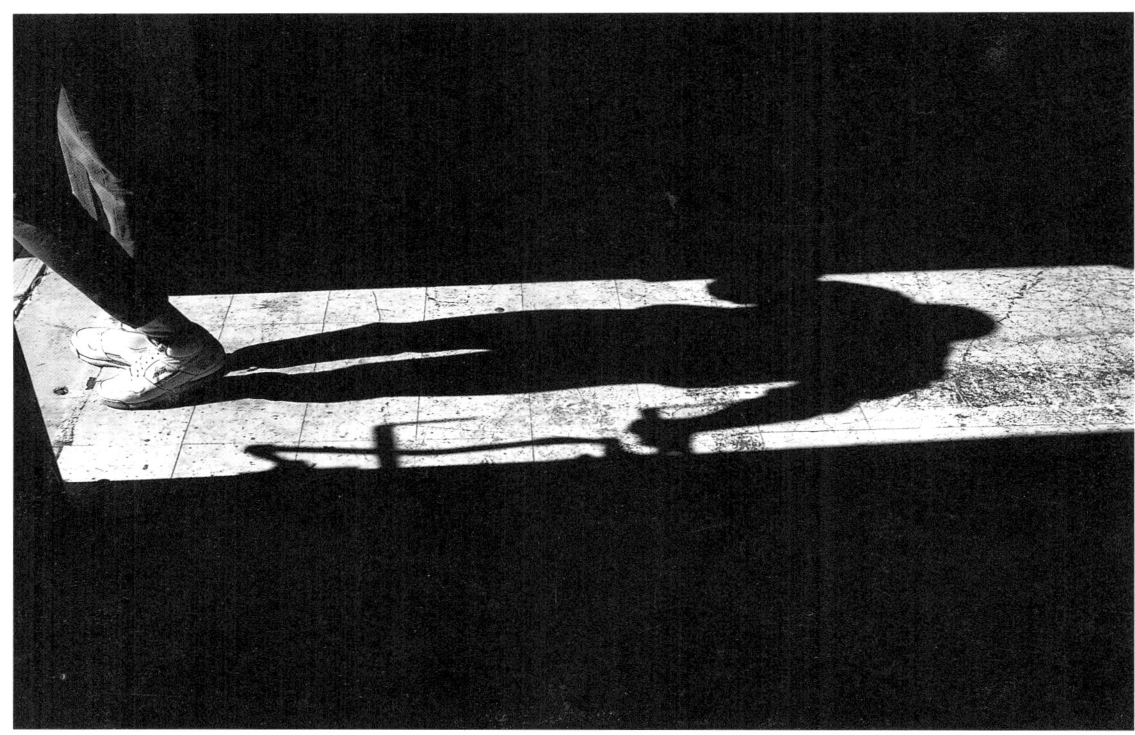

▶▶ *Shattered window*

Daniel Hall, 9
Capitol City Inn,
Washington, D.C.
1989
16" by 20", silver print

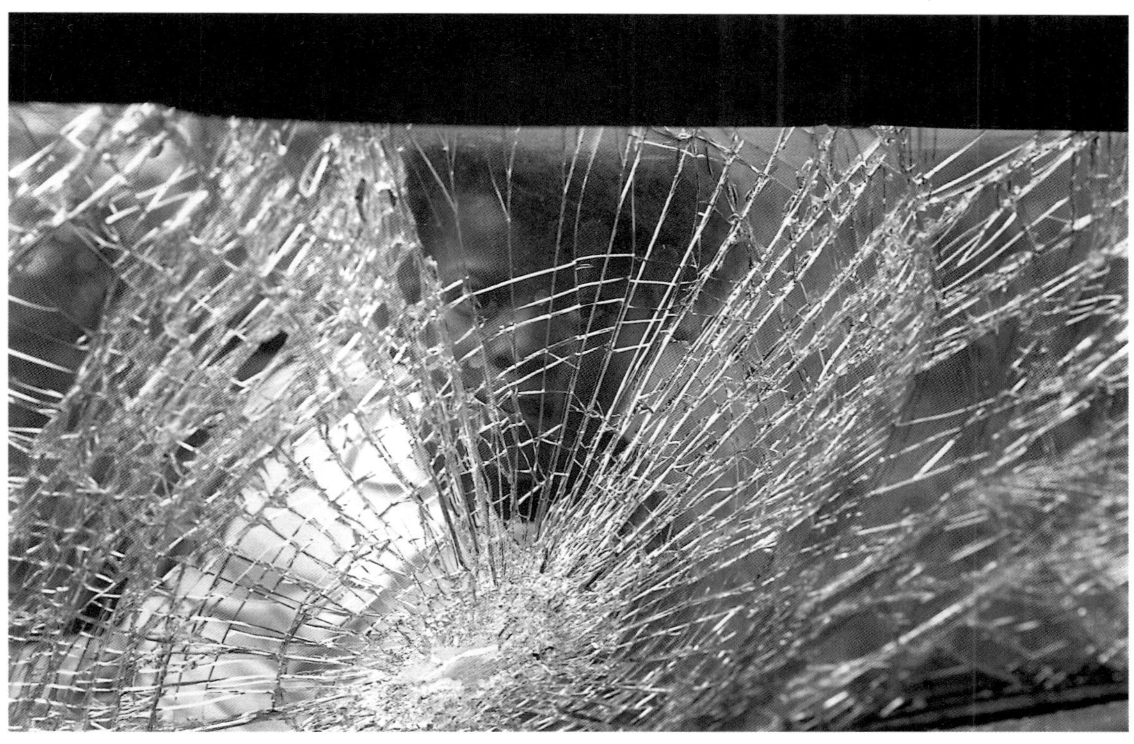

COMMENT FROM SCHOOLCHILD **So many people try so hard to break through, but this barrier is strong and doesn't break too easily. They fall short of their goals and are only able to shatter this barrier.**